Stage Right

Crisis and Recovery in British Contemporary Mainstream Theatre

John Bull

MACMILLAN

First published 1994 by
THE MACMILLAN PRESS LTD
Houndmills, Basingstoke, Hampshire RG21 2XS
and London
Companies and representatives
throughout the world

ISBN 0–333–39596–4 hardcover
ISBN 0–333–39597–2 paperback

A catalogue record for this book is available
from the British Library

Printed in Hong Kong

For Carole and Lydia

Contents

Acknowledgements   vi

1979–1993: A History   vii

Part I

1   Whither Britain?   3

2   The Gamblers' Den   14

3   Private Rooms and Public Spaces   37

4   Enter the Smooth Men   57

Part II

5   Set in Rooms   87

6   Peter Nichols: All My Life in Tudor Manor   105

7   Simon Gray: Bloody Finished at Last   123

8   Alan Ayckbourn: Very English, Very National   137

9   Michael Frayn: Dust and Scaffolding   156

10 Alan Bennett: The Leftovers   178

11 Tom Stoppard: Open to the Public   192

12 Into the Nineties   207

    Notes   220

    Bibliography   227

    Index   243

Acknowledgements

I am grateful to the University of Sheffield for the research grant that made the writing of this book possible, and to the staff of the University of Sheffield and Sheffield City Libraries for their help. In particular I would like to thank Sarah Mahaffy for her encouragement in the early stages of research; as always, Carole Ebsworth for her remarkable skills as a critical reader of the text; and B. Adger for the frequent provision of a fresh view of my ideas. I would also like to acknowledge the work of two critics, Kenneth Tynan and Michael Billington, writers with whom I have not always found myself in agreement but who always seem to be writing about the right issues. I sometimes fantasize about the dialogue that might have been had fortune dictated that their two writing careers had significantly overlapped.

1979–1993: A History

1979

Jan.   Co-ordinated strikes by British Public Service workers result in the 'Winter of Discontent'. 1,500,000 public service workers on 24 hour strike.

Feb.   Shah of Iran deposed. Ayatolloh Khomeini returns from exile and assumes control in Iran.

Mar.   Peace treaty between Egypt and Israel signed by President Sadat and Mr Begin in Washington.
Airey Neave, Shadow Northern Ireland Secretary, killed by IRA car-bomb.

Apr.   Ayotalloah Khomeini declares Iran an Islamic Republic.
Riots after National Front Meeting at Southall, during which 340 people are arrested and Blair Peach, a member of the Anti-Nazi League, killed under suspicious circumstances. Further clashes follow as the Anti-Nazi League mobilize opposition to racism.
Near nuclear disaster at Three Mile Island, Pennsylvania.

May   General Election results in Conservative victory, Margaret Thatcher becoming the first woman prime minister. She announces 'sweeping changes', including anti-picketing legislation, in the Queen's Speech.

June   Presidents Carter and Brezhnev sign the SALT 2 Treaty.

Aug.   Lord Mountbatten killed by the IRA.

Nov.   Iranian students and revolutionary guards seize American Embassy in Tehran.
Decision taken to deploy Cruise missiles in Britain.

Dec.   Zimbabwe National Front agrees to accept arrangements for cease-fire in Rhodesian war.
Russian troops invade Afghanistan.

1980

Jan.–Mar. Strike of British Steel workers.

Apr.	Independence for Zimbabwe.
	Iranian Embassy siege in London.
May	Trade union Day of Action against government's economic and industrial-relations policies.
July	US boycotts Moscow Olympics in protest against Russian invasion of Afghanistan.
Aug.	Unemployment in UK tops 2 million for first time since 1935.
	Formation of the independent trade union Solidarity in Poland, in the aftermath of the Gdansk shipyard strikes.
Sep.	Labour Party Conference votes in favour of unilateral nuclear disarmament.
Oct.	Jim Callaghan resigns as Labour leader.
Nov.	Michael Foot elected as leader of Labour Party.

1981

Jan.	Ronald Reagan becomes President of the USA.
	Datsun of Japan announce plans to open first UK plant.
Mar.	Social Democratic Party formed in Britain, under the leadership of the 'Gang of Four', right-wing ex-Labour Party MPs.
Apr.	Riots in Brixton, South London.
	Hunger strikes by IRA 'H' Block prisoners in Maze Prison, near Belfast. One of the strikers, Bobby Sands, elected MP for Fermanagh and South Tyrone.
May	Bobby Sands dies.
	'People's march for jobs' sets out from Liverpool.
	Mitterand becomes French President.
	Following Labour Party's success in local elections, Ken Livingstone elected chairman of the Greater London Council.
July	Police use CS gas against urban rioters in Toxteth and Moss Side. So-called 'copy-cat' riots in a number of other English cities.
	Poland holds first 'free' elections in a Communist country.
Oct.	British Nationality Bill receives the Royal Assent.
	Socialist Party wins General Election in Greece for first time.

Dec.   Imposition of martial law in Poland.
                UK unemployment reaches 3 million.

1982
Feb.   Sir Freddie Laker's Sky-Train company collapses.
Apr.   Argentinian invasion of Falkland Islands. British task-
                force removes the invaders to the accompaniment of a
                great deal of populist jingoism in Britain.
June   Israel invades Lebanon.
                CND movement re-animated as result of government
                decision to spend more than £10 billion on the Trident
                missile system, and to deploy Cruise and Pershing
                missiles. 250,000 demonstrate in London's Hyde Park
                and 12,000 women join hands around Greenham
                Common Airbase.
Aug.   Poland and Mexico's debts add to banking crisis over
                loans to third world countries.
                Yasser Arafat flees Beirut.
Sep.   Israeli-inspired massacre in Lebanese refugee camps.
                Labour Party Conference votes to expel members of
                Militant Tendency.
Nov.   Lech Walesa freed in Poland.

1983
Feb.   Iran launches major offensive against Iraq.
Mar.   Drought in Ethiopia causing famine affecting more
                than a million people.
June   Thatcher wins surprise re-election in the aftermath of
                the Falklands War and with the aid of the SDP split of
                oppositional voting. She promises a continuation of
                monetarist programme.
                Foot resigns as leader of the Labour Party.
July   £500 million cut in Government spending, including
                £140 million on health.
Sep.   Neil Kinnock elected as leader of the Labour Party.
Oct.   Over 200 members of US and French 'peace-keeping'
                force in Beirut killed by pro-Palestinian terrorists in
                bomb attack.
                Continuing protests against nuclear weapons in
                Europe. Protest in UK centred at the Women's Peace
                Camp at Greenham Common airforce base. Largest

ever anti-nuclear demonstration in London. Huge demonstrations also in West Germany, Italy, Austria, Sweden and Spain.

US troops invade Grenada.

In first General Election for ten years, the Radical Party successful in Argentina.

Nov.   First Cruise missiles arrive at Greenham Common.

US 'peace-keeping' troops in Lebanon in virtual war with Syria.

Dec.   Period 1979–83 slowest for economic growth in the UK since the Second World War.

IRA car-bomb attack on Harrod's store in London.

1984

Jan.   Conservative rebels join Labour Party in opposing 'rate-capping' of local authorities deemed to have set too high rates by central government.

Staff at GCHQ, Cheltenham, deprived of union membership.

Feb.   Muslim forces capture western half of Beirut.

First Japanese Nissan car plant announced for UK.

Mar.   Miners' strike starts. Intensive picketing closes nearly all pits.

European summit meeting in Brussels breaks up after British complaints about size of contributions.

Sarah Tisdall jailed after admitting leaking information about Cruise missiles to press.

Arts Council announce fundamental shift in arts funding, diverting £6 million from London to the regions.

Apr.   Police siege of Libyan Embassy in London after PC Yvonne Fletcher killed by machine-gun fire.

Diplomatic relations with Libya broken.

May.   292 pickets charged with obstruction at Strathclyde. Miners' strike intensifies.

Four and a half billion wiped off share values as Stock Exchange has worst fall for a decade.

Biggest ever UK trade deficit.

June   Government defeated in Lords over plans to abolish Greater London Council.

July   National Coal Board declares 20,000 miners redundant.

	Pound at record low against the dollar.
	Dock strike.
Sep.	Rioting in black townships near Johannesburg.
	Clive Ponting charged with leaking information to the press in connection with allegations about the sinking of the *Admiral Belgrano* during the Falklands conflict.
Oct.	IRA bomb at Grand Hotel, Brighton, during Conservative Party Conference.
Nov.	Reagan re-elected as US President.
	British Telecom privatized.
Dec.	500 killed outright and thousands injured after toxic gas leak at Union Carbide plant at Bhopal.

1985

Jan.	Sterling begins year at record low against the dollar, and continues to slide. Financial markets in turmoil.
	Oxford dons vote not to award Thatcher an honorary degree.
Feb.	Clive Ponting acquitted of breach of Official Secrets Act.
	Panic in city as pound continues to fall and interest rates continue to rise.
	National Union of Mineworkers rejects new formula for return to work.
	Spain opens gate to Gibraltar.
	Sir Peter Hall announces closure of one stage, job cuts and his own departure from the National Theatre as a result of financial crisis.
Mar.	Miners' strike ends after nearly a year. The return to work is marked by marches and banners.
Apr.	President Nimeiry of Sudan overthrown by military coup.
	National Health prescription charges raised from 40p to £2.
May.	Lloyd's investors face underwriting debts of at least £130 million.
	Conservatives lose control of nine councils in local elections.
	Fire at Bradford City Football ground kills 56.
	Riot at Heysel Football Stadium, Belgium, with 38

dead. English clubs banned from European competitions.

June   Bank of England criticised by government for failing to act to prevent the £248 million collapse of Johnson Matthey Bankers.

Cortonwood Colliery, the threatened closure of which started the miners' strike, is to shut with loss of 10,000 jobs in Yorkshire.

TWA flight from Athens to Rome hijacked by Shi'ites.

July   Landslide victory for Robert Mugabe in Zimbabwe.

Greenpeace flagship, *Rainbow Warrior*, destroyed by agents of French Secret Service in New Zealand.

State of Emergency declared in South Africa.

Band Aid Concerts in London and Philadelphia raise £50 million for Ethiopian famine relief.

Sep.   Riots in Handsworth and Brixton.

Lebanese militia destroy 12 Christian villages near Sidon.

Oct.   For the first time in England rioters fire shots in major flare-up on Broadwater Farm estate in Tottenham.

All UK blood donations to be automatically tested for AIDS virus.

Dec.   Government pulls UK out of UNESCO.

Remaining Ulster Unionist MPs in mass resignation in protest at Anglo-Irish agreement.

1986

Jan.   Sikh militants destroy Golden Temple of Amritsar.

Michael Heseltine resigns after Westland Helicopter rescue bid fails to gain government acceptance.

Rupert Murdoch moves News International offices from Fleet Street to Wapping. Start of bitter, year-long mass picketing, with frequent violent scenes and allegations of brutality by pickets and police.

UK unemployment at record level of 3,204,900.

Feb.   After losing election to Cory Aguino, President Marcos of Philippines flees country.

Mar.   South African State of Emergency suspended after 229 days and 757 deaths.

Apr.   US warplanes attack Libya.

Lebanon in 10th year of civil war.

	Greater London Council and other metropolitan authorities abolished.
May.	Reagan renounces SALT 2 treaty.
	Violent scenes on Wapping picket lines.
June	John Stalker suspended from the police whilst conducting investigation of 'shoot to kill' policy in the RUC (Royal Ulster Constabulary).
July	State of Emergency declared in South Africa.
Aug.	Stock Exchange has record one-day fall of more than £4 billion.
	Sellafield nuclear reprocessing plant shut down temporarily as radioactivity found to be above safety limits.
Oct.	Stock Exchange 'Big Bang' day a disaster as computer fails.

1987

Jan.	Terry Waite, Archbishop of Canterbury's special envoy, kidnapped in Beirut.
	Chinese students demonstrate in Beijing.
	Sir Ernest Saunders resigns as Chairman of Guinness as Department of Trade and Industry continues investigation into Distillers take-over.
	Details of sale of British Airways announced.
Feb.	Reagan announces continuation of Star Wars project.
	British Gas sold off.
	Print unions end year-long dispute at News International offices at Wapping in face of legal proceedings.
	Nine animal rights terrorists jailed for total of 37 years for bomb attacks.
Mar.	288 people killed as *Herald of Free Enterprise* sinks off Zeebrugge.
	Worldwide attempts by British government to prevent publication of Peter Wright's *Spycatcher*.
	President Reagan accepts full responsibility for diversion of funds to Contras.
May.	37 crew die when *USS Stark* hit by Iraqi Exocet missile in Gulf.
June	Thatcher wins third General Election, a victory fuelled by the creation of a credit boom and rising interest rates by Nigel Lawson, Chancellor of the Exchequer.

	State of Emergency continued for further year in South Africa.
July	Tension grows in the Gulf as US flags are flown on two Kuwaiti tankers.

Irangate sessions in USA.

Thatcher promises abolition of present rates system (for new and bitterly contested 'poll-tax'), and complete shake-up of Education programme.

Sep.	USA and Russia agree to cut numbers of intermediate-range nuclear missiles. It is revealed that Chernobyl nuclear disaster cost USSR £200 million.
Oct.	Sir Jack Lyons and Gerald Ronson charged with theft in aftermath of Guinness scandal.

'Black Thursday' as £50 million wiped off value of shares in London, part of worldwide collapse of Stock Markets in biggest financial crisis since the time of the Great Depression.

Nov.	32 killed in King's Cross tube fire in London.

11 killed by IRA bomb at Remembrance Service in Enniskillen.

Dec.	Israel acts to halt rebellion amongst Palestinians in the Gaza Strip, at least 20 people killed in clashes.

1988

Jan.	Margaret Thatcher becomes longest serving Prime Minister of century.

Liberal Party votes to merge with Social Democratic Party.

Feb.	Comic Relief (television-oriented charity day of comic acts) raises nearly £7 million for famine relief.

Gorbachov signals willingness to remove Russian troops from Afghanistan.

Mar.	Lieutenant Colonel North and Admiral Poindexter indicted over Irangate affair.

Iran accuses Iraq of using mustard gas to kill 4000 Kurds.

Three IRA terrorists shot dead by security forces in Gibraltar. Gun and grenade attack by IRA during their funeral in Belfast.

June	BBC broadcast of Nelson Mandela's 70th Birthday

	concert at Wembley criticized by South African government.
July	Iran accepts UN resolution calling for end to war with Iraq.
	167 oil-workers killed in fire on North Sea rig Piper Alpha.
	Paddy Ashdown elected leader of new Social and Liberal Democratic Party.
Aug.	IRA bombs in Northern Ireland and on mainland a continuation of enlargement of terrorist activities.
Sep.	Russian troops sent to Armenia to deal with ethnic disturbances. State of emergency declared in Nagormo-Karabakh. Gorbachev reorganizes Politburo.
	Sport Aid (another post-Band-Aid charity appeal) raises several millions to help under-privileged children.
Oct.	Plans for the privatisation of British Steel and Coal Industry announced.
	President Pinochet defeated in first free elections in Chile for 15 years.
Nov.	George Bush defeats Michael Dukakis to become US President.
	State of emergency declared in Soviet republic of Azerbaijan.
Dec.	Gorbachev pledges to substantially reduce numbers of Soviet forces. 70,000 people killed in Armenian earthquake.
	275 people killed in terrorist-bombed crash of Pan Am plane over Lockerbie, Scotland.

1989	
Jan.	Hungarian Parliament approves formation of independent and opposition groups.
Feb.	Vaclav Havel imprisoned for incitement in Czechoslovakia.
Mar.	State of Emergency in Alaska as damaged tanker *Exxon Valdez* leaks 11 million gallons of crude oil into sea.
	First contested elections for 70 years in USSR.
Apr.	'Poll-tax' introduced in Scotland, resulting in widespread protest.

	95 people killed at FA Cup semi-final in Sheffield.

95 people killed at FA Cup semi-final in Sheffield.

Pro-democracy demonstrations in Beijing spread to other Chinese cities.

June   More than 1000 people killed as troops clear pro-democracy demonstrators from Beijing's Tiananmen Square. Widespread arrests follow.

Solidarity wins majority of free-contest seats in Poland.

July   Bill for privatization of water receives Royal Assent.

Aug.   P. W. Botha replaced by F. W. de Clerk as South African President.

Sep.   Bomb detonated outside Liberty's store in London in protest against the publication of Rushdie's *The Satanic Verses*. Its author remains under a death threat.

Hungary opens its border with Austria.

Oct.   Nigel Lawson resigns as Chancellor of Exchequer, and is replaced by John Major.

Nov.   Nationwide demonstrations for reform in East Germany. Berlin Wall pulled down.

Criminal charges brought in connection with 1987 Blue Arrow rights issue.

UK government announces abandonment of plans to privatize nuclear industry.

Dec.   Labour Party supports EC Social Charter.

Start of involuntary repatriation of Vietnamese boat people from Hong Kong.

US troops invade Panama to depose General Noriega.

Communist Party's legal monopoly of power ended in East Germany and Czechoslovakia. The freed Havel becomes President of Czechoslovakia.

State of Emergency declared after riots in Romanian city of Tinisoara. President Ceauşescu flees and is executed.

1990

Jan.   Unrest throughout Russian 'republic' states.

Feb.   Clashes increasing in intensity between ethnic Albanians and the Serbian authorities in Yugoslavia.

Nelson Mandela released from prison.

Mar.   Anti-Poll Tax riots in Trafalgar Square, a part of continuing national opposition to scheme.

Gorbachev elected President of Soviet Union.

Apr.	'Poll-tax' implemented in England.
	Rioting at Manchester's Strangeways Prison.
	21 local authorities 'rate-capped'.
	Government statement confirms attempted sale of 'supergun' to Iraq.
June	First free elections since 1946 in Czechoslovakia.
Aug.	Iraqi troops invade Kuwait.
Sep.	Allied forces begin preparatory build-up around Iraq.
	World oil prices at record level.
Oct.	West and East Germany reunified.
	Britain enters European Exchange Rate Mechanism (ERM).
Nov	After organized campaign within her party Margaret Thatcher resigns as Prime Minister.
	Widely agreed on all sides that Britain is in the grip of a major recession.
	Announcement of dissolution of Warsaw Pact.
Dec.	As Russian crisis worsens Gorbachev given wider executive powers.
	Helmut Kohl elected President of unified Germany.
	ANC President Oliver Tambo returns to South Africa after 30 years exile.

1991

Jan.	Soviet troops, sent to the Baltic republics to quell unrest, kill 14 civilians in Vilnius.
	UN deadline for removal of Iraqi troops from Kuwait passes without response, and US launches air attack over Baghdad. Start of Gulf War.
Feb.	South Africa announces abolition of remaining apartheid laws.
	IRA launches mortar attack on Prime Minister's Downing Street residence during meeting of War Cabinet. IRA bombs at London railway stations.
	Lithuania votes for independent status.
	In Operation 'Desert Storm', allied land forces advance to remove Iraq presence from Kuwait. Following its success a ceasefire declared.
Apr.	Gulf allies parachute aid to Kurdish refugees on Turkish border with Iraq. US troops enter Iraq to set up refugee camps.

	Michael Heseltine announces the abolition of the controversial 'poll-tax'.
May.	Rajiv Ghandi, ex-Prime Minister of India, killed in bomb attack.
	Ethiopian People's Revolutionary Democratic Front take control of Addis Ababa.
June	Boris Yeltsin voted President of Russia.
	Croatia and Slovenia declare independence from the federal republic of Yugoslavia, which is sliding into civil war.
July	New York court finds two founders of the collapsed Bank of Credit and Commerce International guilty of fraud on the scale of at least $5 billion.
	Presidents Bush and Gorbachev sign the Strategic Arms Reduction treaty.
Aug.	Beirut hostage John McCarthy freed after more than 5 years captivity.
	Gorbachev relieved of all duties, as Yeltsin assumes control. Attempted coup fails. Estonia, Latvia and Moldavia declare independence. Soviet government and KGB formally disbanded.
Sep.	Unemployment at 2.4 million, highest figure for two years.
	Beirut hostage Jackie Mann released.
Oct.	Bush and Yeltsin agree on halving of numbers of armed forces.
Nov.	Israeli and Palestinian representatives meet for talks for first time since 1967.
	Newspaper mogul Robert Maxwell disappears at sea, and subsequently evidence of his misappropriation of funds comes to light.
	Terry Waite and Tom Sutherland released from Beirut captivity.
Dec.	IRA bombs in London stores.
	Ukraine votes for independence. Soviet Union disbanded. Gorbachev resigns.
	Terry Anderson becomes last American hostage in Beirut to be released.
	Agreement reached on European Maastricht Treaty on economic and political union. John Major successfully presses for British opt-out on single currency and

Social Charter clauses.

Kevin Maxwell, son of Robert, is issued with writ over an estimated £40 million misplacement of pension funds.

1992

Jan.   President Gamsakhuria of Georgia flees from his burning Parliament in Tblisis. Civil war and battle with South Ossetian separatists continue all year.

Following withdrawal of Red Army troops, territorial fighting between Armenia and Azerbaijan. 'Liberalization' of prices in Russia.

Serbian and Croatian forces continue to fight for military and territorial supremacy in disputed Dalmatian and Slavonian parts of Croatia. European Community recognizes Slovenia and Croatia.

Mar.   Clashes in Sarajevo herald the start of the most extensive war in Europe since 1945. Despite UN and EC peace initiatives more than half a million people killed in the fighting by the end of the year. Europe's largest post-war migration of internal refugees resulting in dispersal of hundreds of thousands of Bosnians to Croatia and western Europe.

This dispersal adds fuel to the racial violence and nationalist chauvinism that grows in strength throughout western Europe, and particularly in what had been East Germany, through the year.

Apr.   John Major leads Conservative Party to an unexpected victory in General Election, the fourth consecutive defeat for Labour.

Long-serving Italian premier Andreotti loses power in Election.

53 people killed and $1 billion worth of buildings destroyed in Los Angeles riots following not guilty verdicts on policemen filmed beating black motorist Rodney King.

June   Danish referendum votes against implementation of Maastricht Treaty.

In France farmers and truckers successfully blockade roads for a month in protest against EC agricultural reform proposals.

Sep.   Black Wednesday as pressure from the foreign
            exchange markets causes the pound to plummet. The
            Government raises interest rates, removes sterling
            from the ERM, allowing the pound to float, and
            slashes interest rates; all within a day.
Oct.   Government announce plans for closure of 31 coal
            pits, an announcement followed by strong and orga-
            nized protest, and a climb-down, legally enforced,
            whilst a report is prepared.
Nov.   Bill Clinton defeats George Bush in US Presidential
            election.
Dec.   Edinburgh   Euro-Summit   on   Maastricht   Treaty
            attempts to patch up differences.

1993
Jan.   Compromise proposals on pit closures announced by
            UK Government, but national protests continue.
Feb.   US, backed by UK and France, in missile attacks on
            Baghdad.
            Savage fighting continues between Serbian and
            Bosnian forces, as evidence of atrocities mounts.
            Privatization plans announced for British Rail and
            London Underground. Hospital waiting lists at record
            high. Unemployment at 3 million.

            what does not change/is the will to change

        what also is unchanged/is the resistance to change

Part I

1
Whither Britain?

From behind a Perrier and a desk consisting of a thick sheet of glass perched uneasily on top of a square pillar made of the same concrete as the exterior of the National Theatre, Sir Peter Hall contemplates the end of the 'Whither Britain' school of drama: 'I think it's over, and I don't know what's going to happen next'.

(Sir Peter Hall, 1984)[1]

In October 1968 Alan Bennett's first play, *Forty Years On*, opened at the Apollo Theatre in London. The modest success it enjoyed doubtless had something to do with Sir John Gielgud's participation in a contemporary play – as did the author's appearance in the production shortly after his association with the highly successful satirical revue *Beyond the Fringe* had finally ceased.

The action surrounds the annual play at Albion House, 'a public school on the South Downs', and from the outset it is apparent that the connection between the health of the school and the state of the nation is always uppermost in the playwright's mind. Albion was the symbolic location for a divided Britain for the poet William Blake, but the divisions in Bennett's are quickly established as very different. This is no Albion of potential revolution, but a rather run-down locale for the traditional education of the male ruling class; and if the analogy is to be made with the decline of the country at large, then it is done from the perspective of that same ruling class. It is a view from the bridge and not from the boiler-room.

That the school has lasted beyond its time is seen in the set for the Assembly-Hall where the action of the play takes place – 'a gloomy Victorian Gothic building, with later additions, a conglomeration of periods without architectural unity . . . dingy and dark and somewhat oppressive'. Albion House, like the Britain that will be depicted by Bennett, is an amalgam of ill-assorted styles, the old merged uneasily with the new, cold and unwelcoming.

And it is not only the building that is seen as out of key. Once the general atmosphere of school-life has been established – a chapel bell is heard, as are sounds of a distant cricket match and of boys learning by muttered rote – the proceedings are opened by the never named Headmaster (Gielgud) addressing the audience, ostensibly the parents present to witness the annual school play. His address is full of nostalgia for a past world, opening with a memory of the first time he had stood in the hall, as a schoolboy on Armistice Day in 1918; but the nostalgia is continually undercut by the noisy evidence of modern war technology:

> That was my first term at Albion House as a school-boy, and now I am Headmaster and it is my last term. It is a sad occasion . . .
> (*A jet aircraft roars overhead temporarily drowning his words, and he waits.*) . . . it is a sad occasion, but it is a proud occasion too. I can see now some of the faces on that never-to-be-forgotten November morning, many of them the sons of old boys who, proud young trees for the felling, fell in that war. And in many a quiet English village there stands today a cenotaph carved with their names, squire's son rubbing shoulders with black-smith's boy in the magnificent equality of death.

It is an opening wonderful in its absurdity, an attempt to get a purchase on the mythical world of a 'Merrie England' where class antagonisms disappear in a rural union against the foreign foe. In every way this man's days as leader of the school are evidently numbered. And predictably on this, his final day, he will continually find his efforts to evoke the supposed values of a past Golden Age thwarted by his liberal successor, Franklin – in charge of a drama production that will largely be concerned to debunk the heroes of the Headmaster's world, and shortly to take over the school.

In the long opening speech of the Headmaster the prevailing tone is very much like that of Bennett's parodied clergyman in *Beyond the Fringe*, and indeed the whole play, which has the structure of a series of loosely connected revue sketches, clearly owes much not only to that show but to memories of his contributions to late-night BBC TV satirical shows of the same period. 'Thirty years ago today, Tucker, the Germans marched into Poland and you're picking your nose.' It is an essential part of what Bennett is about that his Headmaster should be given, what is in effect, a virtuoso performance at the beginning. We are, of course, meant to laugh at his words but to feel at the same time a sense of warmth towards him. The pointed interruptions of his speech about the values he associates with the 1914–18 War by the jet engines that proclaim the imminence of further wars certainly undercut what residual seriousness there is in his theme; but like Addison's Sir Roger de Coverley, the Headmaster is presented as essentially harmless. Ideologically disposable in his eccentricity, it is his *manner* rather than his *matter* that assumes importance. The warmth created for this redundant figurehead comes in part from the clear sense that the character knows himself to be playfully at odds with the contemporary world.

And it is this that gives the real edge to the Headmaster's objections to what he regards as Franklin's tinkering, as he sees it, with the official history of England from 1939 to the present day that is to be the subject of the Albion House Dramatic Society's play, *Speak for England, Arthur*:

Franklin: Have you ever thought, Headmaster, that your standards might be a little out of date?

Headmaster: Of course they're out of date. Standards always are out of date. That is what makes them standards . . . All these years I have been at Albion House, years which have seen the decay of authority, the decay of standards, the slow collapse of all I hold most dear . . . Mark my words, when a society has to go to the lavatory for its humour, the writing is on the wall.

Franklin: You are a different generation, Headmaster.

Headmaster: So are you, Franklin. However daring and outspoken you are, to the boys you are a master, and all your swearing and your smut, your silk handkerchiefs and your suede shoes can't alter that. We're in the same boat, Franklin, you and I.

It will be the pessimistic wit of the Headmaster, sometimes self-conscious and sometimes not, that will reach the audience and not the liberal optimism of Franklin, who is never allowed any real degree of self-analysis. They are both captains of the same sinking boat. The difference is that the Headmaster possesses the certainty of an historical role that will ensure his continuation of control until the bitter end; while Franklin believes the vessel to be recoverable if only he can muck in with the 'men' – who anyway are actually gentlemen – thereby abandoning any pretensions to leadership. His attempts to demythologize the Headmaster's reading of past history, with its rosy vision of the classes pulling together in an ill-defined common interest, founder on his inability to understand that the institution he wishes to inherit (the traditional educational tool of the ruling classes) has been built precisely on the bricks of the Headmaster's mythology. Remove this, and you remove with it the justification for exclusivity.

Viewed in this light then, *Forty Years On* begins to look very much like the cenotaph for the past invoked by the Headmaster in his opening speech. Its world has passed, and is only briefly recoverable in comic terms. But its humour is uneasy, frequently inviting a patronizing belly-laugh at the expense of the characters, then occasionally daring the audience to risk a sympathetic response towards the redundant leader.

What is most peculiar about this production is that it should have occurred in 1968 of all years. For, although there were many other playwrights whose earliest work dates from this period, intent on depicting the decline of Britain as an imperial nation, Bennett is virtually alone in doing so from a perspective that embraces, however hesitantly, the values of that past 'glory'. Philip Hope Wallace thought *Forty Years On* the funniest play of the year but even he, a surprisingly unradical theatre critic for the *Guardian*, could not escape its nostalgic tone, going so far as to compare it with Noel Coward's *Cavalcade*.[2]

For, in as much as it is ever possible to place a precise date on changes in theatrical mood, 1968 represents a key moment, a year that produced what was to become an entire generation of new theatre practitioners, one of whose prime concerns was precisely to open up the debate about Britain's past, but in a manner quite declaredly hostile to that of Bennett:

> After 1968, the rise of the political theatre movement marked a distinct change in the use of history towards a more politically self-conscious and radically revolutionary socialism and Marxism. History was now carefully appropriated as part of the armoury of the left-wing political theatre, and the supplanting of personal by private history was also ... now clearly identified as an ideological concern.[3]

If it can be loosely described as a 'whither Britain' play, to borrow the words of Sir Peter Hall, the then chief administrator of the National Theatre, *Forty Years On* is certainly not characteristic of its kind. Its prevailing tone is one of nostalgia for a cosily remembered past, not of that kind of questioning criticism that Hall clearly has in mind, and which was to be a dominant theme of contemporary drama for the next ten years or so. Although this nostalgia is frequently comically deflated, the overall effect of the piece offers comfort rather than discomfort to an audience that it is assumed would place itself on the right rather than the left ideologically. In this context it seemed, and still seems, an historical curiosity. *Forty Years On* is a period piece, and its period is evidently not that of late 60s' Britain. A direct comparison will help.

The following year another new playwright, Howard Brenton, had his first London production with *Revenge* at the Royal Court Upstairs. Towards the play's conclusion the failed would-be super-villain Hepple has a vision of the immediate future of the country:

Funny. My dreams of a criminal England, it's all come true with the 1980s. The casino towns, the brothel villages, the cities red with blood and pleasure. Public life the turn of a card, the fall of a dice. The whole country on the fiddle, the gamble, the open snatch, the bit on the side. From Land's End to John O'Groats the whole of England's one giant pin-ball table. The ball running wild. Glasgow, Birmingham, Leeds, Coventry, London, Brighton. Wonderful.[4]

Even out of context, it is easy to see that this apocalyptic vision of decline has nothing in common with the elegiac despair of Bennett's Headmaster. If the end is nigh, well then Hepple will embrace it in a celebration of anarchistic criminality, a dance on the grave of all that is understood as civilization by Bennett's protagonist. There is no place in Brenton's play for either the conservative nostalgic or the liberal progressive. That there is room in Bennett's for both does not help it much, for there is quite simply nowhere to go, no direction that might point a way to the future. If *Revenge* declares itself for the 'bang' of final disintegration, *Forty Years On* promises only the 'whimper' of continuing decline.

The ideological position offered by *Revenge* could be found in many forms in much of the new drama post-1968, but it was not the only version of the state of the country offered by the new generation of writers. As I have suggested in *New British Political Dramatists*, the next sixteen years would see a vast plethora of drama ranging from the consciously provocative *avant-garde* to the far-reaches of consciousness-raising of '*agit-prop*' activity.[5]

> Keith Peacock catalogued the range well in 1991: During the 1970s this radical treatment of history was intended to achieve a number of political aims. These were variously to convince ordinary people that they could be agents of their own destiny; by means of iconoclasm to demythologise bourgeois history; to suggest the reasons why, during the post-war years, socialism had not won the hearts and minds of the British public; to present history in Marxist terms as one of class conflict; and to utilise dramatic form in order effectively to achieve these ends.[6]

A listing of these plays would be impressive and would certainly include John McGrath's 7:84 production of *The Cheviot, The Stag and the Black Black Oil* (1974); Trevor Griffith's *The Party* (1974) and *Comedians* (1976); David Edgar's *Destiny* (1976) and *Maydays* (1983); Caryl Churchill's *Top Girls* (1982) and *Serious Money* (1987); Peter Flannery's *Our Friends in the North* (1982); Howard Brenton's *The Churchill Play* (1974), *Weapons of Happiness* (1976) and *The Romans in Britain* (1980); David Hare's *Knuckle* (1974) and *Plenty* (1978); as well as Brenton and Hare's collaborative *Brassneck* (1973) and *Pravda* (1985). In 1979 Brenton calculated that about 700 new plays had been performed in Britain since 1965 (roughly equivalent to the total produced in the great Elizabethan/Jacobean period 1582–1618). 'Well over half of these would be more than interesting to read and worth staging to an audience now. And what is the drift, the chorus of this explosion of new work in the theatre? It is socialist'.[7]

What is important to stress is that in the 1970s and early 80s it was the various strands of this kind of political drama that appeared to be winning the battle for supremacy, moving from fringe venues to take over the subsidized mainstream in a way that could not have been envisaged when *Revenge* first opened. The significance of the development was well summed up by Brenton when his *Weapons of Happiness* became the first new play to be commissioned for the National Theatre in 1976:

I know I'm in an exposed position but someone's got to go in first and start doing something . . . If the National is to be in any sense national, then it's got to be about England today and that means new writing. You can go on forever as a playwright earning your living in cultural cul-de-sacs playing to 30 people a night: I now want to be tested on a big scale and that means using the kind of money and resources that only the National or the RSC can provide.[8]

What Brenton had in mind in talking then about 'England today' is far removed from the concerns of Bennett as expressed in 1968. In the opening speech of *Forty Years On* the Headmaster had talked of the perpetuation of tradition represented by the continuation of the school, 'this Albion House, this little huddle of buildings in a fold of the down, home of a long line of English gentlemen, symbol of all that is most enduring in our hopes and traditions'. By the end he talks of a no longer secret garden, now invaded by the vulgarity which rips up the flowers and bestrews the lawns with rubbish. We might compare this with Brenton's very different account of the same Home Counties gardens in *How Beautiful with Badges* (1972) – 'Nature? It's all got up by the bourgeoisie. Camouflage. No fishing or boating. Keep out, trespassers will be prosecuted. Barb-wire round the bluebells.'[9] – or with the Doctor's wife's connection between her dreams of a surburban garden and the harsh reality of political prison camps in *The Churchill Play*.[10]

The headmaster's final words are delivered from the lectern:

To let. A valuable site at the cross-roads of the world. At present on offer to European clients. Out-lying portions of the estate already disposed of to sitting tenants. Of some historical and period interest. Some alterations and improvements necessary.

Appropriately, the depiction of the loss of Empire, and the potential loss of sovereignty with the imminent entry into the European Community, is given in the language of the property developer – not interested in the political heritage of the old, only in the economic advantage of the new. The future as seen by the Headmaster, and ambivalently the playwright himself, lies not with the liberal pretensions of such as Franklin, but with the sharp prac-

tices of the new materialism, with the 'unacceptable face of capitalism' as it was memorably labelled by a Conservative Prime
Minister.

Why then start with this admittedly rather slight first stage
effort at all, a play that, furthermore, insists on its connection with
a theatrical world that had supposedly been destroyed by the first
new drama wave of the latter 50s and 60s? Well, apart from its
significance as precisely an anomaly, further interesting facts about
the play's stage history can be added.

As a result of his steadily increasing reputation as a writer – a
reputation that owes as much to his television work as to his
stage plays – Bennett's play was revived in 1984, opening at the
Chichester Festival before transferring to London's West End,
where it enjoyed a longish run into 1985 at the Queen's Theatre.

Popular press reviewers found the revised play uncomplicatedly
funny – uncomplicated because they neither sought nor found any
contemporary relevance in it – treating it simply as a light comedy
like any other. More sustained critical attention was less kind. The
reviewer in *Plays and Players* found much to admire in its verve,
but was not very impressed with its argument or its structure:

> Alan Bennett's first play . . . for all I know, was intended to
> deliver a short, rabbit punch firmly in the neck of its audience
> . . . Today, its strained prurience is likely to give a gentle stroke
> along the funny bone, and not much more . . . the sketches . . .
> seem to shoot furiously wide of the mark, or of any mark that
> means much to us right now.[11]

David Roper's remarks strike the right note – not wishing to first
build up the rather slight play's significance before easily knocking
it down – but they were not representative of the general audience
reaction. There was no consensus that it 'shot wide of the mark';
rather, an ideological predisposition to accept the validity of the
Headmaster's rhetoric. If the response was a little uncertain at
times, this was because Bennett's occasionally unambiguous ridiculing of the man – his confusion between T. E. and D. H.
Lawrence, for instance – did not square with the generally sympathetic portrayal they were being offered. There is little doubt that
Bennett originally intended to write in the confusion – an expression of his own ambivalent feelings towards the world-view that
the Headmaster represents. The particular audiences that flocked

to the revival – a revival, remember, that had started at the very heart of bourgeois Britain, at the Chichester Festival – both wanted and were invited to empathize with the Headmaster's reactionary views. For them the ridicule raised rather different problems than it had in 1968. In this context both the recasting and the timing of the revival are crucial.

In place of the theatrical Knight, the part of the Headmaster was played by Paul Eddington (Franklin in the original production). In his creation of the role, much of the school-masterly authority of Gielgud had disappeared, and his Headmaster was now a far less formidable figure, inviting and getting considerable sympathy. Still absurd, he had become less of a stereotype and more of a rounded character, oozing pathos at every pore. In Eddington's interpretation he became a kind of charming modern Quixote, a little ridiculous no doubt, but thoroughly likable and tilting at now fashionably liberal windmills to the delight of an enthusiastic stalls audience.

By 1984 Eddington presented a complete contrast to Gielgud. Throughout the 70s, which included a London run in Alan Ayck-bourn's *Absurd Person Singular*, he was best known for his work as the wryly professional, anti-liberal protagonist in BBC TV's highly popular situation comedy, *The Good Life*, in which he appeared alongside Felicity Kendal, Penelope Keith and Richard Briers, three other stalwarts of the contemporary West End mainstream. Indeed, his next stage appearance was to be with Felicity Kendal in the London revival of Tom Stoppard's *Jumpers*, and prior to *Forty Years On* he had been in Michael Frayn's *Noises Off* (1982), a shallowly witty piece of behind the scenes repertory comedy that graced the stages of many a provincial Rep and amateur theatre in subsequent years. He was established as a leading exponent of light comedy and was much in demand by many of the writers I shall be considering in the course of this book.

It was entirely in keeping that the 1984 Royal Command Variety Performance (an annual charity-raising spectacular of comedy and music of an unusual degree of blandness, recorded in front of a live audience, including members of the Royal Family, for later television transmission) should have included a long extract from Bennett's play, with Eddington presenting an amalgam of pieces from the Headmaster's speeches. This was the first time that drama had been included in the show and it was presumably in part a response to the actor's popularity; but the appropriation of the role as a comically sympathetic enactment of nostalgia was given a special edge by its placement in this populist screening – made more acute by the lingering resonances of the jingoistic posturings of the British Prime Minister, Margaret Thatcher, during the last sad gesture of British Imperialist endeavour, the Falklands invasion crisis of 1982.

It is clear that something had changed between its first and second London runs. Whereas in 1968 it had seemed something of an historical anachronism, by 1984 many of its ambivalently articulated attitudes towards past values and traditions struck a more responsive chord. That the screening occurred during the miners' strike – carefully presented by the tabloid press as an unpleasant reminder of trade unionism's power to hold the country to ransom, and fought by Thatcher as a virtual re-run of the Falklands conflict – effectively created a political scenario for its deployment. That there might have been a temptation for parts of the audience at the revival to identify the Headmaster's nostalgia with that of the Prime Minister herself for that of a selectively recalled Victorian 'Golden Age' is entirely possible; but it is the past as seen through the eyes of such as Harold Macmillan rather than those of Margaret Thatcher that is really evoked by Bennett's play – the setting of sun on distant colonies, the sound of cricket being played on lushly kept greens, and not the urgencies of the modern world of monetarist economics. So that if it had seemed out of its time in 1968, it should have appeared doubly so sixteen years later – to be enjoyed by audiences who would have sought as much contemporary relevance as had been looked for, say, in a Whitehall farce of the 1950s.

That this was not the general audience response raises important issues. I have posited three kinds of reaction to the revival, and it must be admitted that in my reconstruction of the audience, a properly sociological examination of responses to the play would doubtless have found evidence of all three. I have talked of a popular press reaction, treating the play as an ideology-free play; of a more serious level of analysis, seeing the play as raising ideological problems; and of a general audience response, not necessarily seeing the play as an ideological construct, but nevertheless responding sympathetically to at least one element of the play's ideological structure, its anti-liberal posture and the convenient nostalgia afforded by the Headmaster's denial of class warfare in a vision of national unity.

Now, none of these is in any sense the 'correct' line. A play may be many things to many people, and in the final event is created in the dialogue between performance and reception. But what it is safe to assume is that the majority of the audience who went to see the revival did so with a firm sense of what to expect, of what they would, literally, *make of it*. That this was possible by 1984 derives not only from individual access to Bennett's other work, but from the clear sense that by this date his work could be subsumed into a larger body of work which agreed on a general sense of the function of theatre; and which did so, furthermore, in a conscious stance against the kind of political theatre I discussed in *New British Political Dramatists*. Tom Stoppard once expressed a jokey jealousy to Howard Brenton about the amount of 'denim' the latter attracted to his plays, and the distinction between jeans and lounge-suits is not without point.

What we are faced with then is the growth of two distinct and hostile theatrical traditions, both of which are sufficiently defined to attract partisan audiences whose sense of the social function of theatre is so different as to make them mutually exclusive. The creation of both dates from the late 60s but, inevitably, that of the conservative mainstream has its roots in the earlier British theatrical tradition, whereas that of the new political theatre, with its general distaste for tradition, does not. That a battle between the two camps should occur was inevitable, for the theatres both subsidized and non-subsidized are areas of potential occupation. In *New British Political Dramatists* I traced the rise of modern political theatre. In this book I will consider the recovery, both of territory and of 'health', of the mainstream.

My concern will be both with why the recovery should have taken place and, more interestingly, how the mainstream was historically so well able to fill the vacuum afforded by the effective removal of political theatre from the arena; as well as what forms this new mainstream has taken. The first question is the simpler and will be considered in the next chapter, which will consider events from 1979 on. The second set of related questions are more complicated, and will occupy the rest of the book. For answers to them we will need to first look briefly at the real nature of the so-called 'Theatrical Revolution' of the 1950s and its aftermath.

2

The Gamblers' Den[1]

If you are drowning in a large municipal swimming-pool,
should you question the motives of the life-saver or the kind
of life jacket he throws you? Is a national lottery, which might
provide a few of the many millions needed to bring the great
cultural stock of theatres, museums and galleries up to standard, the answer for the arts? The news that John Major has
asked the Treasury to draw up proposals for such a lottery
indicates that culture is on the Government's agenda – as a
problem which it wants to dispose of in a massive national
flutter. There could not be a better example of the cynicism to
which we have sunk than that this device should be hailed as
a panacea. 'What is aught but as 'tis valued?' . . . The answer
is that culture is valued as a commodity whose survival
should be ensured not through the national conscious will but
the lurch to the gamblers' den.

(Nicholas de Jongh, 1991)[2]

It all starts in 1979 with a General Election, the result of which has
had a significance for British political, economic and cultural life
only rivalled by that of the very coming to power of the Labour
Party in 1945. Indeed, this comparison is particularly apt, for in
both instances the assumption of power was accompanied by a
conscious intent of change that would challenge the otherwise
largely consensual nature of post-war government. In many ways,
the programme initiated by that first Thatcher administration, and
continued waywardly but insistently ever since, was based on the
deconstruction of that post-1945 structure that has largely shaped,
for better or worse, the subsequent state of the nation. Very little
has been the same since, and the British theatre is no exception.
The roots of the theatrical crisis and the direct cause of its continuing malaise must be seen as a direct result of wider government
monetarist policy, as must the particular ways in which it has
developed.

The success of the Conservative Party in that General Election and the formation by Margaret Thatcher of the first of three successive administrations, plus that of her successor John Major, has had momentous consequences for Britain. Of course the problems facing Britain cannot be isolated from those of the world at large, but clearly the particular nature of the government's attempts to directly affect the economic base of the country have created a rather different situation to that in most of the wider industrialized west. The manufacturing base of the country has been progressively savaged – ten years into Thatcher's rule it had shrunk by 20 per cent, and the process continues. Programmed unemployment continues unabated and, despite attempts to doctor the statistics, has reached 3 million again in 1993. The privatization of public state assets continues apace, and what is left of the dwindling British revenue from North Sea oil continues to be squandered. The general sense of malaise is reflected in the uncertainties of the Stock Exchange and the banking and currency markets. The increasingly inadequately state supported areas of education, health and social welfare have borne the brunt of the long period of resultant public spending retrenchment, and to single out theatre as a particular victim – along with all the other national cultural institutions, libraries, galleries, orchestras, etc. – is, of course, to argue a particular case. But to see the way in which the theatre has responded to the situation is to understand a great deal about the very nature of the ongoing crisis.

For, just as the national malaise has proved a selective one – particularly in the first ten years – so too the theatre has undergone a mixed reaction to the changing economic climate. The destruction of the manufacturing base had a far more profound effect initially on the north than the south, and whereas unemployment hit hardest at the traditional working-class areas involved in the older manufacturing industries – all but eliminating the production of steel and coal, for instance – there was plenty of new money to be played with during the first two Thatcher administrations, most of it to be found in the south of the country. And it is for this reason that in this chapter I will be concentrating largely, though not exclusively, on the theatre in London; for the capital city is, in the light of an increasingly centralist government policy, more than ever the heart of both the political and the theatrical nation.

That British theatre through the 1980s was in a state of crisis is undeniable. But it is a crisis with a changing history, and one that has not proved all-embracing. Reviewing Peter Shaffer's *Amadeus* in the first issue of the revamped *Plays and Players* (October 1981) – the temporary disappearance of which is in itself evidence of the essentially economic nature of the crisis – the editor, Peter Roberts, welcomed its appearance at the National Theatre. 'With so many West End Theatres having gone dark this summer or occupied with little more than a couple of actors and a budget set, it is good to see the full panoply of the NT's resources lavished on the spectacle-hungry West End public.'[3] Leaving aside for a moment his enthusiastic embracement of *Amadeus* at the National, Roberts' distinction between the non-subsidized 'West End' theatre and the subsidized sector is crucial. What is interesting is that at this point he sees the crisis as one that affected the former rather than the latter. This was to change quite rapidly.

If it was true that the non-subsidized theatre felt the squeeze of the new monetarism first, it was nevertheless the better able to make the necessary adjustments. Michael Billington in late 1985:

> The language in which we discuss the arts has been debased. We no longer talk of subsidy: we speak of investment . . . The Society of West End Theatres has got its act together and now markets and promotes commercial product with great efficiency. In 1983 there were 37 West End theatres open: in 1985 there were 43. In 1983 gross box-office revenue was £66.5 million: in the first nine months of 1985 it was £69.5 million.[4]

The distinction that Billington makes here between the notions of subsidy and investment in the arts is crucial. The commercial West End theatres of London were, after all, well used to providing a product. They had been doing so, under the control of a small handful of theatre-owning impresarios, since before the 1939–45 War. They were in business precisely to make money, and thus in perfect harmony with a naked government policy that preached loss of public support under the guise of individual self-sufficiency, and an exclusive concern with profit-making under that of individual self-improvement. A theatre that relied on support from public funds to offer a rather more varied dramatic programme would increasingly find itself in the same queue, and with much the same begging-bowl, as the educationalists, the doctors, and the like.

Billington goes on to point to the significant increase in overseas tourist attendance – a result largely of the then weak state of the pound – as a key factor in the improvement in West End theatre fortunes. And this should not be underestimated. By 1988–9 overseas earnings from culture- and arts-related tourism had risen to £6 billion (compared to the £4 billion per year at the time at which he is writing). Of this £80.8 million was directly accounted for by overseas earnings from theatrical performances, a figure which is put into perspective by the fact that the two most important entrepreneurs, Andrew Lloyd Webber (of the Really Useful Group) and Cameron Mackintosh, were responsible for productions that grossed £14.5 and £8.9 millions respectively.[5]

The proliferation of plays by American dramatists in the subsidized London theatres in the 80s must then be seen neither as an accident nor as a result of some kind of rediscovery of cultural connections. The Royal Court Theatre had already embarked on an arrangement of mutual benefit with the American Joe Papp Company, and other subsidized companies soon realized the advantages of a transatlantic link. In 1988, Terry Hands, the Artistic Director of the Royal Shakespeare Company, defended himself in the face of what John Vidal described as the 'experience of having had almost every critic in the land slate the production, the concept (or both) of nakedly courting the Americans' with the musical *Carrie*. He stressed a new economic reality in the subsidized theatre, in which private sponsorship must play a part, as must a more sophisticated awareness of the make-up of their audience.

'Americans make up 17.5 per cent of our audiences. We've been to America 36 times, we've had two theatres built by Americans and I'm not going to sit in a toffee-nosed manner saying that we're not going to do American work.'[6] The much abused production of *Carrie* involved a deal that guaranteed it against loss, put £200,000 into the RSC's depleted reserves, allowed for a 10 per cent investment in the New York production, and gave the company 1 per cent of the box-office take.

Billington's choice of language acts as a further cue. If theatre were to be regarded as a product then its audiences would be its consumers, and as admission prices rapidly rose so the less successful consumers – the unemployed, the low-waged and the politically disaffected – would perforce stay away; and the increasingly better-off audiences would demand a drama that reflected and, indeed, celebrated their financial success.

This is nowhere more evident than in what was the major development in London theatre in the 1980s, the mushrooming of lavishly staged and expensive home-grown musicals which saw London take over from New York as the Musical Capital of the world for the first time this century. Less than six months after Billington wrote there were sixteen musicals on offer or announced in London; six years later there were twenty.[7] It was a development started in the West End arenas that the subsidized RSC and NT were quick to capitalize upon with productions of *Guys and Dolls* and *Les Misérables*. Sheridan Morley that year:

> Musicals always thrive in thin times. What was true for Busby Berkeley in the Hollywood 1930s has been proved true again as *42 Second Street* comes back to us 50 years later. An audience that has trouble finding the money for its tickets nevertheless likes to see where its money has gone, and huge sets or lavish costumes fulfil an escapist need. They also pose no real challenge.[8]

And certainly, looking at the sold-out notices for *Cats*, *Les Misérables*, *Aspects of Love*, *The Phantom of the Opera*, *Miss Saigon*, *Starlight Express*, etc. through the 80s and into the 90s, it is difficult not to be impressed by the magnitude of their success, and still more by the way in which they have come to embody what is now commonly taken to be the point of theatrical activity.

For these shows have but one object, the production of profit. These and other British-produced musicals played, and continue to play, not only in London, but in a number of American locations, across Europe, in Australia, and in Japan. The first four listed above alone accounted for 41 per cent of the total number of seats sold for Broadway productions in 1990.[9] To catalogue their financial success, and in particular the personal fortunes being made by the two most important figures of the new entrepreneurial theatre, Andrew Lloyd Webber and Cameron Mackintosh, is to realize just how important the word 'industry' has become in relation to the oft-used phrase, entertainment industry.

The fortunes being made are colossal. In five years *Les Misérables* has made £1.8 million in profit in London alone; in under ten years *Cats* has made £15.7 million. Average weekly payments for *Miss Saigon* total £46,000; for his directorial work on *Phantom*

Hal Prince draws £8000 in London alone – and he has five other *Phantoms* busily minting it in other corners of the globe. Cameron Mackintosh is reckoned to be worth £65 million and Andrew Lloyd Webber £60 million. And we shouldn't forget the humble touts, some of whom are now estimated to earn £250,000 a year – with profits of £100 per ticket it's a plausible sum – and they pay no tax.[10]

The prevailing tone of all these offerings is one of social irrelevance, of an unwillingness to discuss, or an unconcern with, contemporary political issues. That the lavish account of life at the bottom of the heap in nineteenth-century France, *Les Misérables*, should start life at a subsidized theatre is merely ironic; and, despite its title, *Miss Saigon* is as little concerned with the Vietnam War as its predecessor, *Evita*, was with Argentinian politics. They are what the period has seemed to demand, undemanding product posing, as Morley says, 'no real challenge'.

Where then might this sort of challenge have previously been thought to have come from, and what has happened to it? Without answers to these questions it will be difficult to explain either the presence or the significance at the subsidized National Theatre of *Amadeus*, a play which, by any account, would seem to fit perfectly the formula demanded by the West End. Tim Brown on a 1986 revival of the play:

> Nobody with any respect for money could fail to admire this piece of merchandise. *Amadeus* is the pinnacle of that English export trade you might call Tony Award drama, and the high point of the Peter Shaffer sales graph.[11]

How then had a play such as *Amadeus* found a National venue? It follows from what I have said already that the commission derived essentially from the expectation of profit, but it is not as simple as this.

In *New British Political Dramatists* I traced the development of a generation of politically committed playwrights whose earliest work dates from the late 1960s. In that book I distinguished between two separate, though frequently related, strategies – that of an *agit-prop* movement formulated along the lines of traditional class-based Marxist analysis (and most usually hostile to conventional theatrical venues), and that of a self-conscious *avant-garde*:

It is apparent that this division of political theatre into two camps is no historical accident. Although they share the common ground of disillusionment with, and removal from, Labour Party politics of the sixties, and the 'revolutionary' experience of 1968, there is at heart an ideological separation. The *avant-garde* occupied the counter-culture intent on by-passing the discourse of orthodox political debate, whilst the *agit-prop* groups remained essentially a part of activist class struggle.[12]

From this internal struggle there emerged an increasingly defined political theatre by the late 1970s, intent not only on dramatizing political debate but, more importantly from our present considerations, on politicizing the very institution of theatre itself. Leftist theatre – those more 'purist' practitioners of the *agit-prop* tradition notwithstanding – proved only too willing to move the action from the fringe and alternative theatre circuits and to advance into the camps of the enemy, the subsidized theatres which had been seen at the outset as the entrenched shrines of establishment ideology.

With the greater availability of Arts Council funding and the development of the major subsidized theatres, principally those of the National Theatre, the Royal Court and the Royal Shakespeare companies, as well as the many new provincial repertory theatres and studios that had been planned in the financially rosier years of the 60s, a battle for the middle-ground inevitably ensued – away from the Arts Labs, the Pub theatres, the Working Men's clubs and the University and College studios of the early years of the 'alternative' theatre. The protagonists were on one hand the varied representatives of the politicized theatre and on the other what we can label the mainstream, a perfect latter day product of which would be Shaffer's *Amadeus*.

I use the language of warfare and occupations advisedly, for it was always seen by playwrights and critics alike as a battle for space. Howard Brenton summed up the sense of confrontation well when talking about his 'capture' of the National Theatre to stage *Weapons of Happiness*:

David [Hare, the director] and I regard ourselves and our cast and our production team as an armoured charabanc full of people parked within the National walls – we've brought our own concept with us because we want consciously to use the National facilities to show off our work to its best advantage.[13]

That was in 1976, and for a few years it had looked as though the forces of the left, whilst they were never going to be able to fully consolidate their position, would be able to continue the process of attrition. That same year Clive Barker spoke of the essential contradiction of a left-oriented theatre seeking to locate itself increasingly within the institutions of the establishment, but he did so in terms that still suggested some grounds for optimism:

> Working inside the establishment is always a contradictory process. The basic compromises necessary to present politically committed work inside an alien system will mute, if not silence, the radicalism of the dramatists. On the other hand the system will have to change to accommodate them.[14]

And, although writers of the *agit-prop* tradition such as John McGrath stayed away from the conventional theatres – occasional forays to the Royal Court excepted – others were increasingly happy to be welcomed in from the cold. Another early *agit-prop* adherent, David Edgar, had three simultaneous London productions running the year of the 1979 election; whilst Belts and Braces (an offshoot of McGrath's 7:84 Company), entered the 80s with a long-running West End production of their previously toured adaptation of Dario Fo's *Accidental Death of an Anarchist*, which was seen by an estimated total audience of half a million.[15] Indeed, an impressive list of committed drama in occupation of new territory could easily be compiled, mostly large-scale plays dealing with major public and political issues.

But although it was possible for a committed writer such as David Hare to come to prominence through essentially the same path as a solidly mainstream writer such as Michael Frayn – and in both cases the support of the dynamic impresario Michael Codron was vital – the West End was never to play a major part in the occupation. The Royal Court was able to transfer a play to the commercial theatre from time to time, continuing its practice of subsidizing its other productions – as it did with David Hare's *Teeth 'N' Smiles* in 1976, for instance – but this was not common. It was the subsidized theatre, both in London and in the provinces, that allowed writers, companies and directors the money, space and resources to stage large plays about public issues. The importance of this can hardly be overstressed for, if it then afforded venues for leftist theatre, it was also completely vulnerable when the inevitable cuts in central government-inspired spending came.

It is nonetheless tempting to misinterpret the kind of importance that can be attached to the very visible presence of leftist theatre. There was no time when committed drama came close to dominating the output of either London or provincial theatre, where, when contemporary plays were on offer at all, the predominant emphasis was on safely uncontroversial theatre, conventional both in argument and in format. However, what the work of this new generation of writers did briefly was to complete the process that had been started in the earlier theatrical 'revolution' of the mid-50s of driving a wedge between a serious drama tradition of debate and one that, more and more, retreated into the security of theatre as mere entertainment, escapism or leisure consumption.

That it could do so is itself a reflection of the general tenor of intellectual and political debate in Britain from the late 60s to the late 70s; for, although a new right was quietly coming together, there was, even with the advantage of hindsight, very little evidence of this on a cultural level. The spectrum had admittedly become a very wide one, but the major dynamics of debate remained largely on the left throughout those ten years. And it is for this reason, in particular, that the presence of large numbers of committed plays in the repertoires of the acknowledged locations of cultural excellence – the National Theatre and Royal Shakespeare companies' various stages most importantly – was so significant. Their presence in the flagships of national and international cultural prestige guaranteed a degree of incorporation into the discourse of what remained predominantly an establishment-dominated culture – which is what British theatre has always been; and this in turn produced a rippling-out effect, as these and other plays by this loose grouping of committed writers found productions in provincial, regional and educational venues; and, equally importantly, as television companies were then persuaded to offer commissions that brought the debate to a far larger audience.

From 1979 on, however, the situation was gradually altered. Jenny Topper was then co-artistic director at the Bush Theatre in Hammersmith, a venue dedicated to the production of new work. The 1991 recall of her reaction to the Election result could be repeated endlessly. 'When Margaret Thatcher first got in we sat around trying to predict what would happen, scaring ourselves . . . One of the things we predicted, which has happened, is the theatre has not remained immune. And then almost on the instant people got less emotionally generous. You see how cold they are about the numbers of unemployed, about the people sleeping on the streets – that is a huge emotional shift that has occurred.'[16] The defeat of the Labour Party and the return to power of the Conservatives would not necessarily, in itself, have led to such alterations. And certainly the similar reversal of Labour Party fortunes at the end of the previous decade had had no such effects.[17] For, just as the commercial theatre largely defined itself in a way that took little account of parliamentary struggle, so committed drama regarded the efforts of successive Labour administrations as reformist and irrelevant to the larger political struggle. What was different about the first Thatcher administration, and increasingly obviously so as the first victory was followed by a second, rendered possible by the combined effects of the Social Democratic Party's vote-splitting defection from the Labour Party and the after-effects of the rhetoric of the Falklands campaign, was that the terms of reference had changed.

For the first time since the 1945 Labour administration – many of whose policies leading to the formation of the modern Welfare State were to be especially under threat – the broad consensus of successive governments on how the country should be governed was seriously questioned. The election of a new administration was accompanied by a firm promise to change the entire structure of state; a promise that for once was worth more than the paper it was printed on. The political implications of the new monetarist policy of cuts in public spending in all areas – the health service, education and the provision of publicly owned housing, as well as the arts – were far-reaching, and the first and obvious impact on subsidized theatre was on its potential repertoire. It did not initially have an immediate effect on the kind of plays being written for it. The first impact was on the economic structure of subsidized theatre, enforcing from without a change in the criteria by which plays were chosen for production.

The new administration immediately instituted what were effectively cuts in Arts Council funding at national and regional levels, and many of the 'alternative' companies faced large or even total cuts in subsidy. And it had been the Arts Council that had been the chief source of funding for productions by new writers. Like so many features of the modern Welfare State, the origins of the Arts Council go back to 1945, and the creation of a Committee for the Encouragement of Music and the Arts. From these humble beginnings it soon evolved into the Arts Council, initially under the chairmanship of the economist Keynes. By 1968 rigorous attempts were being made to throw off its elitist tag – although the vast majority of its funding still went, and continues to go, to the perceived major centres of 'artistic excellence', the Royal Opera House, the National Theatre, the RSC, etc. – and a new-activities sub-committee was formed. As a direct result increased sums of money were made available from this period on for more regional and fringe activities, and this had obviously beneficial results for drama of all kinds.[18]

However, this very strengthening of the sphere of influence of the Arts Council has made it particularly vulnerable to direct intervention by a government anxious to curb both the amount and the areas of its patronage. The brief reigns of Norman St-John Stevas and Lord Gowrie, both supposedly sympathetic to the arts, notwithstanding, the message was clear. Culture was a commodity in the market place like anything else and, as in industry, lame ducks would go to the wall.

And lame ducks, both actual and potential, there were as the financial squeeze took hold. At the beginning of 1981 the prestigious National Youth Theatre presented two plays by Barrie Keefe, *Killing Time* and *Gotcha*, at their base in London's Shaw Theatre. As they were performing these plays, both of which addressed contemporary youth issues, Camden Town Council was discussing the likelihood that both this company and the Dolphin Theatre Company, the other user of the Shaw, would have their Council support withdrawn, as a direct result of the loss by both companies of Arts Council funding (a matter of £15,000 a year in the case of the NYT).[19]

In the years that followed the story would be repeated many times. Many venues, both in outer London and in the rest of the country, relied primarily on funding from a mixture of Arts Council and local Council sources. Initially, the effect was worse outside than within London, which not only retained the Labour-controlled Greater London Council still willing to make such support available where possible, but also received from the Arts Council, even after excluding the money given the national companies, as late as 1984 more money per head than the rest of England. Twice as much as Yorkshire, for instance where, in Sheffield, the Crucible Theatre spent the 80s and early 90s tottering from one financial crisis to another, culminating in the resignation of its artistic director, Mark Brickman, in 1991 after just one year in the job, a result of his refusal to accept yet further financially inspired reorganizations of the theatre's production programme. The same year it was known that York's Theatre Royal, the Bristol Old Vic (which had already gone dark in 1989), Richmond's Georgian Theatre, the Birmingham Alhambra, Plymouth's Theatre Royal, and Wigan's Pit Prop Theatre Company were all under threat – as were many others – Newcastle's Gulbenkian studio was about to close; and the Liverpool Playhouse was threatened with bankruptcy and the introduction of the Official Receiver, a victim of the way in which the Arts Council and local councils had been 'encouraged' to shrug off responsibility from one shoulder to another. The chief administrator John Stalker:

> We have lost £250,000 a year in subsidy since 1988. The Arts Council has reduced its subsidy dramatically to persuade the local authorities to increase theirs.

The dilemma was a result of the new strategy of 'parity funding' in which the Arts Council demanded that any subsidy should be matched by equal local funding, a policy that netted £1.7 million in 1990 from local authorities alone.[20]

But such a strategy was in practice extremely difficult to sustain. Local government was put under the same pressure as the Arts Council to make financial cut-backs and, in London even more than elsewhere, the breaking-point occurred in 1986 with the politically motivated demolition of the large metropolitan authorities, recognized by Thatcher as a threat to the government's centralist domination of resource allocation. The abolition of the Greater London Council immediately threatened the existence of both the Riverside Studios and the Lyric in Hammersmith, both of which concentrate on non-West-End theatre.[21]

For every theatre in the country in any way reliant on subsidy, the 1980s were a constant struggle for survival. The Young Vic theatre is a salutary example. First founded in 1970, it rapidly established itself as a forcing-ground for young acting talent and a venue that actively sought a youthful audience. Through the 80s it struggled hard to continue, and certainly would not have done so without the continuing support of the actors Vanessa Redgrave and Timothy Dalton. In 1988 it was still managing just to keep its head above water, sustaining its stated policy of playing to essentially youthful audiences at prices they could afford. But David Thacker, the artistic director, was only too aware of the problems inherent in the Company's policy:

> The affordability of the Young Vic is a bone of contention. There is a relatively small Arts Council grant of £225,000, but up to 90% of the audience come on £3.75 concessionary tickets. Well and good . . . but the trouble is that if your whole purpose is to play to people in this bracket, you have substantially reduced your box-office possibilities. Other theatres with ticket prices triple that will obviously get three times the income if they sell out, so I would argue that if the Arts Council is serious about funding this theatre because they believe that it is important for someone to play to young audiences, then they should compensate us . . . Otherwise we'll be forced to put on plays that don't appeal to the young just to survive.[22]

Ironically, as Thacker spoke in 1988, the Young Vic's studio theatre was preparing for a residency by the country's leading Asian theatre group, Temba. Three years later Temba had lost its South London base after the axing of its £55,000 grant by Wandsworth Council; following the loss of such important companies as Foco Novo after the removal of Arts Council support.

But by this time the Young Vic was itself in trouble. Faced with a £100,000 bill for necessary repairs, it launched a public appeal in 1990. It did so after the Arts Council had issued a statement saying that it was 'deeply concerned', hoping that the appeal would be successful since it had no reserve funds of its own with which to help them.[23]

The Arts Council's response is indicative of a general move away from an emphasis on direct funding, to one on personal fund-raising, and in particular to a reliance on corporate patronage. The larger companies, in particular, were not slow to pick up on the message. By 1992 the Royal Shakespeare Company had organized a three year deal worth £2.1 million with the Royal Insurance Company, the Royal Court Theatre had £1.2 million from Barclays Bank to support their 'New Stages' venture, and British Telecom (a creation of the brave new world of privatization) were stumping up £1.5 million for the RSC touring productions and for the Northern Ballet Theatre.[23] Corporate patronage of cultural events currently totals some £57 million a year, about 10 per cent of the entire budget of the Office of Arts and Libraries, and has resulted in a quite new attitude to the subsidized theatre, which is now dominated by what Michael Billington describes as 'the arrogance of these modern Medicis':

> But the point that hits me is that sponsorship is divisive. What has already corroded sport is beginning to afflict the arts: the creation of a two-tier audience . . . Sponsorship has its uses for funding extra initiatives. But I resent its centrality, its capriciousness, its divisiveness, and its overweening demands.[25]

Billington is writing in response to his own recent experiences in the theatre, but more particularly to the fact that British Telecom had decided to sponsor a commercial tour of Agatha Christie's repertory stand-by of many years, *Witness for the Prosecution*, rather than an RSC tour of Shakespeare's *Richard III*. But the political implications of the enforced presence of sponsorship in the subsidized sector are actually far more serious than those involved in a choice between a lowbrow or a highbrow touring production, and are inherent in the very possibility of outside agencies exercising control over the theatre at all. For, just as the government is able, via the Arts Council, to halt the activities of what might be thought of as unsuitably subversive companies such as 7:84, it is difficult to imagine a multinational company fronting the production of a play that was, let us say, overtly critical of the workings of multinational capitalism.

Meanwhile, as British Telecom was agonizing over whether to promote Agatha or William, Gay Sweatshop, the leading gay theatre company in the country, and the company for which Martin Sherman wrote *Bent*, continued to struggle for its very existence, a result of the Arts Council's refusal in 1991 to consider subsidizing it other than on a show-by-show basis.[26] Billington's notion of a 'two-tiered' model extends to much more than simply the audience. The dramatic world away from the possibilities of sponsorship has become bleaker and bleaker every year since 1979, though there is no doubt that the situation worsened considerably after the third of Thatcher's successes and its sequel, the first electoral victory of John Major.

The urge by successive Conservative administrations to look directly to the private sector for substantial portions of future income has meant that the sponsored production is now a commonplace, as is the increasingly oppressive use of aggressive ad-agency publicity campaigns. Sometimes the two converge. Paul Tyler in 1988:

The Government, understandably, is very keen on promoting arts advertising as part of its policy of encouraging self-help. Under the arts marketing scheme of 1987, a company could apply for a grant to match money which they had persuaded a private sponsor to donate to an original advertising idea. Still rankling, Don Keller [the marketing manager of the English National Opera] recalls how the ENO's tabloid ad was turned down, whereupon Shell decided to finance the whole thing.[27]

The then Arts Minister, Richard Luce, pursued this theme of private initiative against public spending. In the 1987 review of British Theatre, Michael Billington saw little but gloom:

What troubles me is the vulgarity of the prevailing ethos, the assumption that commerce is the prime criterion of artistic value. Richard Luce in a post-election speech said that 'the only real test of our ability to succeed is whether or not we can attract enough customers . . .' By that yardstick, *The Mousetrap* is the greatest play of the century.[28]

At the end of 1988, Richard Luce made available a video, *Marketing the Arts: Foundation for Success*, to accompany a study-pack. It is easy to see that this is not the kind of territory that might operate as a source of funding for a politically committed group such as 7:84, and generally to that entire theatre tradition that had chosen consciously to strive for new kinds of audience. In the summer of 1988, John McGrath indeed resigned from his own 7:84 Company as a direct result of what he saw as unwarranted attempts at interference with production details by the Scottish Arts Council. Starved of funds, the fringe companies are less and less able to experiment. Already by 1985 Martin Hoyle saw significant change:

In some respects the Fringe is merely the commercial theatre writ small, with lesser resources and less access to central outlets.[29]

In the provinces, the regional theatres found themselves increasingly unable to support a company for the traditional repertory season, and more and more use was perforce made of touring companies that were themselves already under direct pressure from the funding bodies to come up with safely commercial products; and then further pressured by the potential host itself, in need of a full house.

In 1988, Bill Pryde resigned from his post as Artistic Director of the Cambridge Theatre, one of the most prestigious Arts Council funded touring companies. His explanation – 'artistic restrictions have made my position untenable' – was by then a familiar one. Robert Hewison:

> For Bill Pryde, the effort of trying to match his company's creative endeavours with the artistic taste of theatrical managers has become too much. He says that financial pressures have made the venues 'timid'. 'They can no longer afford for every show not to be a box-office success, there is no room for artistic risk-taking. I am worried by the fact that regional audiences are not only being starved of new plays, but are not now being offered modern classics such as Pinter or Bond.'[30]

Since then things have steadily worsened. As it became increasingly apparent that the consumer boom that had been generated to ease the third Conservative victory in 1987 was leading into the worst and most sustained economic crisis in Britain since the 1930s, even those possessors of the new money of the early 80s selective 'boom' began to find life less comfortable. The south belatedly began to feel the full effects of the monetarist experiment, and public spending was cut yet further.

The Royal Court struggled through the decade, caught in the constant struggle to balance its books against a shrinking percentage subsidy from the Arts Council. In February 1989 a new play opened in its Theatre Upstairs. *A Hero's Welcome* by Winsome Pinnock was set in the West Indies in 1947, and is concerned with the efforts of its three main female protagonists to struggle free of the poverty that is their joint lot. It proved to be a prophetic theme, for after this production the Theatre Upstairs went dark, and the arena that had proved so important as a testing-ground for new talent – including Jim Cartwright's first performed work, *Road* (1986) – was lost.

It is certainly not the end of what had already been a long battle. In 1984 the administrators of the theatre were talking publicly, and more plausibly than before, about the strong possibility of the imminent closure of both the mainhouse and studio theatres, a response to impending Arts Council cuts. That they were then able to keep going was because of a new financial link made with Jo Papp's Public Theatre in New York, by which the two theatres would exchange productions.[31] And all around as Britain moved into the second half of the 80s there was evidence of retrenchment on a massive scale. Provincial repertory theatres steered increasingly clear of new and contentious work, retreating into safe revivals, and a standard seasonal fare of an examination-prescribed Shakespeare text, an Alan Ayckbourn comedy, a rock opera (preferably *The Rocky Horror Show* or a Lloyd Webber offering), and the most recent sequel to *Equus* as the liberal thematic play of the year was posted in foyers all over the country.

That it was still possible as late as 1983, however, for David Edgar's huge and seminal epic, *Maydays*, to be staged by the RSC at their prestigious new Barbican site, is perhaps as good an indication as any of the time lapse that occurred before the full effects of government policy were felt. But if this was the product of a still very much committed writer, its subject matter is indicative of a great deal of rethinking already being undertaken on the left. For its title not only refers to the historical continuity of socialist history (May Days), but to the International Distress Signal (Mayday). Questioning the entire state of contemporary European socialism in the context of its wider history, it suggested the need for a re-examination of many of the basic premises upon which the play's most developed protagonist, Martin Glass, had first constructed his political world around 1968; at the same time as Edgar and the rest of the new generation of committed dramatists. And when we add to this the play's concern with the movement – dramatized in the development of the play's three main and related protagonists – from differentiated versions of socialist commitment to various right-wing stances, it is apparent that Edgar is himself only too aware of the changing political perspective. Not, however, that the play embraces their moves at all.

Maydays is a play very much of the 80s, in that it points to an overall uncertainty of response on the left, both tactically and analytically, to the new situation. The left, and what of its theatre has found a stage since 1983, except in relation to specific issue-related questions such as the new feminism and the nuclear industry, has found itself increasingly in a state of disarray. It is a disarray, incidentally, that may be more than symbolically dated from the defeat of the long-lasting miners' strike of 1984/5, a battle successfully and bloodily won by the Thatcher government against what had been the most militant of the trade unions. This doubt has in itself caused a weakening in the fervour of committed drama, much of which has looked more to past battles than to current struggles of late.

Generally then, the policy of economic retrenchment for all the Arts has had a sharp and growing impact on the sort of theatre on offer in the country. By 1985 the Barbican, which had offered *Maydays* a home only two years earlier, were staging their sell-out *Les Misérables* in the main-house, whilst a season of plays by Howard Barker, a committed writer who produced a quite dazzling array of work in the 80s, was relegated to the Pit, a rehearsal room only belatedly and inefficiently converted into a studio. The same fate had already befallen Peter Flannery's huge political epic, *Our Friends in the North*, when it arrived in London in 1982 and, even more astonishingly, Trevor Griffiths' first stage play since *Comedians* (1975), *Real Dreams* (1986) was also only offered the Pit.

Griffiths' position in the 80s is instructive. A writer far more interested in the dramatic and political potential of television and film, he found his efforts in that decade almost entirely in vain. The Government White Paper of 1988, *Broadcasting in the 90s: Competition, Choice and Quality*, represents but a further move along the already established lines that see public terrestrial broadcasting increasingly aware of government constraints on the selection of programmes to commission and screen, and forced more and more to bend in the direction of the exclusively commercial.

There has been a marked decline in the amount of television drama, a move away from the televised play to the filmed blockbuster series. And even these are increasingly produced with an eye to the international market. Furthermore, international co-productions, however good in themselves, necessitate the dramatization of general social concerns accessible to a cross-cultural audience, and will rarely allow a directly political discourse. Sponsorship of programmes has become almost commonplace: Beamish Stout, who have latterly been 'associated' with the highly successful, and internationally marketed, *Inspector Morse* series, for instance, have increased their British sales by 150 per cent. And the new entrepreneurial innovation, satellite television – with its heavy reliance on the screening of sport, pre-existing films and regurgitated programmes from the terrestrial channels – has done nothing to encourage new writing. Anthony Howard concluded of government policy towards broadcasting, 'Only in an Orwellian *Nineteen Eighty-Four* society should it be necessary to make sure that only one TV diet is available – and that of popular, uniform pap'.[32]

In a decade that saw the BBC under fire for screening Alan Bleasdale's *Monocled Mutineer* (1986), and the cancelling of a considerable number of productions, including the 'postponement' of Ian Curteis' play about the Falklands War the same year, Griffiths' own experience is perhaps unsurprising. Questioned by Sarah Dunant in 1992, the night before the opening of *The Gulf Between Us* at the West Yorkshire Playhouse in Leeds, the writer listed the reasons why he had apparently been silent as an established voice of the left during the last momentous decade:

> I was working on a play about the ANC in South Africa, I was working on an anti-war film, I was working on a film called *Fatherland*, which was about somebody coming out of Eastern Europe, East Germany, in the early 80s, I was working on *Tom Paine* . . . The fact of the matter is that I made these plays. They were never actualized in production . . . As far as you're concerned I was invisible in the 80s. . . . I wrote a play in the summer, *God's Armchair*, which the BBC did not deign to do because it made a judgement that the people between 14 and 17, the target audience, did not need to know the things I was talking about.[33]

The relegation of his 1986 play to the Pit takes on more significance when it is put into the context of the effective silencing of Griffiths as a writer with comments to make about public contemporary issues. It will help to push the point further. Why was it that the Barbican was unable to offer a place in its main auditorium for the work of writers of proven stature, while at the same time it could stage *Les Misérables*, the original staging costs of which were estimated at £1 million? The answer lies back on the other side of the subsidy coin.

Successive governments' insistence on self-suffiency in business and industry, and on a policy of non-support for what are labelled 'lame ducks', has been extended straightforwardly to the theatre. And this, of course, means the generation of subsidy from the private sector to offset the loss of revenue from central government sources. In the subsidized arena this has resulted primarily in an increasing reliance on corporate patronage, but also in a new kind of relationship with the commercial theatre and its controllers.

At the time of his death in 1990 the Australian Robert Holmes à Court had financial interests in 13 London theatres. He had earlier attempted unsuccessfully to 'raid' Andrew Lloyd Webber's Really Useful Group, already owned two of the theatres housing the current sold-out musicals and was about to acquire two more. Four of those musicals were produced by Cameron Mackintosh Overseas Ltd, and four of them were composed and the rights owned by Andrew Lloyd Webber.

The RSC was only able to stage *Les Misérables* because Cameron Mackintosh agreed to put up £300,000 with a similar figure from Mackintosh's own 'angels'. The RSC's agreement to match this figure was in fact only a notional one, which allowed the company 50 per cent of any subsequent profits for a comparatively small outlay. This commercial patronage not only made the production feasible, but shielded it until it could transfer into the West End theatre – where the resultant long run is the only thing that can guarantee real profit for theatre companies intent on the rapid turnover of new plays and classic revivals.[34]

Now, it is difficult to imagine Cameron Mackintosh and what is now an effective mafia of theatre producers believing that there might be any commercial point in supporting plays by writers whose work would be seen as hostile to the very ethos of such financial activity, and this raises a further point. Increasingly, the possibility of commercial transfers to the West End began to dictate policy in the subsidized theatre. Why take a risk when a suitable market product can be packaged, and the possibility of financial failure hedged by private support?

The National Theatre too is not above such considerations. Alan Ayckbourn is easily the most produced contemporary playwright in Britain. His plays certainly do not need the subsidized support of the National to survive; all are guaranteed a London airing. Such is the new economic climate that the National needs Ayckbourn more than Ayckbourn needs the National; thus his *A Chorus of Disapproval* (1985), for instance, was opened at the National before transferring to the unsubsidized Lyric as a moneymaker; and the likes of Griffiths and Barker have lost out twice.

Not that the commercial theatre has been without its troubles in the last five years. In 1987 it was calculated that a play by Peter Shaffer, with just three main actors and a few extras, would cost approaching a quarter of a million pounds to stage in London; which meant that, in order to attract the necessary investors, not only would a long run be essential but the first three months would have to do extremely good business. That the risk was then taken was, of course, a direct result of Shaffer's proven track record in the commercial theatre, but the relationship between the subsidized and non-subsidized theatre could offer an attractive alternative to taking a risk on a less obviously bankable writer. For about £75,000 the proven classic hit, Arthur Miller's *A View From The Bridge*, could be transferred from the National.[35]

But the possibility of such transfers as a source of revenue for both the subsidized and non-subsidized sector was in itself threatened by the difficulties encountered by the National and the RSC in mounting transferable productions at all. Michael Billington in 1987:

> The blunt fact is that the private sector depends very heavily on the public sector both for its product (16 West End shows currently started in subsidized houses) and its personnel (actors, directors, designers). By slowly dismantling the subsidized structure ... this government is, in fact, gradually cutting off the pipeline to the West End. A depleted RSC, a thinned-out, part-time, safety-first regional theatre, a static Fringe where new ventures stand minimal chance of getting subsidy is not only bad in itself. It is also commercially short-sighted and could mean that in a decade's time we have the worst of both worlds; an artistically impoverished West End producing only mega-musicals and a depressed subsidized sector living off its memories.[36]

By 1990 Billington was able to write ironically of the London commercial theatre, 'I begin to hunger for the days of epic plays with four characters',[37] and already, in May of 1987, the whole of Shaftsbury Avenue had gone briefly dark.

The effects of this unhappy relationship between the subsidized and non-subsidized sectors can be seen then both in the ideological choice of plays selected for production – well-established classics and safely commercial work being at a premium – and in the permitted size of the potential productions, a point that David Edgar made well as early as 1985:

> The danger is that the great tradition of post-war British dramaturgy – that series of plays anatomizing the nation's decline, from *The Entertainer* and *Chips With Everything* via *Saved to Comedians*, *Plenty* and *Pravda* – is in danger of extinction because plays on social issues tend to require larger casts than those on personal subjects.[38]

Edgar has at least been fortunate enough to have three productions mounted at the National/RSC since then – and has thus fared better than most – but the biggest theatrical success of the 80s for him came with the 1980 adaptation of Dickens' *Nicholas Nickleby*, gratefully embraced by the RSC as a considerable money spinner on its American tour.

One of the National's auditoria was dark as a result of underfunding for half of 1985 – surely an unthinkable situation in a National Theatre – and Brenton has been proved largely correct in his supposition that his and Hare's *Pravda* of that same year would be the last large-cast play there for a long while. Almost alone among the writers I considered in *New British Political Dramatists*, David Hare has continued a steady relationship with the National Theatre but, significantly, his plays have been small-cast affairs, considering the political through the ostensible framework of the private and the domestic. Even so, the first of these productions, a double bill of *The Bay at Nice* and *Wrecked Eggs* (for which just four actors were needed) of 1986, was tucked away in the Cottesloe Studio, whilst *Brighton Beach Memoirs* played in the main Lyttelton Theatre – this the new play by Neil Simon, a stalwart of the American mainstream who can scarcely thought to be in need of a subsidized production.

The kind of theatre I considered in *New British Political Dramatists* was intent on using the full resources of subsidized theatre – producing plays with enormous casts, and dealing with large public issues. The overall strategy was concerned with moving the theatre away from the psychological intimacy of domestic drama, enclosed by walls that separated the characters from any larger public or political role and into a vast and epic consideration of historical and political events and issues. British theatre through the 80s and into the 90s has not consisted entirely of a diet of musical extravaganza. Alongside, and usually ignored by the political theatre, there has developed a new mainstream geared to adapt in format to the changing economies of production, and thematically concerned with a middle-ground eschewed by the committed drama. The writers most in evidence both as writers and translators are such as Alan Ayckbourn, Alan Bennett, Michael Frayn, Simon Gray, Peter Nichols and Tom Stoppard, all in their various ways with their eyes fixed firmly on a theatrical tradition hostile to all that is represented by the work of Edgar, Brenton, Griffiths, et al.

This new mainstream is important not just because of the space it came to occupy in the years post-1979 but because of the way in which it sought to redefine the model of serious theatre. It comes from the kind of theatre previously more associated with the playhouses of Shaftsbury Avenue than the major subsidized arenas; from a theatre tradition well used to supplying less financially crippling small-cast plays for a commercial theatre. Now it was to find its historical moment, and with it an increasingly frequent welcome into the subsidized sector with all the resultant potential for enlarging the stage scope of its activities.

The various shapes this new mainstream has assumed, the subject matter it has taken as its own, and the strategies it has adopted will be the main theme of this book. It is a theatre tradition with a very different history from that of the opposing political tradition, and its origins are to be found at the time of the first drawing up of the lines of opposition – back in the 1950s with the earlier modern theatrical 'revolution'. The connection may be made quite neatly by reference to the 1992 production of John Osborne's *Déjà Vu*, a sequel, 36 years later, to the seminal *Look Back in Anger*. In the programme Osborne commented on the link in a characteristically unamused fashion:

> When I see successful revivals of old-time Shaftsbury Avenue kitsch, I wonder why I bothered all those years ago at the Royal Court. But then theatre is a eunuch to fashion, and remains so.

3

Private Rooms and
Public Spaces

The reason why Absurdist plays take place in No Man's Land
with only two characters is primarily financial.

(Arthur Adamov, 1963)[1]

The enthusiasm with which events at the Royal Court Theatre and
the Theatre Royal, Stratford East, were seized upon in the mid to
late 1950s had a dual edge to it.[2] It was provoked by the emergence of a considerable wealth of new writing talent certainly, but
the rush to acknowledge this new talent served to underline the
general sense of malaise that permeated the British theatre. Whilst
there was no general agreement on the import or significance of
the work of writers such as John Arden, Brendan Behan, Shelagh
Delaney, Ann Jellicoe, John Osborne, N. F. Simpson and Arnold
Wesker, almost desperate attempts were made to force these and
other writers into some kind of movement. But what was undeniably apparent was that *something* was happening and that, for
better for worse, a concerted attack on the entrenched values of
Shaftsbury Avenue theatre was being mounted.

What is more, there was a widespread feeling that such an attack
was not before its time, a feeling by no means restricted to theatre
audiences. It was immediately apprehended as a part of a larger
cultural movement, as yet further influence of a new spirit of excitement and risk after the long years of austerity and safety. Indeed,
it was highly appropriate that the ultimate box-office success of the
play that can still quite rightly be claimed as the starting-point for
it all, *Look Back in Anger* (1956), should have been ensured only
after an extract from it had appeared on television. For it would be
via television and the brief renaissance of British Cinema in the
early 60s – with films such as *Saturday Night and Sunday Morning,
Billy Liar, The Loneliness of the Long-Distance Runner, Room at the Top,
A Kind of Loving* and *This Sporting Life* – that this new spirit was to
be most apparent. And, although screen adaptations of stage

successes such as *A Taste of Honey* can be evidenced, it is significant that all the titles listed above started life as novels rather than plays. *Look Back in Anger* itself was better known to the general public as a film starring Richard Burton than as the Osborne play that guaranteed the initial success of the Royal Court experiment. Paradoxically, a turning away from all that the British theatre had come to represent – and towards the more democratically representative dramatic media – was an important constituent of the larger movement of which the new drama was felt to be but a part.

The new drama was rapidly presented by the newspapers and television as but one element in a complete package of freshly articulated attitudes towards class, sex, youth, culture, the accumulation of material goods, social conformity and so on – an urgent stimulus demanding reaction of some kind on all sides. If there were three voices to denigrate – or more likely to dismiss – it for everyone to praise, well, that did not much matter. Whether it would prove in time to be a theatrical revolution or simply a three-day wonder, it was unmistakably a sign of life in an institution that appeared to all those outside the immediate circle of family and friends to be in its death throes.

It was in response to this sense of a new theatrical spirit that *The Observer* announced a competition for new playwrights. When the winning entries had been staged, the plays, including N. F. Simpson's *A Resounding Tinkle*, were published. The competition's organizer, Kenneth Tynan, had long been the most scathing critic of contemporary theatre, and his remarks in the 'Preface', setting out his intentions, leave the reader in no doubt as to how he viewed the situation in 1958:

> We wanted eyes that were focused, ears that were bent, on the turbulent world around us; we hoped to answer Arthur Miller's charge that the English theatre was 'hermetically sealed off' from contemporary life. The idea was to challenge a belief ultimately held by most English audiences, that reality stops at the stage-door and has no business on the boards themselves, since 'we get enough of that kind of thing in everyday life without going to the theatre for it, yours faithfully, "Forty Years a Galleryite"'.[3]

More than thirty-five years on, it is hard to take seriously the claims made for much of the new drama, but it was not surprising that from the outset attempts were made to create out of it a coherently realized movement with conscious aims – and with a consensus on the need for a new kind of theatre, and thus ultimately for a new kind of society. For, although it would be hard now to substantiate this sense of a cohesive movement, it is not difficult to see why the attempts should have then been made. British theatre had become historically time-locked, endlessly and nostalgically recreating a world that if not past was rapidly passing. Tynan's 1954 construction of the main characteristics of the mass of British drama then will serve in place of a deal of laborious and unnecessary analysis on my part:

> If you seek a tombstone, look about you; survey the peculiar nullity of our drama's prevalent genre, the Loamshire play. Its setting is a country house in what used to be called Loamshire but is now, as a heroic tribute to realism, sometimes called Berkshire. Except when somebody must sneeze, or be murdered, the sun invariably shines. The inhabitants belong to a social class derived partly from romantic novels and partly from the playwright's vision of the leisured life he will lead after the play is a success – this being the only effort of imagination he is called upon to make. Joys and sorrows are giggles and whimpers; the crash of denunciation dwindles into 'Oh, stuff, Mummy!' and 'Oh, really Daddy!'. And so grim is the continuity of the thing that the foregoing paragraph might have been written at any time during the last thirty years.[4]

The single most characteristic feature of British drama from the end of the First World War to the mid-1950s was its commitment to an essentially unchanging sense of the social function of 'serious' theatre and of its appropriate dramatic forms. But if this perpetuation of a dramatic tradition had originally reflected accurately enough the dominant cultural concerns of its times, it was increasingly clear that it was not doing so post-1945. Viewed with the advantage of historical hindsight, the theatre 'revolution' of the mid-1950s comes as no surprise.

The earlier drama's resistance to change can be seen not only in its unwillingness, or inability, to adapt to internal cultural and political developments, but in its reluctance to come to terms with external, continental influences. Thus, whilst its *matter* was drawn largely from the environments of an identifiable audience, the drawing-rooms et al. of the upper middle and professional classes, its *manner*, whilst frequently literary, was studiedly non-intellectual. Tynan (again!) may have put the case more vociferously than others, but few contemporary theatre-goers could have mounted much of a lasting defence against his words of 1954:

> The bare fact is that, apart from the revivals and imports, there is nothing in the London theatre that one dares discuss with an intelligent man for more than five minutes. Since the great Ibsen challenge of the nineties, the English intellectuals have been drifting away from drama. Synge, Pirandello, and O'Casey briefly recaptured them, and they still perk up at the mention of Giradoux. But – cowards – they know Eliot and Fry only in the study; and of a native prose playwright who might set the boards smouldering they see no sign at all.[5]

Furthermore, what dynamism the theatre then possessed derived entirely from the brilliance of its wit, the cleverness of its plot organization. It was inward-looking, self-obsessed, reflecting an insularity that was both class and geographically based. Its central concern was with questioning the details of a settled moral order – with the ruling classes of England securely at its centre – and not with subjecting the very foundations of this moral order to examination.

The failure of the theatre to respond to the challenge put it in an increasingly entrenched position. The attempt by such writers as Terence Rattigan to discuss larger social and moral issues was always doomed by the limitations of social locale imposed upon them by the established theatre. The traditional audience was well satisfied with both the level and the narrowness of the debate – but this audience was looking ever more non-representative of the changing order of society. So, however complacently it might view the situation, a crisis point had been reached, and had the British theatre not belatedly moved towards the articulation and analysis of a larger social milieu it would have reverted to the essentially irrelevant cultural role it played throughout most of the nineteenth century – and from which it was rescued by, amongst others, George Bernard Shaw, in the wake of the continental 'revolution' usually associated with the influence of Ibsen.

In the mid-1950s a number of factors combined to (apparently) threaten the perpetuation of this consensus – factors which served, for instance, to move playwrights such as Rattigan and Noel Coward from positions of central importance to ones of passing historical interest within a matter of a few years. As Britain recovered slowly from the effects of post-war readjustment – in the wake of the 1945 Labour government institution of programmes of Social Welfare and Educational Development, and in the direct context of the new prosperity of the Macmillan era – the possibility of social mobility became less a theoretical and more a practical issue. The emergence of a new mass culture, in opposition to the values of a minority, elitist culture, demanded the creation of appropriate models of the new discourse over the entire cultural and entertainment spectrum.

That this was slower to happen in Britain than in the USA is in large part economic, but it stems also from the supreme importance placed on registers of language as badges of class in Britain – a fact only too apparent in the exclusive world of the earlier drama. In the USA, 1955 had been the year of *Rebel Without a Cause*, of James Dean and the growing articulation of a teenage culture; the year of *Blackboard Jungle*, 'Rock Around the Clock' and the start of Rock 'n' Roll. One year later in Britain the very non-adolescent Jimmy Porter, still hooked on traditional jazz, and articulating clearly his regrets for the passing of the brave old causes, was being heralded as the voice of the new generation! The difference is acute. Bill Gaskill in 1961:

> You have to remember that up to 1956 working class parts were always comic, that actors never used a regional accent in a straight part, and that plays did only depict one section of society.[6]

Indeed, much of the early impact of Harold Pinter's early plays, for instance, derived from the deployment of a variety of proletarian accents no longer with the comfortable – and comforting – intention of comic patronage, but with the conscious aim of posing a direct threat to the possessors of the language most usually heard from those people on stage and seated in the theatre. It was an important component in the clash between the old and the new, finding an early expression in Arnold Wesker's *The Kitchen* (1958) and *Roots* (1959), and accounting fairly clearly for the first reactions to Osborne's *Look Back in Anger* – perceived as the voice of the rebellious young against the settled old.

In addition, as the old ties of Empire began to drop away in the early years of the 'Cold War', so Britain found itself increasingly forced to abandon its isolationist position – this particularly after the Suez fiasco – and starting to think of itself as part of a larger continental entity. In theatrical terms this move can be conveniently illustrated by two crucially distinct 'invasions' – that of Epic Theatre, and that of Absurdist Theatre. From the outset the two were seen as ideologically opposed and, once the dust had settled on the immediate controversy, there gradually emerged two defined camps, each intent on fighting for the middle ground – the territory of the major theatres – that stood between them. It was to be a long struggle.

The first of these invasions, that of Brecht and Epic Theatre, dates from around the time of the first, highly influential visit of the Berliner Ensemble to London in 1956 – with *Mother Courage, The Caucasian Chalk Circle* and Brecht's adaptation of Farquhar's *The Recruiting Officer, Trumpets and Drums*. News of the impending visit was given by *The Times* on June 4 in the same edition that announced that public interest in *Look Back in Anger* was such that it was to receive additional performances.

> The last place in which to be insular is the theatre, which is seldom so full of ideas that it can afford to disdain inspiration from other lands, so that is good reason to welcome the announcement that Mr Bertolt Brecht is shortly to bring his Berliner Ensemble from East Berlin.

The prim tone of the announcement continues as the correspondent goes on to quote the Berliner production's programme notes to 'explain' the political content of *The Recruiting Officer* before gratefully lapsing back into the more familiar territory of the contemporary British drama critic: 'Fortunately the production's bark is worse than its bite and the production and playing in Berlin were found to be a delight from start to finish.'

This was not actually Britain's first introduction to Brecht. Three of his works had been performed in the 1930s, and his plays and theoretical pronouncements on a political theatre had been available on a piecemeal basis, and even occasionally discussed in intellectual and political circles, for some years previously. Post-War, a production of *The Caucasian Chalk Circle* had been mounted at Stretford.[7] But the first major professional production of one of

his plays came as late as 1955, with a rather unsatisfactory production of *Mother Courage* at the Barnstaple Festival of Arts –
unsatisfactory largely because very belatedly Joan Littlewood
bowed to pressure from Brecht to play the lead as well as direct.
Productions were at first rare enough for *The Times* to carry an
announcement in September 1956 that the first English staging of
Galileo would be by Birmingham University Guild Theatre Group.
1956 also saw *The Threepenny Opera* at the Royal Court, *The Chalk
Circle* at RADA, *The Exception and the Rule* at the Unity, and *The
Good Woman* at the Royal Court. *Mother Courage* was at the Unity
in 1958; *The Exception and the Rule* was broadcast on the BBC Third
Programme in February 1959. In the same month *The Threepenny
Opera* opened at the Court Theatre, later transferring to the
Aldwych; whilst in June of that same year the BBC Third Programme broadcast the first English production of *Puntila*. In
addition, there were just three professional provincial productions
of Brecht in the 50s, and that is it. It is not an impressive list given
the amount of ink that has been spilt discussing the supposedly
enormous influence that they had.

Subsequently productions – good, bad and mostly indifferent –
of Brecht's plays began to appear with a reasonable regularity
through the 1960s. So that it is not surprising that that generation
of committed writers whose earliest work dates from the late 60s –
rather than, as so frequently claimed, that generation whose
earliest work dates from the mid-50s – should have inevitably
been heavily influenced by both his theory and, more importantly,
his practice. Although as recently as 1974 one playwright of this
committed generation, Howard Brenton, was still anxious to deny
any such influence, an influence which has become increasingly
obvious in his work *after* this date:

> I think his plays are museum pieces now and are messing up a
> lot of young theatre workers. Brecht's plays don't work, and are
> about the thirties and not about the seventies, and are now
> cocooned and unperformable.[8]

Thus, strenuous efforts by critics to fit John Arden's early plays
into an 'epic' tradition notwithstanding, Brecht's direct influence
on the theatre of the 1950s in Britain was fairly negligible, and
chiefly concerned with a new understanding of the use of stage
space – perhaps best exemplified in the work of the RSC on

Shakespeare's History Plays at Stratford and in London after this date. It is true that for directors such as Bill Gaskill, who was to play a formative role in the development of the Royal Court, Brecht's was a seminal influence; and indeed in 1962 he regarded his work on *The Caucasian Chalk Circle* as the most important event in his career to date.[9] More generally, however, Brecht's work was ignored or misconstrued by the British theatre.

Arguably, the main reason for this failure to come to terms with the 'epic' tradition in immediate terms was that an essentially intellectual/political debate about the theory was never properly assimilated into performance. There was evidence certainly of a theoretical debate amongst theatre critics – and even *The Times* carried an uncertain article on 'Piscator and Epic Theatre' on 29 January 1957 – but little evidence of an acceptance into the theatrical canon. What is clear is that the adherents of Brechtian theory totally failed to take into account the very different political and theatrical conditions that prevailed in Germany and Britain. Martin Esslin in 1966:

> The critical reaction to the productions the Ensemble brought to London . . . was on the whole lukewarm; but the impact on the theatrical profession all the more profound. Ironically, however, because hardly anyone in the English theatre knows any German, this impact chiefly manifested itself in those spheres that remained unaffected by the language barrier: in stage design and lighting and in the use of music . . . Hence, the English style of acting already being cooler and more Brechtian than Brecht's own company's, most of his polemics against the heavy German style (and that after all is what his insistence on non-identification and alienation is really concerned with) are totally inapplicable to English conditions.[10]

The predominant urge on the part of politically committed writers and directors at the time was towards social naturalism, towards an articulation of the disaffected voices not previously heard on the stage; a concern with the local and the regional, rather than the larger world-views of Brecht's mature plays. Where the attempt was made the result was usually a version of the large-scale historical drama – Osborne's *Luther* or Robert Bolt's *A Man For All Seasons*, for instance – where only the size, and not the dialectical structure has been borrowed. And in this context the influence of the work of first Arthur Miller and then Tennessee Williams that was beginning to find its way across the Atlantic prompted a further urge towards naturalism.

It is worth spelling this out quite bluntly. Whereas in the 1970s the theatrical *avant-garde* allied itself with the progressive epic model, that of the 1960s not only looked away from the epic but did not even see that as the primary opposition. *Avant-garde* theatre of the 60s defined itself against the dominant mode of naturalism – a naturalism heightened by the increasing importance that television and cinema were to play in the development of drama – and took as its guiding light that other simultaneous continental invasion, that of the Theatre of the Absurd. This, as we will see, though thought exciting and innovatory, could be more easily subsumed into the existing native tradition – subsumed or even subverted.

The Absurdist tradition was far more suited to adaptation by the British theatre, bringing with it as it did an insistence on an essentially non-political content, sufficient shock value to be presented as a novel development and a succession of small-cast and cheaply staged pieces which proved a temptation to even the most timid of managements. Thus it was that when Sir Laurence Olivier eventually put a toe into the water, it was with Ionesco's *Rhinoceros* rather than *Galileo* – which opened at the Royal Court in April 1960, a production of the play having been previously broadcast on the Third Programme in August of the previous year. The Royal Court production played to capacity audiences, matched only by Wesker's *Roots* that year, before transferring to the Strand, which had twice the seating capacity. On June 25 *The Times* reported:

> Ionesco's *Rhinoceros*, in which Sir Laurence Olivier is appearing at the Strand Theatre, had packed the theatre so regularly that it had been decided to extend its limited run to July 30 so as not to disappoint too many theatre-goers.

As well as Olivier, the production had Orson Welles as director, so public interest was not too surprising, but that it should have attracted these two in the first place gives some indication of the way the Absurdists were capturing theatrical ground in the early 60s. For contemporary audiences the Absurdists offered the thrill of the new and the continental within a recognizably middle-class context. The relief on the part of the reviewer for *The Times* on April 28 is apparent when he is able to report that there is 'nothing in the least incomprehensible in the fable'.

This sense of relief is symptomatic of the period, for the Absurdists were then still regarded as a threat to what was taken to be the main concern of the 'new wave', naturalism. It was only in the 60s that the full impact of this invasion began to be felt in the British theatre.

It had all started with the unexpected success of Samuel Beckett's *Waiting for Godot* which opened at the Arts Theatre in 1955 before transferring to compete with the ordinary world of commercial theatre – an event without modern precedent for an *avant-garde* play. Donald Albery of Donmar Productions in 1960:

> I always maintain that *Waiting for Godot* was unquestionably the start of the new wave, better than anything since. It was the first stirring of something new and its nine-month run at the Criterion was unheard of in those days for that sort of thing, not a thriller, or a drawing-room comedy or the revival of a classic.[11]

The point is reinforced when it is realized that Beckett's play took over at the Criterion from a perfect example of the kind of English revue which was to play such a major part in the Anglicization of the Absurd tradition – *Intimacy at Eight* which had played for 551 performances. Throughout the Criterion run, the play continued to be plugged by *The Observer*'s claims: 'it will be a conversational necessity for many years to have seen *Waiting for Godot*.' And all this in the same year that Terence Rattigan's *Separate Tables* (starring Olivier and Vivien Leigh) achieved the longest ever run at the St James's Theatre.

The Arts Theatre had also introduced Ionesco to English audiences with *The Lesson* in 1955, followed there the next year by a double-bill of *The Bald-Headed Prima-Donna* and *The New Tenant*; and in 1957 the Royal Court presented *The Chairs*. The New Lindsey Theatre gave the first public performances of Jean Genet's *The Maids* in June 1956 (based on an earlier private production of 1952); and the following year *The Balcony* (reviewed in the *Manchester Guardian* on 23 April 1957 with a headline, 'New Play Set in House of Prostitutes', the prurience of which sums up well English reserve to these foreign importations) ran at the Arts.

After its successful run at the Criterion, *Waiting for Godot* toured five British cities – an event again without precedent – and in January 1957 The Third Programme broadcast his *All That Fall*. In April *Fin de Partie* and *Acte Sans Paroles* had six performances at the Royal Court, the first of which (under its English title of *Endgame*) reappeared as a part of a double bill there for 38 performances towards the end of 1958. In addition, works by alliable playwrights, such as Max Frisch and Arthur Adamov, were beginning to put in an appearance[12] – the latter making his British debut with *Paoli Paoli*, again on the Third Programme in August 1958.

Now, I have listed these productions to demonstrate one key fact. With the exceptions of *Waiting for Godot* and *Rhinoceros*, the initial impact of the continental Absurdists on the commercial theatre was as minimal as that of Epic Theatre, and a heavy reliance was placed on the Royal Court, the arts theatres and BBC Radio. They were part of a general current of intellectual debate and not initially integrated into the general theatrical tradition. This point is reinforced when we recall that both these commercially successful productions started life in the non-commercial theatre, only later transferring. Their real influence on the development of English theatre came via this intellectual debate, producing from native dramatists plays which drew from but importantly altered their terms of reference.

Thus it was that when N. F. Simpson's *A Resounding Tinkle* was first performed at the Royal Court (as a Sunday play without decor), *The Times* reviewer was able perceptively, and I suspect with relief, to report on December 3 that 'the author . . . is interested only in the comic possibilities of a method that has been used to graver purpose'. It is important to stress this lack of immediate interest in the Absurdists on the part of the commercial sector because otherwise a completely distorted picture of the wider spectrum of British theatre will be given – and indeed has been given frequently in the past.

Absurdism may not have found an immediate welcome into the commercial theatre, but it did immediately find itself involved in a violent debate. It was a debate that was initially located in the pages of the 'quality' newspapers and in such in-houses periodicals as *Encore* rather than in the theatres, but its implications were increasingly to affect the development of British drama more directly. From the outset the supporters of Epic and Absurd

Theatre saw themselves engaged directly in battle. The most famous contemporary manifestation came in the published dispute between Tynan and Ionesco, in which the lines were drawn between a politically committed theatre and an Absurdist tradition that sought consciously to absent itself from political struggle. In his reply to Tynan's original attack in *The Observer* Ionesco was firm in his dismissal of ideological concerns in the theatre:

> A work of art has nothing to do with doctrines.... A work of art which is only ideological, and nothing else, is useless, tautological, inferior to the doctrine which it expresses ... An ideological play is nothing more than the vulgarization of an ideology. In my opinion, a work of art has a system of its own, its own means of direct apprehension of reality.[13]

The premises of this dispute are concerned ultimately with a clash between an optimistic (however problematically so) and a pessimistic (however excitingly expressed) view not only of the potential of the theatre to effect social and political change but of society at large to undergo such change. Although many Absurdists such as Adamov underwent a modification of this latter position – and even Ionesco in his *Rhinoceros* conjured directly with ideology – the predominant vision of life offered in Absurdist drama was of despair, of the impossibility of effecting change in a world which possesses the means to achieve its own destruction. This did not mean that their plays were devoid of humour, far from it as any half-way decent production of Beckett's *Godot* will demonstrate. But the news generally is bleak, and the emphasis is moved away from a social world of communication and public affairs to an inner one of pain and irreversible decay. Ionesco summed up his intent well in *The Physician's Panorama*:

> If the theatre is to be relevant today, it has to be a witness ... of our spiritual disintegration ... [The writer] has to show, to suggest this disintegration, by a language that is disintegrated, by situations that are in themselves disintegrated ... Social reality is that of unauthentic, two-dimensional hollow man. The theatre must turn its attention inwards.[14]

The 1963 Edinburgh Festival played host to a session of the International Drama Festival in which Martin Esslin (who had recently published his seminal *Theatre of the Absurd*), Arden, Pinter, Wesker, Joan Littlewood and Bernard Levin pursued the theme. Perhaps surprisingly, Arden rejected the idea of theatre as a tool of change; less surprisingly, Pinter dismissed completely the relevance of the Chairman's (Esslin) key distinction between the two camps; completely unsurprisingly, Levin vigorously attacked all supporters of a 'committed theatre'.[15] But it is difficult to miss the point that from 1956 until about this date the terms of this debate/quarrel were central to all discussion about a theatrical *avant-garde*.

And that it was principally still a part of an *avant-garde* debate is important. Critical reception to many of the early Absurdist productions in Britain was usually hostile or at best baffled. There are other problems, however, inherent in the relationship of such plays to their audience. Interviewed in 1962 the ex-Absurdist, Arthur Adamov, was able to accept Beckett's status as a major dramatist even though he disagreed with his philosophy, but when he turned his attention elsewhere he was unrepentant in his hostility:

> It is the theatre of Ionesco I am really against: the sort of writing which makes a great to-do about being critical of something – let us say, the *bourgeoisie* – but is actually designed to be TOTALLY acceptable to those it is ostensibly criticizing. A bourgeois audience can go to an Ionesco play, enjoy it, and say to themselves, 'Look, that's us – how funny!' when they should be saying, 'That's us – how terrible!'. They go away amused and self-congratulatory at being able to take a joke against themselves in good part, when they should be shattered at the truth which has been revealed to them.[16]

To argue in this way is to accept that Absurdist theatre, despite all its protestations about political non-involvement, is in fact a political theatre; and that its argument with the committed tradition should be redefined to incorporate this sense of a political difference. And indeed, as we shall see, the British adaptation of the Absurd tradition did precisely latch onto its political potential.

Its initial intellectual attraction was then that it offered a dramatic way-in to a world that might be hostile to the conventions of realist drama but which agreed on the area in which the disagreement should take place. Ionesco's world is indeed a nightmare vision of the life and culture of the French *bourgeoisie*, and its terms of reference seemed attractive to a British theatre audience dedicated to a non-progressive political perspective. Absurdist drama offered a circular, unchanging (bleak maybe but frequently comically so) development of plot. And in so doing it not only influenced British drama, but struck a responsive chord with events that were already taking place in the native theatre. Pinter's early plays were frequently claimed to owe much to the Absurdists, as in this review of his 1959 double bill of *The Dumb Waiter* and *The Room* at the Royal Court:

> What can already be applauded are his successes in finding minutely observed English personages to fill a structural framework borrowed from the continental *avant-garde*.[17]

Indeed, he has always acknowledged his early debt to Beckett but was surprised to be told in 1960 that *The Birthday Party* owed much to Ionesco since, 'when I wrote it . . . I had only seen only one of his plays, *The New Tenant*'.[18] But such affinities, and claims of affinities, are to be expected in this case. A more extreme example will help.

No one I think has claimed that Osborne was influenced by Beckett in writing *Look Back in Anger* – and I certainly do not intend to initiate such a move. But examination of the structure of *Waiting for Godot* does reveal some similarities to that of Osborne's play. If, as been said, in *Godot* nothing happens twice, then in *Look Back in Anger* nothing can be said to happen three times. Two plays which are so clearly different in style and in the theatrical traditions from which they draw, nonetheless share a comparably circular action in which nothing changes, nothing can be done, and in which the articulation of boredom becomes the most meaningful activity of the day. In both cases the characters are isolated from an outside world, Beckett's waiting for something which will not happen and Osborne's for something that possibly already has. That Osborne's characters should do so in a naturalistically realized urban dwelling whilst Beckett's do so on an ill-defined roadside leading to and from nowhere should not blind us to the fact that the two writers share a rhetoric of despair that leaves both plays unresolved other than in a general consensus to continue, to survive. For what else is there? No 'great causes' and no Godot.

It is in this insistence on the supremacy of an inward-looking vision that Absurdist drama found most purchase in contemporaneous developments in British drama. Writing in 1962 about the possibility of bringing drama to a new audience with his Centre 42 project, Wesker used a telling metaphor of modern living in his article entitled 'One Room Living':

> You might say that a house keeps a man sheltered from the wind and the rain, but if the man lives in one room only, then we could safely assume that the quality of that sheltering was a bit mean, a little meagre . . . To have lived and never stirred beyond one room; this to me is desperately sad, this is a lunatic waste of life.[19]

The inhabitants of post-war drama had virtually all effectively lived their lives on stage within a single room. And however much the new generation of writers may have wished to challenge the values of the earlier drama their characters too continued largely to so exist. Pinter's very first play was *The Room* and the dominance of the theme of the invaded room in his work is a critical avenue so well explored as to need no elaboration. The epic tradition proposed an opening up of the action, away from the dramas and traumas of the domestic hearth or the individual psyche and into a world of publicly disputable places. And it is to this development that the new mainstream as it emerged was most demonstrably opposed.

What continental Absurdism offered was a new infusion of ideas, one that allowed a critique of, an attack on even, the conformity and security of its 'respectable' audience without ever threatening the ultimate sanctity of the nuclear family unit with the threats heard off-stage from the large public places of the 'committed' tradition. To deny that this involves a political stance is to twist the concept of politics beyond all reasonable limits.

If, as I have argued, neither Absurd or Epic Theatre at first made any great inroads into the predominantly naturalistic mode, it will be useful to briefly consider the relationship as it developed between 'new wave' naturalism and the drama of the conventional commercial theatre it opposed. In 1967 John Russell Taylor, having heralded the new drama movement of the 1950s in his *Anger and After* of 1962, set himself the task of depicting the development and the decline of the serious mainstream that had been destroyed 'with results both good and bad for British drama today'. His book, *The Rise and Fall of the Well-Made Play*, is an epitaph for the standard well-crafted stage play as it had been developed in France and brought to Britain in the nineteenth century – continually evolving, changing and adapting, until it had reached the end of its particular road under the control of its last masters, Noel Coward and Terence Rattigan. Its final manifestation for Taylor was in the kind of Loamshire play attacked by Tynan earlier in this chapter:

> The well-made drawing-room comedy was above all a theatrical pattern based on a social pattern; essential to its effect was the imaginative presence of a rigid convention of behaviour against which everything done by anyone (in certain classes, at least) would always be measured and judged.

In his final chapter Taylor describes how the theatrical revolution of the 50s has finally destroyed the tradition before suddenly throwing the assertion back at his reader, wondering whether the 'well-made play' really is a thing of the past and going so far as to invoke Pinter as evidence of its perpetuation. 'What else is *The Birthday Party* but a well-made drawing-room comedy complete in every detail, except that the exposition is left out altogether?' Now this is a rather disingenuous remark, as Taylor himself realizes, going on immediately to point out the importance of the removal of exposition. But his next example of continuity is more telling. In invoking Arden, to which he could have added the names of Osborne, Wesker and virtually every other practitioner of the 'new wave' drama, he lays casual stress on a central point. The language, themes and settings of the new drama might be different, but all the new naturalists derived their theatrical structure from precisely the same format of the well-made play that the commercial theatre continued to perpetuate. Naturalism did nothing to threaten the model.[20] A similar point had occurred to Rattigan late in life, albeit rather more sadly:

> It's a bit of a joke to think of the writers whose names were used to belabour me. John Osborne and Harold Pinter, for example. Two superb craftsmen, both writers of exceptionally well-made plays. They'd be annoyed if anyone suggested otherwise.[21]

Taylor's carefully placed reservation was apparently lost on one of these two modern 'craftsmen', however. In a review of the book which allowed him a characteristically splendid swipe at the state of British theatre, its critics and its management, Osborne finds that reports of the death of the thing are somewhat exaggerated:

> The direct descendant of the 'well-made' play (that is to say, where you can point out the joins) is the Hugh and Margaret Williams play. True, it is a pretty sucked-on fag-end to have to pick out of the West End gutter but there are 2 running presently and doing very nicely no doubt.[22]

The two plays he is referring to were *The Flip Side* and *Let's All Go Down the Strand* and 'very nicely' they were indeed doing. In November 1967, after a long West End run, *The Flip Side* was sold for a New York production for a figure approaching £100,000, whilst Twentieth Century Fox had bought the film rights for an initial £40,000 rising to £100,000 dependent on the length of the Broadway run.[23]

Osborne's choice of these particular plays is a telling one, for the husband and wife team had had a steady stream of highly successful West End productions since the early sixties – the ever-ageing husband taking the male romantic lead until his death in 1969. *The Grass is Greener* (1960) was set in the traditional country house and possessed a butler who is trying to write a novel, a Lord who is attempting to run the place as a going concern and a wife who is described predictably as 'younger than Victor and beautiful by any standards'. *The Irregular Verb to Love* (1961) was set in a 'comfortably furnished' sitting-room opposite Regent's Park Zoo, and its plot is set on its pointless way with the reappearance of a mother who has just been released from prison after bombing a furriers as a protest against animal suffering.

The productions followed a traditional pattern, opening out of town in suburban and Home Counties try-outs before enjoying the accolades of the West End audience. The world presented is one which links them with all that had supposedly been destroyed by the 50s 'new wave', and all the emphasis is placed in the acting editions on costumes and decor rather than on motivation. It is a world of wealth, status and wit, all of which are seen as inevitably linked. The description of the setting for *Past Imperfect* (1964) will give a good sense of what is on offer:

A room on the first floor of a private house in a London square otherwise given over to offices and embassies. The room has been furnished by someone of immense wealth and with a knowledge and love of beautiful things. It retains the atmosphere of the eighteenth century despite the telephone, Dictaphone and other office equipment placed on a desk which was once the property of the regent.[24]

The room is that of Lord Flint, an actively anti-Communist peer, and the description places him, and the play, carefully. Although securely linked to a past of wealth, good taste and aristocratic privilege, the room overlooks offices and embassies and is thus in contact with the world of contemporary affairs, both economic and political. The traditional decor is balanced by all the paraphernalia of a modern business office, and we are clearly intended to see Lord Flint not as the impossible freak that he is but as a perfect amalgam of the old and the new. The plot involves the inducement of a heart attack after he has been seduced into marriage by a young (and yes extremely beautiful – in this instance Susan Hampshire who was then 22 against Hugh Williams' 60) secretary, who is in reality a Communist agent. The play allows the Williamses a long digression into direct political polemic in which Magna Carta and the inventor of Rugby Football are invoked in the cause of traditional values; and of course Lord Flint recovers in time to utilize all his charm and wit to woo his wife away from her silly political notions, and all ends happily.

What the Williamses found was a marketable formula which retained the structure and setting of the traditional 'well-made play' and imposed upon it elements of plot which *almost* dragged it into a contemporary world. Their plays always ended with the world put back to rights, the fleeting independence of the female characters abandoned in a sensible desire to comply with the will of the paternalistically conceived male leads. Although the general tone is anti-socialist – the then Labour Prime Minister, Harold Wilson, is described in *Let's Go Down the Strand* as 'that awful Mr You-Know-Who', for instance – their plays flirt with fashionable (or trendy as they would then have been called) ideas, and increasingly so as Britain moved into the late 60s. But in every case the 'grown-ups' were seen, by the last act, to come to their senses and to return to the domestic status quo. *Let's All Go Down the Strand* concerns a struggle between a mistress and a wife, and

The Flip Side is about real wife-swapping. In the later plays there is much talk about smoking 'pot' and a general flirtation with elements of the permissive society for the safe titillation of its Home Counties audience for whom, one assumes, that this would have been about as near as they were to get to the age of Aquarius!

My reason for dwelling on these plays is to stress that they are far more representative of the state of British theatre through the sixties than the adaptations of the Absurd that I shall discuss at the beginning of the next chapter. Other names could easily be added, the most notable of which would be that of William Douglas Home who continued the process started with *The Chiltern Hundreds* in 1947 – a country-house comedy with an aristocratic Labour candidate being opposed in an election by his horrified and Conservative-supporting butler. Somewhat out of favour since his success with *The Reluctant Debutante* of 1955, by the end of the 60s he was a hot property once more with a West End audience in search of a few sexual thrills along with its traditional fare. *The Secretary Bird* (1968), with its struggle between a philandering wife and a witty and older husband, was welcomed by Irving Wardle as an antidote to the *avant-garde* excesses of the experimental theatres:

> In the British Theatre's first month of joyous release from censorship the most noteworthy event has been the restoration to favour of William Douglas Home. 'Well,' remarked one of his converts during an interval in *The Secretary Bird*, 'it gives people a change from *Hair*' . . . Light Comedy in recent years has come to imply opportunistic trend-following and shoddy workmanship: thanks to Mr Home, it has now regained some self-respect. *The Secretary Bird* is a sex comedy, and I suppose it is the sort of thing the Open Space Theatre has in mind in its programme note this week on plays for 'tired businessmen'.[25]

Well, yes, I suppose it was, but it is this kind of comedy, along with the formulaic thriller, that continued to dominate British theatre despite all the words generated by the old, and now the new, *avant-garde*. Versions of the kind continued into the 70s, eventually dwindling into appalling farcical romps – *Boeing-Boeing* and *No Sex Please, We're British* being the longest-running examples. But what the 50s revolution had achieved was a separation of its many and varied activities into a serious and dynamic theatrical tradition, cut off from the bulk of commercial theatre – which, whilst it continued to generate income for another generation of writers, actors, technicians, directors and, above all, impresarios and theatre-owning organizations, had lost all claim to the kind of respectable label of real debate still accorded to Coward and Rattigan in their heydays.

It was to be the work of the new mainstream to bridge this gap and to regain a credibility for the traditional against the efforts of an increasingly politicized *avant-garde* in the late 70s. If their initial impetus came from the world of *avant-garde* Absurdism, their theatrical models were to be drawn increasingly from the conservatism of a commercial theatre that continued to retain the formulaic structure of the well-made play. And in this movement there were to emerge a Crown Prince and a Court Jester – Harold Pinter and Tom Stoppard.

4

Enter the Smooth Men

Stoppard often puts me in mind of a number in *Beyond The Fringe* . . . in which Alan Bennett, as an unctuous clergyman, preached a sermon on the text 'Behold, Esau my brother is an hairy man, and I am a *smooth* man'. The line accurately reflects the split in British drama which took place during (and has persisted since) this period. On one side were the hairy men – heated, embattled, socially committed playwrights . . . On the other side were the smooth men – cool apolitical stylists like Harold Pinter, the late Joe Orton, Christopher Hampton, Alan Ayckbourn, Simon Gray and Stoppard.

(Kenneth Tynan, 1977)[1]

When Harold Pinter's first full-length play, *The Birthday Party*, was first staged at the Lyric, Hammersmith, in May 1958 it limped out of the theatre after less than a week with total box office receipts of just over £250. The lack of public interest was paralleled by the press reactions to the piece, at best baffled and more usually hostile. However, what critical attention the play did receive placed it firmly within an English version of the Theatre of the Absurd, the names of both Beckett and Ionesco being frequently invoked. *The Times* commented on May 21, 'This essay in surrealistic drama . . . gives the impression of deriving from an Ionesco play which Mr Ionesco has not yet written'.

The new school was soon to be peopled with other writers. The following day *The Times* reviewed John Mortimer's first stage productions (a double bill that had moved from the Lyric to the Garrick to make way for Pinter's play):

What Shall We Tell Caroline . . . is more intricate and perhaps even more successful [than *The Dock Brief* which accompanied it], exploiting further a happy vein of almost Ionesco-like inconsequence; indeed, in its tragi-comic reflections on married life it has some resemblances to *The Bald-Headed Prima-Donna*.

The linking of these playwrights may seem somewhat perverse, but by September 24 of that year *The Times* was confident enough to publish an article on the new theatrical 'school'. The writer talks of the new school as being in opposition to the prevalent mode of naturalism – citing Osborne, Peter Shaffer and Robert Bolt as his examples – setting against it a 'comedy of menace' deriving from the influence of Ionesco and including in its ranks Mortimer, David Campton, Simpson and Nigel Dennis. 'Its main distinguishing feature is the spectacle of a violent or extraordinary action involving characters who fail to notice anything queer going on.'

It is possible to detect a certain strain in the yoking together of these various writers, and certainly Pinter and Simpson do not sit very easily together. Whereas Pinter's early work is tight and economical, that of Simpson is unwieldy and awkward. The free-wheeling nonsense of Mr and Mrs Paradock in *A Resounding Tinkle* (1958) proclaimed a piece that was certainly not in the well-made play tradition, and this was followed by a number of shorter plays, including *The Hole* (1958) and *The Form* (1961), but is perhaps best seen in the full-length *One Way Pendulum* (1959) – in which Kirby Groomkirby continues throughout in a vain attempt to train his collection of weighing-machines to sing the 'Hallelujah Chorus' despite all the domestic disruption attendant on his house being converted into a court room for his trial for a series of murders carried out because he likes wearing black.

What then does *The Times* reviewer nave in mind? Well, the generic description, 'comedy of menace', is borrowed from that used by David Campton to describe his *The Lunatic View* of the previous year. The piece had started life at the Library Theatre, Scarborough – where Alan Ayckbourn started his theatrical career, even starting an unsuccessful collaboration with Campton on a children's play, *Dad's Tale*.

The Lunatic View is a four-piece comedy, each self-contained 'lunatic view' concerned with a vision of a progressively disintegrating world. The first, 'A Smell of Burning', is concerned with the minutiae of breakfast time in the household of Mr and Mrs Jones, and it is easy to spot the influence here of *The Bald Prima-Donna*, both in the flatness of their speech and in their shared obsession with the details of their diet:

Jones: The eggs were all wrong this morning.
Mrs Jones: They couldn't have been dear . . .

Jones: Soft boiled. Very, very soft. Pop them into very hot water. Leave them for just two minutes. Then test them. Watch the water drying on the shell. If it dries very, very slowly, they're not done enough. If it dries very, very fast – you've jiggered them again.

Mrs Jones: There was nothing wrong with your eggs this morning.

Jones: Like bullets.

Mrs Jones: There was nothing wrong with your eggs this morning . . .

Jones: Prove it!

Mrs Jones: You had haddock.[2]

And through this presentation of petit-bourgeois absurdity we can look of course to the opening breakfast of Pinter's *Birthday Party*, and beyond that to the derivative meal at the start of Joe Orton's first (radio) version of *The Ruffian on the Stairs* (1964).[3] Into this domestic scene Campton intrudes a minor official from the Town Hall who, without explaining his presence, orders the pair to provide first a hatchet and then a length of strong rope. The couple continue unconcerned, introducing into the dialogue supposedly unconnected snippets from the outside world via their reading of the newspaper – the Hungarian uprising, riots in Cyprus, the Algerian revolution, nuclear missile tests. Meanwhile, a series of explosions are heard and we learn that the Town Hall has been burnt down and the Gas Works blown up. The official, Robinson, discovers that he is in the right house and checks on the drop from the kitchen-window before leading Mrs Jones out. Shortly after he returns in satisfaction, the unquestioning bureaucrat having completed his task:

Robinson: Robinson. You could hardly tell me apart from several million other Robinsons. I go to work at nine, and finish at five-thirty. I live in a semi-detached villa with a small garden in front. I am fond of gardening . . . I am also fond of dogs. I observe the correct holidays. I am not a deep thinker: it is so much better to believe almost everything I am told. I believe there is no such place as home, and beer is best, and the sun never shines on the British Empire.

This depiction of parodied conformity delivered – the term 'semi-detached villa' here being a cue to an expected response, as we will see – he removes a piece of symbolically burnt toast and leaves, musing as he goes, 'Strange that you never notice what is happening'. It scarcely needs the now lone Jones' final words, the repeated 'there ought to be a warning bell', to tell us that we are here faced with a fusion of anti-bourgeois satire and a related anti-bomb message. This conjunction is elaborated in the next two pieces before we come to 'Them' which is set in initial darkness with the moon rising. The two characters, a teacher of physics and higher mathematics and the current Miss Europe, spend the entire scene with their heads covered by paper bags as instructed, believing themselves to be the sole survivors of the post-nuclear holocaust world that we are now clearly in.

It is not then difficult to understand what Campton intended by his phrase 'comedy of menace'. What is less clear is how this could be linked to the rambling excesses of *A Resounding Tinkle*; and, even more surprisingly, the kind of menace on offer in Pinter's early plays. For, although there is a common theme of domesticity disrupted, Campton's play has a centrally conscious and explicit political intent in a way that the work of the other writers cited does not.

Indeed, *The Times* review of *A Resounding Tinkle* (first produced at the Royal Court as a Sunday performance without decor) on 18 September 1957 was able to make the distinction quite easily: 'the author . . . is interested only in the comic possibilities of a method that has been used to graver purpose'. But despite the evident differences the attempt to define a new school became evermore apparent. On 4 January 1960, the same newspaper talked of John Mortimer's announced *The Wrong Side of the Park* as 'one of the most important productions of the New Year', only then going on to talk of the coming double bill of Pinter's *The Dumb Waiter* and *The Room* as by 'another young dramatist . . . well-known to a wide public through his brilliant contributions to the revues *Pieces of Eight* and *One to Another* and also as the writer of *The Birthday Party*'. But two years later the emphasis had been quite altered.

On 22 July 1960 *The Times* set out to put the record straight in a general article on the state of the theatre:

> Two years ago *The Birthday Party* was thought so obscure that the critics despaired of it; today *The Caretaker* is a solid commercial hit, and Mr Pinter, without concessions, one of our most popular television dramatists. Not so long ago *A Resounding*

Tinkle was one of the Royal Court's less patronized ventures; this year *One Way Pendulum* became a notable West End success.

Phrases like 'commercial hit', 'popular television dramatist' and 'West End success' point to the way in which this new drama was beginning to make inroads into the commercial arena, although the writer is still at pains to argue in *avant-garde* terms, insisting on Ionesco and Beckett as a way of approaching Pinter and Simpson's work. But in the same year, David Parry's *Stuff and Nonsense* and *The Trouble With Our Ivy* was seen to be influenced by Pinter, as was Desmond McCarthy's *The Waiting Room* the following year: 'it is . . . rather as though several of Pinter's characters had been set loose in the fog-bound waiting-room from *The Ghost Train*'.[4]

By 1961 the school was sufficiently well established for *The Times* of July 6 to talk of Arthur Kopit's new play at the Lyric Hammersmith, that had first housed *The Birthday Party*, as a parody. 'The full title of what appears to be intended as a hilarious skit on the Ionesco school of Playwrights is *Oh Dad, Poor Dad, Mumma's Hung You In the Closet And I'm Feelin' So Sad*'. The term 'Ionescoique' had been coined in France in 1958, but by now 'Pinteresque' had joined the critical vocabulary and, after the success of *The Caretaker* (which opened at the Arts Theatre in April 1960 before transferring to the Duchess) there is a clear sense of this new school as having Pinter at its head.

He was actually to share a billing with Campton and James Saunders in 1961, under the general title *Counterpoints*, as indeed he did with many of the other writers who were increasingly confidently identified as part of his 'school'. Already in 1960 the revue *One To Another* had consisted of two pieces by Simpson ('Gladly Otherwise' and 'Can You Hear Me?'), four by Mortimer ('Triangle', 'Cleaning Up Justice', 'Collector's Piece' and 'Conference'), as well as two by Pinter himself ('The Black and the White' and 'Trouble in the Works').

Interestingly, his contribution to *Counterpoints* was *A Night Out* – the nearest Pinter had then got to writing a naturalistic play – which had already been screened on BBC Television the previous year when it had been the most watched programme of the week with an estimated audience of about 18 million. It was his work as a contributor to that traditional English theatrical form, the revue, and to the coming medium, television – and not his work for the stage – that really brought early recognition for Pinter.

An important distinction needs to be made, however. What all Pinter's early plays have in common is the vigorous deployment of a language that is not that of the middle classes who populate just about all of the other plays, or of the audiences that watched them. Robert Kidd in 1970 applauded Pinter 'for his raids on the resources of the British-English language . . . For almost the first time, vernacular English – meaning working class English – started to appear outside (so to speak) quotation marks'. The one exception amongst his early plays was *A Slight Ache* of 1961 which was originally part of a triple bill with pieces by Simpson and Mortimer. Here the characters are of the middle classes whose angst would form the staple diet of all Pinter's work after *The Homecoming* (1965, RSC at the Aldwych), and versions of which almost entirely account for the variety of characters in the work of the playwrights with whom he was associated. It is this middle area of the social milieu that would become the exclusive concern of the English Absurdists, and which would be picked up again as the mainstream regrouped post-1979.

In the second half of the 60s Joe Orton was virtually alone in continuing an adaptation of the Absurdist tradition that retained any real sense of menace. The influence of Pinter on his early work was always apparent – one of the most comic instances of the influence coming with the opening of the 1966 television play, *Funeral Games*, where the detective, having broken into the house of a defrocked priest, announces to its surprised occupant, 'My name is Caulfield. I've broken into your house'.[5] But, by the time of *The Homecoming*, Orton saw his own *Entertaining Mr Sloane* as an influence on Pinter.[6] The finest embodiment of Orton's deployment of menace in the Absurdist tradition was in *Loot*, which properly played is not the easy comic romp that it is too frequently taken for. As Charles Marowitz rehearsed its first production in 1966, Orton's stage version of *The Ruffian On The Stairs* – a play heavily indebted to Pinter's early work – was staged as half of a Royal Court Sunday bill with Howard Brenton's *It's My Criminal*. *The Times* review of Brenton's play on August 22 serves perhaps too well to demonstrate how, by now, almost any new development in the theatre would be fitted into the established school. In any account of his work, the figure of Beckett would not loom large, but the reviewer is undeterred:

Brenton seems to be suggesting that to wait for Godot is a foolish waste of time because Godot is only a meaningless heap of blankets in an invalid chair, and that anyhow, those who wait for him do not know what they want from him. This seemed to be what Mr Brenton was telling us, but as his symbols were provided with no ascertainable relationship to life, he may have meant something quite different.

Now, I have made such use of *The Times* partly because it was then virtually the only British newspaper to consider the contemporary theatre in any real detail; but mostly because of the way in which it reflects the voice of the establishment – which is exactly how *The Times* saw itself – coming to terms with something potentially dangerous, and recognizing with relief that the movement could be contained and incorporated back into the terms of the official, politically non-radical, discourse.

The easiest way of pointing to the significance of this distinction is to turn eastwards, to see how Absurdism was transmuted behind the 'Iron Curtain'. As part of the 1964 World Theatre Season at the Aldwych, The Polish Contemporary Theatre Company included a double bill of Slavomir Mrozeck's *What A Lovely Dream* and *Let's Have Fun*. Interestingly, that same year his *Tango* was published in an English version adapted by Tom Stoppard. *The Times* reviewer of May 5 duly noted the affinities of the double bill to Ionesco and Pinter, but rightly saw no political significance in the pieces: 'The plays move along with an acrobat's frightening sure-footedness along the tightrope on one side of which is comic fantasy and on the other callously observed black comedy.'

And indeed it is hard not to believe that permission had been granted for the cultural exportation of these productions precisely because the Polish government thought they were so politically safe. But such plays did nevertheless go against the still officially 'encouraged' mode of socialist realism and, although Absurdism took longer to take root in the eastern bloc, once it had done so it developed in quite a different way from its British counterpart.

The following year *The Times* carried an article on a season of plays by Ionesco and Beckett at the Theatre of the Balustrade in Prague. Noting that 'the Czech public had to wait for Godot for more than a decade', the writer went on to talk of the very recent emergence of a 'home-grown, yet strangely vigorous Theatre of the Absurd'.[7] The work of John Grossman at the Balustrade was examined in more detail later that year, and a breakaway from the strict didactism of socialist realism observed. That is to say, that by 1965, versions of Absurdism constituted an important part of the counter-movement to official state culture in a way that was never to be the case in Britain. 'The Stalinist theatre addressed itself to abstract man. The problem was that abstract man did not go to the theatre.'[8]

It was at the Balustrade Theatre that John Grossman directed Vaclav Havel's first staged play, *The Garden Party*, in 1963 – the same year that Tom Stoppard, for whom Havel was later to assume such importance, saw his first work on stage. *The Garden Party* was a perfect example of Absurdism with a specifically political slant, its plot being concerned with the struggle between Hugo, a chess-playing fanatic, and his bourgeois parents who want him to find a career in the world of public bureaucracy. Having successfully conned his way into the Liquidation Office, he is quickly put in charge of its liquidation, and ends the play the perfect bureaucrat but mad.

Unlike for instance Romania, both Poland and Czechoslovakia began to develop an Absurdist tradition with a directly political intent, albeit one usually and necessarily disguised. This was particularly true of the latter country as it moved towards the troubles and the tanks of 1968. 1965 saw Havel's *The Memorandum* performed, and the following year *The Times* was able to report on a 'wind of change in the Czech theatre',[9] leaving its readers in no doubt about the link between the use of the Absurdist tradition to satirize and attack the bureaucratic machinery of state government and the larger urge for reform. One year after the 1968 uprising Irving Wardle talked of the way in which the new Czech drama had been able to offer an oblique criticism of oppression in a way undreamt of by Ionesco:

> Politics are inseparable from the rest of life - and from the sense of history: and any piece that seems to refer to the Russians will probably relate equally to the Hapsburgs and the Nazis. It is a theatre of allegory, metaphor and double meaning.[10]

This sense of the adaptability of the historical drama is made tellingly in Tom Stoppard's *Cahoot's Macbeth* (1979). The Cahoot of the title refers to the Czech playwright Pavel Kahout, who had been forced underground after the Russian tanks invaded in 1968, and Stoppard's play is, amongst other things, an enactment of the circumstances of performance of his work. A private performance of Shakespeare's play in a Czech flat is interrupted by the arrival of a secret policeman who is in no doubt about the subversive potential of the event: 'The fact is, when you get a universal and timeless writer like Shakespeare, there's a strong feeling that he could be spitting in the eye of the beholder when he should be keeping his mind on Verona . . . The chief says he'd rather you stood up and said, "There is no freedom in this country", then there's nothing underhand and we all know where we stand. You get your lads together and we get our lads together and when it's all over, one of us is in power and you're in gaol. That's freedom in action. But what we don't like is a lot of people being cheeky and saying they are only Julius Caesar or Coriolanus or Macbeth. Otherwise we are going to start treating them the same as the ones who say they are Napoleon.'

If History plays, one of the staple diets of Eastern European theatre, could be used in this way, then the Theatre of the Absurd offered even more inviting possibilities. The Absurdist tradition as it belatedly developed there placed an increasing emphasis on the dramatic sense of menace to the individual from the agents of the state (where the History plays could be interpreted as being about the fact of external Soviet invasion of the state as a whole). Its rooms were not invaded by isolated individuals but by representatives of the not always clearly defined authorities with absolute power of life and death. Its literary precursor was Kafka more than Ionesco, and its terms of reference were in stark contrast to the supposedly apolitical stance of its Western counterpart.

As early as 1960, the Polish writer Tadeusz Rozewicz's first play, *The Card Index*, can be seen to be looking directly towards the Western tradition, the Chorus of Elders even intervening at one point to complain that nothing is happening on stage:

> But even in a Beckett play
> someone talks, waits, suffers, dreams,
> somebody weeps, dies, falls, farts.
> If you don't move the theatre is in ruins.[11]

The play's 'hero' is confronted by a series of figures from his past – parents, an ex-mistress, former teachers, etc. – all them vainly attempting to make sense of his life, to provide material for a complete card index (a perfect image of pre-computerized bureaucratic organization) that will have him properly located and accounted for. The text as published had no obvious political content, other than as that of the struggle of a bohemian ne'er-do-well against the representatives of bourgeois society, but the frequent intrusion into his room of unexplained and menacing men must always have allowed a link to be made by audiences with a world of secret police.

This kind of connection was almost never made in English adaptations of the Absurd. A rare exception could be seen in Orton's *Loot* (1967) when Inspector Truscott calls on the suspected Hal, but even here the fact that the policeman is disguised as an official from the Gas Board moves the action nearer to farce than the menace intended by Orton:

> Truscott: (*shouting, knocking* Hal *to the floor*) Under any other political system I'd have you on the floor in tears!
> Hal: (*crying*) You've got me on the floor in tears.[12]

As early as 1963 Martin Esslin cites Rozewicz as one of a number of writers who have created a Polish drama that could 'express political comment in a suitably oblique way'; and certainly by 1980, when I saw a gripping production of the play in Lodz shortly before the declaration of the State of Emergency had driven Solidarity underground, the response indicated that the general allegorical thread of the play would only too easily yield a more material explanation for an audience for whom the arrival of unexplained officials in search of documentation held very different connotations.

In stark contrast, English Absurdism as it emerged in the early 60s placed the emphasis entirely on the comic disruption of bourgeois conformity, and in particular on satirical enactments of the extremities of consumerism – the meaningless drudgery of work as a means to the acquisition of status achieved through the purchase of more and more material goodies. The genesis of Stoppard's *If You're Glad I'll be Frank* (1966) was as a commission for a half-hour radio play as part of a BBC series, *Strange Occupations*, about real or imaginary absurd jobs. It gave Stoppard the idea of a piece predicated on the notion that the telephone time service, TIM, was not a recording but delivered live by a woman trapped at the other end of the phone; and to this could be added Stoppard's consideration of the plight of the man endlessly repainting 'the fourth biggest single-span double-track shore-to-shore railway bridge in the world bar none' in *Albert's Bridge* (1967). Both these early plays are very much in the spirit of theatrical developments in the earlier part of the decade.

The suburban location that was shortly to become Alan Ayckbourn's particular territory was the one most favoured by the English Absurdists intent on the satirization of the aspirations of upward mobility of the new middle classes. One of the most successful of the kind was Giles Cooper's *Everything in the Garden* (1962) which questions the function of work in relation to material status in an extreme manner. Bernard and Jenny Acton are a young married couple, obsessed as always with the acquisition of material goods. To help, Jenny takes a job in a brothel, an occupation it transpires that is shared by all the neighbouring wives. Upon discovering what his wife is about, the husband is at first horrified, but is only too easily reassured:

Jenny: There'll be enough for a new car next week. Two if we did one on H.P.
Bernard: There's no . . . I don't believe it.
Jenny: No what?
Bernard: No room in the garage. How could you do such a thing?[13]

This is by no means an isolated instance of the kind, but a few further examples will have to suffice. In 1960 David Parry's *The Trouble With Our Ivy* was first produced at Hornchurch before transferring to the West End. The central action is concerned with the Chard family's growth of a monster ivy plant in their front garden, an activity planned to block the sunlight from the house of their snobbish neighbours, but one which eventually culminates in the destruction of the entire suburban neighbourhood. This attack on the values of the world of the semi-detached was also to be found in T. M. P. Frisby's aptly titled *The Subtopians*, first produced in 1961, but is probably most excitingly seen in David Turner's *Semi-Detached* of 1960, where amongst other things to crop up in a crowded plot the boyfriend is invited to choose between staying in the semi-detached of the girlfriend's parents and continuing his improvements of the father's model railway-set or running away with her. In talking about the play, Turner twice applies the word 'absurd' to his depiction of the kind of world of suburbia where a man might put down a red drive just to annoy his neighbour:

> I can't reject it lock, stock and barrel and comfort myself with thinking that what I have rejected is wholly deadening and worthless, because I know it isn't. Of course it is absurd, but at the same time it is perfectly serious and worthwhile: it's a matter of what angle you see it from. I see it from both angles at the same time. I accept the paradox and I think I even recognize the truth about myself and the world I live in (and even as I say this I see that the assertion is both true and absurd).[14]

These examples of the domesticization of the harsher edges of continental Absurdism will serve well enough to illustrate the way in which versions of the well-made play initially resurfaced as more serious alternatives to the standard West End fodder in the early 60s. Such plays had in one sense found precisely what the Royal Court craved from the outset, a new kind of audience. But it was one that was less interested in real social change than in seeing its own more humbly middle-class preoccupations enacted on stage – rather than the genteel drawing-rooms of the leisured class of earlier drama. The new audiences were more representative of the wider social base but they were still a part of an established status quo. It was just that the centre of power had in some respects moved slightly downwards. Offering a safe opposition to consumerist values, the attack undertaken by these plays was a cosy one, not threatening the premises of the world it portrayed, simply satirizing some of its dafter manifestations; presenting a mirror, as Jonathan Swift had written many years earlier, in which people might see every face but their own! The bleakness of Beckett's vision was transmuted into surburban banality.

Through the 70s this portrayal moved further and further away from the satiric. Kevin Laffan's *It's a Two-Foot-Six-Inches-Above-the-Ground World* of 1970, for instance, was a comedy, but a comedy in which the domestic problems of contraceptive debate in a Catholic household could receive due consideration. Peter Nichols' *Chez Nous* of 1974 continued his quasi-biographical journeying to the domestic problems of contemporary English settlers in France, and so on.

In this context, it is important to realize the extent to which television was to play a major part in this development. Peter Nichols is now thought of as very much a stage writer, but before the success of *A Day in the Death of Joe Egg* (1967) his output had been entirely concerned with the small screen, where with Granada, ATV and the BBC he had already had 12 plays produced. These three companies, and in particular the BBC with its 'Wednesday Play' series (started in 1963 and continued from 1970 under the title of 'Play for Today') had presented an impressive collection of drama which, if it had a single common link, stressed the need to use the medium as a way of examining the social and domestic issues of contemporary society. It was a philosophy that is perhaps best remembered for Jeremy Seaford's *Cathy Come Home* of 1966 (a play whose screening resulted in the formation of the housing action group Shelter), but is more typically represented by plays like Nichol's *Hearts and Flowers* (BBC, 1970), which is concerned with the domestic turmoil surrounding a family funeral.

The 'Wednesday Play' was certainly more prepared to look unsatirically at the lives of ordinary people than was the English stage at the time, but it was to become an important spawning-ground for writers who would later turn to the stage with a series of dramas of domestic life (as well as Nichols, Michael Frayn made his dramatic debut on television, and the medium was also instrumental in promoting the work of writers such as Simon Gray and John Mortimer). The three companies also played a large part in expanding the geographical base of contemporary drama, with an insistence that there were lives to be examined outside of the metropolis which would be considered because television viewers could not be conveniently marginalized in the way that theatre audiences could. And this connects directly with the major theatrical development of the late 60s and early 70s; the creation of a series of new provincial theatres intent not only on simply replaying past London successes, but on establishing a relationship with their own regional cultures, attempting (with greater or lesser success) to encourage local writers and offering plays with direct regional relevance.

I have already talked about the connection between the Stephen Joseph Theatre at Scarborough and Campton's *The Lunatic View*, and to this could be added, for instance, James Saunders' *Alas Poor Fred* (1960), 'a duologue in the style of Ionesco' as it was described by its author, which was also produced at Scarborough. The point of the connection is both general and specific.

General: in that it is obvious that a theatrical kind that concentrated so relentlessly on the world of the suburbs and provinces was clearly going to find a lot of exposure both prior to and subsequent to London runs in the theatres of the provinces, thus helping in a qualified reanimation of that provincial theatre. Specific: in that Scarborough was where the young Alan Ayckbourn imbibed his early experience of the theatre – and was to remain the launching-pad for his plays prior to a London run – taking in the new English Absurdism along with the established fare of the standard well-made comedies, farces and thrillers that continued to dominate provincial repertory theatre.

Ayckbourn wrote his first four plays for the Scarborough Theatre under the name of Roland Allen, and all of them show the unmistakable influence of the Absurdist tradition. His next play, *Mr Whatnot* of 1963, was the first to be staged under his own name and also the first to get a London run. *The Times* of August 7 reviewed the New Arts Theatre Club production under the heading 'Theatre of the Ridiculous'. Indeed, the piece with which the man who is now easily the most popular of all the playwrights of the new mainstream first received real recognition in 1972 was entitled, suitably enough, *Absurd Person Singular*.[15] A play in which the upward aspirations of the petit-bourgeois proprietor of a General Stores, Sidney Hopcroft, are traced through three successive Christmas parties, culminating in his triumph over the socially superior guests of his first party, a banker and an architect.

Throughout, it is the values of the suburban world of Sidney and his house-proud wife Jane that predominate, even as they are parodied in a manner that owes much to the deflection effected by Absurdism on the dialogue of domestic naturalism. As the Hopcrofts prepare for the party in their kitchen in the first scene the unstoppable Sidney tells his wife, as she continues obsessively to clean, that he has thought up some really good games to keep the party moving, 'some real devils'.

> *Sidney: (He puts his leg up on the table)* Just in case things need jollying up. *(Seeing Jane still wiping)* I don't want to disappoint you but we're not going to be out here for our drinks you know.

Jane: Yes, I know.

Sidney: The way you're going . . .

Jane: They might want to look . . .

Sidney: I doubt it.

Jane: The ladies might.

Sidney: (*chuckling knowingly*) I don't imagine the wife of a banker will particularly choose to spend her evening in our kitchen. Smart as it is.

Jane: No?

Sidney: I doubt if she spends very much time in her own kitchen. Let alone ours.

Jane: Still . . .

Sidney: Very much the lady of leisure, Mrs Brewster-Wright. Or so I would imagine.

Jane: What about Mrs Jackson?

Sidney: (*doubtfully*) Well – again, not a woman you think of in the same breath as you would a kitchen.

The dialogue here is very precisely located in class terms, as indeed are the ritualized struggles within the plot structure. But it is important to notice what has been excluded. It is the small shopkeeper with ambitions who is at the bottom of this social pile. The world of the working class was something that was to concern the new mainstream about as little as it had its precursors, and the centre of interest was normally to remain the various strands of the middle classes whose appropriation of new territory it became the increasing function of 60s new theatre to celebrate, however ambiguously. Where any account was taken of life below this social level, the usual response was one of continuing patronage or outright condemnation of a world of manual labour, trade unionism, et al. Peter Hall's 1964 production of *Eh?* by Henry Livings (another playwright who was quickly assimilated into the new school with, in particular *Nil Carborundum*, 1962) is a case in point. The central character, work-shy Valentine Brose, is found a job in a works' boiler-room with a door that plays 'Chanson d'Amour' every time someone enters, and a Tannoy system that broadcasts personalized messages of warning and encouragement 'Big Brother' style. The absurdity of the location is reinforced by the nature of the 'work' that he is required to do, simply pressing a button to start and stop the machine each end of his shift. It is, he is assured, a job that is not really a job at all.

Price: A chimpanzee could do what I'm going to ask you to do, Mr Brose . . .

Valentine: I know what you want me to ask: why don't you . . . no, I can't, it's daft . . . oh well, all right, here goes: why don't you get a ch . . .

Price: You could perform the entire operation with your left elbow, eyes shut and in two minutes flat.

Valentine: Is it paid by the hour?

Price: Your *presence* will be required midnight to eight a.m. six nights a week. You will be paid eight pounds three and six. It will be your business to supervise this boiler, in which you will find no shred of effort is required: there's no labour in this works, only productivity: not busyness, business. What the devil's he whistling about?

Mrs Murray: I guess he thinks he's getting eight pounds three and six for his Sunday off and he's wondering how he can wriggle out of the other six days.[16]

The limpness of the characterization and the easy nature of the targets are characteristic of the early 60s' adaptations of the Absurd. That such a lightweight piece should have found a production in the prestigious RSC, still not overkeen on staging contemporary work at this point, is an indication of how seriously the various strands of English Absurdism were being taken. Although Valentine can be considered to some extent as a version of the bohemian rogue figure, the major energies of the play are directed towards a ridiculing of the world of demarcated labour. The fact that this play was to become Peter Hall's first filmic venture (under the new title *Work is a Four-Letter Word*) adds further emphasis on the seriousness that such a play was then accorded.

The boiler-room here presented as an absurd fantasy might well have figured perfectly seriously in a piece of social realist drama (as an industrial equivalent to Arnold Wesker's *The Kitchen*, perhaps). Interestingly, *The Times* review (16 February 1961) of his earlier *Stop It Whoever You* (Arts Theatre) had made such a connection in order to argue precisely for the hostility of Livings' work to that represented by Wesker:

One way to receive this rude North Country farce. . . . is to assume that it is intended as a skit on the New Drama. On the basis of this possibly false assumption it might be held that the skit, even with the public lavatory substituted for the kitchen sink, is hardly good enough for its subject.

And still as late as 1970, in *The Ffinest Ffamily in the Land*, Livings continued in what seemed by then an undeniably patronizing way, parodying the middle-class pretensions of his working-class family.

Pinter himself, having been declared the leader of this new school (by acclamation and not by intent), moved away quite rapidly from the kind of models that allowed for the creation of such a role. By the 70s his work was to be enshrined in the canon of official culture almost as soon as it hit the stage. Both *Old Times* (1971) and *No Man's Land* (1975) were staged at major subsidized venues – by the RSC at the Aldwych and by the National Theatre at the Old Vic – and together they confirmed what was already evident from the second half of the 60s, that the playwright had moved the social base of his work, if not the particular treatment he gave it, back to the world of the professional middle classes that his earliest plays had so refreshingly confronted. With his departure it became harder and harder to sustain the illusion that a continuing movement existed. His real importance in this context was to be that his status as world-renowned playwright in a theatre that was increasingly looking towards the political arena in the 70s meant that some small claim could be made for the perpetuation of a serious mainstream tradition. For most of the other British playwrights I have considered in this chapter the period from the late 60s on proved bleak as their particular brand of suburban satire looked increasingly tame and irrelevant in the face of the more politically and dramatically abrasive plays on offer; although for some, John Mortimer in particular, television became the natural medium to which to turn.

What this development on Pinter's part meant was a movement of his work away from a perceived original stance as a part of an *avant-garde* and towards an assimilation into a world of highbrow culture. The significance of this move is illustrated well by the very different ways in which non-populist theatre critics still largely continue to distinguish between the drama of Pinter and Ayckbourn. Pinter is regarded as a cultural icon, whereas Ayckbourn's concern with the despair of rather less culturally elevated beings has led to him being largely dismissed. Michael Billington in 1983:

Alan Ayckbourn is popular. He is prolific. And he writes comedies. For all those reasons he is still, I believe, seriously underrated.[17]

And at this point the figure of Tom Stoppard intrudes itself. In 1967, just one year before what I located as the starting point of the new political theatre, *Rosencrantz and Guildenstern Are Dead* had its first professional production, by the National Theatre Company at the Old Vic. It was a first stage production quite different in its impact from that of Pinter's *Birthday Party* nine years earlier. It enjoyed enormous success, immediately guaranteed Stoppard a major place in theatre history regardless of what might follow, and proclaimed a theatrical strategy not only quite different from, but self-consciously hostile to, that shortly to be developed by Brenton, Edgar, Griffiths, et al.

I used to feel out on a limb, because when I started to write you were a shit if you weren't writing about Vietnam or housing. Now I have no compunction about that . . . *The Importance Of Being Earnest* is important, but it says nothing about anything.[18]

The Oscar Wilde play alluded to by Stoppard is in fact central to his own *Travesties* (1974), which also contains glancing echoes of at least eight Shakespeare plays. Indeed the title of this later play is, in itself, a key to Stoppard's work up to this point, which places an obsessive reliance on borrowings from, references to, and parodies of earlier theatrical work. That the base text in *Rosencrantz and Guildenstern* was *Hamlet* helps to place Stoppard's play more precisely as, amongst other things, a piece of playfully classic 'deconstruction' within the very portals of the company most responsible for the continuing enshrinement of the Bard. Comparison might be made with Alan Ayckbourn's use of John Gay's eighteenth-century box-office hit, the balladic *Beggar's Opera*, which is being rehearsed in his *A Chorus of Disapproval*, which opened in Scarborough before transferring to the National Theatre and winning the *Evening Standard* 'Comedy of the Year' award in 1985.

That *Rosencrantz and Guildenstern* was able to find such immediate success was in no small part due to the pioneering work undertaken by Pinter & co. Unlike *The Birthday Party* it found itself in a theatre whose audiences were fully primed to expect and savour permutations of Absurdism. By 19 June 1964 *The Times* was able to claim that *The Birthday Party* and not *Look Back in Anger* 'is the ur-text of modern British drama'. It was a connecting thread stressed about *Rosencrantz and Guildenstern* by Charles Marowitz, who described it at the time as an 'existential comedy whose ur-text like *The Caretaker* is *En Attendant Godot'*;[19] and its borrowings from, and general reference to, Beckett's play are too apparent and too well documented elsewhere to need further elaboration here. However, perhaps the most interesting single connection is with an earlier version of the play, which had ended with another pair of attendant lords being woken,[20] thus emphasizing the pattern of repetition, of nothing ever being changed or being changeable, that is central to Absurdist theatre; and that, in itself, opposes the central tenet of political theatre as defined by Brecht, that man 'is alterable and able to alter'.

But the apparently overnight success enjoyed by Stoppard in 1967 is deceptive, and to present him in this way is to ignore the way in which his development can be seen to be related quite closely to the kind of English Absurdist theatre I have been discussing. He wrote his first play, *The Gamblers*, in 1960, a play he described to Kenneth Tynan as '*Waiting For Godot* in the death cell – prisoner and jailer – I'm sure you can imagine the rest'; the same year he wrote *A Walk on the Water*, a play so influenced by Arthur Miller and by Robert Bolt's *Flowering Cherry* that he was subsequently to refer to it as *Flowering Death of a Salesman*.[21]

This, his first full-length play, was transmitted by ITV in 1963, and when it was eventually staged in London in 1968, reworked and with the new title of *Enter a Free Man*, the influence of *The Birthday Party*, as for so many plays of the period, was only too apparent. In 1964 BBC Radio broadcast a fifteen-minute play, *The Dissolution of Dominic Boot*. A brief summary of the plot will give a good indication of its indebtedness to the English Absurdist tradition. Dominic Boot is in a taxi. Realizing that he cannot pay the fare, he has the driver take him round London while he unsuccessfully attempts to get sufficient money, all the time increasing his debt on the taxi-meter. At the end of the play he is sacked by his boss, whose secretary hails a passing taxi, telling the hapless, jobless and broke Dominic 'Come on, you can drop me off'.

That same year he travelled to West Berlin with a number of playwrights, including James Saunders, whose absurdist exercise *Next Time I'll Sing to You* – a hit of the 1963 London theatre season

– is 'the British play that seems most behind *Rosencrantz and Guildenstern Are Dead*' according to one recent critic.[22] And certainly, a play that opens with two characters discussing what they are doing on stage with more than a sideways glance towards *Godot*, has a very obvious connection with the opening gambits of Stoppard's protagonists:

> *Dust*: Where's Rudge? Late. He was late last night. (*He looks at his watch.*) We were scheduled to begin five minutes ago.
> *Muff*: We 'ave, mate.
> *Dust*: What?
> *Muff*: I've kicked off already. He's not written himself in for another ten minutes.
> *Dust*: Every night the same excuse.
> *Muff*: You say that every night.
> *Dust*: And you say that every night.
> *Muff*: And you say –
> *Dust*: I'm not going to argue the point. I have a wife waiting for me, I trust this is realized.
> *Muff*: Every night you say –
> *Dust*: *Exactly*. Night after night the same circular dialogue, round and round we go.[23]

To reinforce the connection, it was James Saunders who suggested that Stoppard turn the first, burlesque, version of the play into a full-length piece. And interestingly, in view of the later specific connections between Stoppard and the Czech theatre, it was James Saunders who would translate Vaclav Havel's 1987 play *Redevelopment; or, Slum Clearance*.[24]

Later in 1964, BBC Radio broadcast another short Absurdist piece, *M is for Moon Amongst Other Things*; in 1966 *If You're Glad I'll Be Frank*; and in 1967, after the first success of *Rosencrantz and Guildenstern*, *Albert's Bridge*. It wasn't until 1968 that Stoppard first had a play produced that had started life in the commercial theatre, the play that, with *After Magritte*, was to become a regular stand-by in the amateur theatre of the 70s, *The Real Inspector Hound*.

This last play is an affectionate parody of the kind of country-house murder mystery that had refused to die in the post-war theatre. In Stoppard's version, murder takes place both on and off stage, as the play is publicly watched, and commented upon, by two rival critics, Moon and Birdfoot. In the first scene they watch the caricatured home-help as she answers the phone on stage; her response draws in all the clichés of the model, a fact that does not go unnoticed by the critics:

> *Mrs Drudge*: Hello, the drawing-room of Lady Muldoon's country residence one morning in early spring . . . Who did you wish to speak to? I am afraid there is no one of that name here, this is all very mysterious and I'm sure it's leading up to something, I hope nothing is amiss for we, that is Lady Muldoon and her houseguests are here cut off from the world, including Magnus, the wheelchair-ridden half-brother of her ladyship's husband Lord Albert Muldoon who ten years ago went out for a walk on the cliffs and was never seen again – and all alone, for they had no children.
> *Moon*: Derivative, of course.
> *Birdsfoot*: But quite sound.

This was not by any means new territory, even in modern terms, and the introduction of populist theatrical forms into a non-populist context had ample precedent; a point made by *The Times* on 13 June 1963 about Henry Livings' Royal Court debut:

> One assumption it is high time we discarded is that farce and melodrama are poor relations of comedy and tragedy. In fact the idea seems already to be on the way out, thanks to a handful of modern playwrights who have treated the forms with the respect they deserve. No one has helped more than Henry Livings to restore farce to the serious theatre; and now, in *Kelly's Eye*, he has dived in to rescue melodrama.

The key phrase here is 'serious theatre', a term deployed to drive a wedge between a perceived highbrow drama and the supposedly lowbrow entertainments which, as I argued in the previous chapter, continued to provide the basic theatrical fodder in the West End. The country-house murder was to receive parodied homage from other new writers – most notably in Antony Shaffer's *Sleuth* (1970) and *The Case of the Oily Levantine* (1979); and Simon Gray's *Stage Struck* (1979) – and the related country-house farce parody has resurfaced most successfully in recent times with Michael Frayn's *Noises Off* (1982), the last two being productions

of Michael Codron, a figure of vital importance in the development of the serious mainstream.

Frayn's piece, like *The Real Inspector Hound*, contains a play
within a play – in this case three versions of the same opening
scene of an awful example of stock repertory production, the
fictitious *Nothing On*, seen from in front of and behind the set, in
final rehearsal and in performance, as the lives of the actors
collapse in a mirror-image of the chaos on stage. The action in
Frayn's play also starts with a home-help taking a stage telephone
call:

> *Mrs Clackett*: Hello . . . Yes but there's no one here love . . . No,
> Mr Brent's not here . . . He lives here, yes, but he don't live
> here right now because he lives in Spain . . . Mr Philip Brent,
> that's right . . . The one who writes the plays, that's him, only
> now he writes them in Spain.

And so on, as the familiar figure of the comic char is once again
wheeled out, as it had been so many times in post-war rep, but
now only made possible by the self-consciousness of the parody.
As early as 1973, Alan Bennett had Mrs Scrubb, his stage char in
Habeus Corpus, present herself to her audience in terms that placed
her carefully within the tradition: 'I represent ye working classes.
Hoover, hoover, hoover'. Stoppard's work from this period right
through to the mid-70s continued to draw heavily on the influence
of the Absurdist tradition, a usage which by the time of *Jumpers*
(1972) and *Travesties* (1974) – first produced by the National
Theatre and the RSC respectively – had developed into an
extended exercise in wit and ingenuity for the audience to puzzle
away at. Manner had almost entirely taken over from matter, and
Stoppard's mainstream contemporaries did little to suggest any
alternative mode of address.

What this meant was that any sense that the English Absurdist
school had had originally of being a part of a self-conscious *avant-
garde* was rapidly eroded. It was not its willingness to experiment
that ensured its growth, but its capability of being reassimilated
into the mainstream. It moved the social parameters of British
theatre without seriously questioning or challenging the overall
order, and it offered the excitement of new theatrical tricks that
could be easily be welcomed into the conservative theatrical establishment.

It is but a short jump to the success of, for instance, Peter Shaffer's *Equus* (National Theatre 1973), a play that is in part a logical development of a career that had started in 1958 with *Five Finger Exercise*, and had included the Absurdist experiments *The Public Ear*, *The Private Eye* and *Black Comedy*. For *Equus* is a perfect model of how the peripheral experimentation of the new drama could be brought back into the general structural demands of the mainstream. Interestingly, it is one of the last plays to be considered by Christopher Innes in his impressive survey of the *avant-garde* published in 1993. In a last chapter, 'From the Margins to Mainstream', he describes the significance of the play's global success in the context of the process of the incorporation of *avant-garde* theatrical strategies by the mainstream:

> *Equus* was a worldwide success. The *avant-garde* approach had, as it were, arrived, but in a watered-down and conventional form.[25]

One of its immediate predecessors in the liberal drama stakes was Peter Nichols' *A Day in the Death of Joe Egg* (1967), a comedy about the family life of a spastic child. The terms in which it was praised by Irving Wardle at the time point to the way in which the reassimilation has become an established fact:

> What the play confirms is that it is still possible for a dramatist to know who he is talking to. Peter Nichols has observed the speech habits, social attitudes, and ideological confusions of the British sixties, and on his stage presents our own image. This is not *avant-garde* writing: it is addressed to the general civic conscience, and it endows the random audience with the sense of a common human bond.[26]

By the following year, however, the same critic is to be found complaining that contemporary British comedy has become formulaic once more. He cites 'plays like Simon Gray's *Wise Child* . . . which re-style yesterday's *avant-garde* tricks for today's commercial audience'.[27] This, Gray's first stage play, of 1967, was described by another critic thus:

> Is he, one wonders, simply trying to write a black comedy after the manner of Joe Orton? Or is he inviting our sympathy for a

trio of misfits who are curiously dependent on each other for
their survival? Or is he perhaps indulging himself in a bit of
fashionable, baroque nastiness?[28]

What these two different reactions to the play emphasize above
all is a clear uncertainty about whether this new offering is to be
thought of as a part of an *avant-garde* or a mainstream theatre.
And certainly the play, which offered a battery of racist, anti-
semitic and sexist smears amidst a plot conjuring with transvest-
ism and homosexuality in a manner still heavily dependent on the
Absurdist tradition for its dialogue patterns, seemed a very
peculiar thing to be discovered on the late 60s London commercial
stage. By 1969, however, his *Dutch Uncle* – another post-Absurdist
romp – was directed by Peter Hall for the RSC at the Aldwych.
Thereafter, Gray's plays would rely on the wit and ingenuity of
their only too articulate characters for their effect; not only concentrating exclusively on the world of the educated middle classes
but frequently considering directly the very places of their education – the University (in *Butley*, 1971, and in *The Common Pursuit*,
which was first directed by Pinter in 1984) and the Public School
(*Quartermaine's Terms*, 1981).

But the play which best represents this new concentration on
the conscious display of wit is Christopher Hampton's *The Philanthropist* of 1970, a piece that Stoppard in 1977 said contained his
favourite line in modern English drama; 'I'm a man of no convic-
tions – at least I *think* I am'.[29] As Hampton recalled in 1991, the
genesis of the play came from his interest in creating a contemporary opposite to the figure of Alceste in Molière's *Le Misanthrope*:

> It occurred to me that in the climate of abrasive candour which
> characterized the late 1960s, Alceste would have been quite at
> home: whereas his opposite, a man concerned above all to cause
> no offence and be an unfailing source of sweetness and light,
> would very likely succeed only in raising hackles wherever he
> went . . . As a setting which might be a modern equivalent of
> Molière's world, in which clever and envious people with a
> startling amount of leisure time sit around demolishing their
> colleagues, thoroughly insulated against any external pressures
> or upheavals, the university naturally suggested itself. Nowa-
> days, no doubt, the bubble has burst and universities are as

subject as the rest of us to the harsh rigours of market forces; but in 1968, as campuses erupted all over Europe, Oxford seemed as sleepy as ever, cocooned and self-regarding.[30]

Hampton's account of the general tone of the play captures well its oppositional stance to the kind of political theatre that was to be spawned post that 1968 eruption; and its emphasis on dialogue as a medium of witty banter, rather than of either psychological or political definition, will allow it to serve as a model of its kind. The play's central character, Philip, an emotionally detached lecturer in philology, might usefully be compared with the figure of George, the intellectually tortured Professor of Moral Philosophy, in Stoppard's *Jumpers* of 1972, his first full-length play after *Rosencrantz and Guildenstern* – in that, however wide apart their analysis of the world and their reaction to that analysis might be, both characters are united in emphasizing the supremacy of manner over matter in their discourse.

But a play that has a first scene that opens with a character, John, delivering what is apparently a somewhat melodramatic suicide speech, immediately revealed to be an extract from his own play, is evidently looking backwards as well as forwards. In this first scene, the would-be playwright's friends discuss his manuscript, wondering in particular about the continual appearance of a window cleaner called Man:

Don: Well, I take it that he has some allegorical significance outside the framework of the play. I mean I don't know if this is right, but I rather took him to signify England.
John: No, no, erm, in point of fact he signifies man . . .
Don: Hence the name.
John: Yes . . .
Philip: I thought he was just meant to represent a window cleaner . . . Under the circumstances, I think you've integrated him into the plot very well.
John: Thank you. (*He seems displeased.*)
Don: I always think the beginning and the end are the most difficult parts of a play to handle, and I'm not sure you've been entirely successful with either . . . I can't really say that I like that Pirandello-style beginning. It's been done so often, you know. I mean I'm not saying that your use of it isn't resourceful. It is. But the device itself is a bit rusty.[31]

The reference to Pirandello, a writer of direct relevance to Stoppard's own theatrical games, is significant, and certainly it is increasingly Pirandello rather than Beckett or Ionesco who assumes a major importance as an influence. Throughout its London run in the 80s, Michael Frayn's *Noises Off* was described by *Plays and Players* as a piece in the spirit of the other playwright, and many other examples of borrowings and parallels could be adduced. Indeed, a revival of his *Rules of the Game* was playing at the Theatre Royal, Haymarket, and on a national tour while Frayn's play was running – and, interestingly, this and his *Six Characters in Search of an Author* had been staged as part of the World Theatre Season at the Aldwych in 1965.

But the reference to the playwright acts both as a cue to the fact that we are here in the familiar, if parodied, territory of plays about plays, and as a deliberate unpreparation for the conclusion of the first scene when John places a gun in his mouth and actually commits suicide.

Mention elsewhere in the play of off-stage slaughter stresses the debt of this self-styled 'bourgeois comedy' of manners to the Absurdist tradition. We learn that the Prime Minister and the best part of the Cabinet have been machine-gunned to death by 'an elderly and rather corpulent lady wearing one of those enormous tweed capes . . . and sucking Glacier mints', and later that Braham Head, a novelist who has been 'forced to abandon the left wing for tax reasons', has taken umbrage because he is not one of the twenty-five eminent English writers on the hit-list of FATAL, the Fellowship of Allied Terrorists Against Literature, who have already claimed one victim.

By this time, however, the *direct* influence of Absurdism was beginning to fade. Its use in *The Philanthropist* is actually rather peripheral, allowing for a few additional on-stage jokes, and no longer central to the plot in a way that it had been in Hampton's first play, *When Did You Last See My Mother?* (first staged professionally in a Royal Court Theatre Sunday production in 1966), for instance. After *Travesties* (1974), Stoppard would be less easily fitted into such an English school, and Pinter's work from *Old Times* (1971) on was taking his version of serious mainstream theatre into quite different territory.

The adaptation of continental Absurdism had originally allowed for a satirical concentration on the preoccupations of the English middle classes. Although strains of the original spirit continued and continue to be felt (in Ayckbourn's later work, for example), its central importance lay in redefining the social preoccupations of the new drama as a mirror, distorted or not, of the changing theatrical audiences. Satire gave way to a playfulness, an insistence that even, or perhaps especially, in serious theatre nothing is serious – in a conscious if defensive opposition to the new political theatre. By the 80s it was able to move on again, confident in its access to an audience for whom the anxieties and aspirations of bourgeois life were no longer the stuff of satire or parody, but ideologically central to a modern world as redefined by the new monetarist economics. From 1979 on the new mainstream found itself not only the better able to survive in the new market, but culturally more in tune with what seemed to be the rapidly changing orthodoxy.

What this meant was that in practice a new serious mainstream was not a direct product of the politics of the 80s, though it was certainly moulded and shaped by those politics. By 1979 a clear sense of a definable mainstream already existed, with a history and now quite clearly with a future. That it already existed, and in particular that it had succeeded in finding an identification of audience with subject, means that it must be regarded in itself as evidence of the general cultural and social move that was to facilitate the new politics.

When the Conservative Party formed the first of four successive administrations following the electoral victory of May 1979, the London commercial theatre was already well stocked both with plays that looked back to the earlier Absurdist roots and with variants of the new mainstream. There were revivals; of Joe Orton's *What the Butler Saw* and of James Saunders' *Bodies*. Alan Ayckbourn had two plays in production, *Bedroom Farce*, which had transferred to the Prince of Wales from the National, and *Joking Apart*, which had opened earlier at the Arts Theatre Club in 1976, was on at the Criterion. Tom Stoppard's *Dirty Linen* was in its third year at the Arts Theatre, and his *Night and Day* – which heralded a new direction in his work – had recently opened at the Phoenix. Brian Clark's *Plays and Players* '1978 Play of the Year', *Whose Life is it Anyway* continued at the Savoy, and his new play, *Can You Hear Me at the Back*? was in rehearsal at the Picadilly.

Of course this is not the whole story, although there is not one example of committed drama in the commercial theatre to offset the balance. Elsewhere things continued much as they had done for years. There were four formulaic thrillers (including the still present *Mousetrap*); *No Sex Please We're British* continued to run, and was joined by *Happy Birthday*, an offering from the same team that had brought the West End the long-running 'sex' comedy *Boeing-Boeing*. There were 14 musical shows and reviews, mostly catering for versions of the nostalgia market – with *Beyond the Rainbow*, *Chicago*, *The King and I*, *Elvis* and *A Day in Hollywood*, *A Night in the Ukraine* – though two of them pointed the way things would go in the 80s. Andrew Lloyd Webber's *Jesus Christ Superstar* was in its seventh year at the Globe, whilst his new musical, *Evita*, was approaching its first anniversary at the Prince Edward.

However, as good an indication as any of the state of serious theatre would be given by a consideration of the productions both current and announced at Britain's National Theatre in June 1979, just one month after the Conservative victory. The only uncomplicatedly new play on offer was Simon Gray's *Close of Play*, directed by Harold Pinter who had a new production of his 1978 piece *The Betrayal* on at the Lyttelton. There were revivals of Congeve's Restoration Comedy *The Double Dealer*, of Somerset Maughan's *For Services Rendered*, and Bernard Shaw's *The Philanderer*. In addition there were versions by Tom Stoppard of Arthur Schnitzler's *The Undiscovered Country* and by Michael Frayn of Tolstoy's *The Fruits of Enlightenment*. The remaining production, at the Cottesloe, was an adaptation by Michael Herr of *Despatches*, a stage version of the Vietnam War novel.

Now, it would be dangerous to put too much weight on this single sampling – and ironically Howard Brenton's updated version of *The Churchill Play* was playing at the RSC's Warehouse as the new furniture was being moved into 10 Downing Street – but a distinct sense of a new mood in the theatre is unmistakable. The epic stages of 70s political theatre have apparently disappeared, and in their places are displayed a series of rooms, rooms inhabited by representatives of those sections of society who apparently stood to gain most in the brave new world of monetarist experiment. It would be a good moment to consider the nature of those rooms and of the activities that they frame.

Part II

5

Set in Rooms

Well you could say that there are two kinds of plays – those set in rooms and those outside rooms ... There is a huge divergence in the ways of looking at the world amongst playwrights who write inside and outside rooms.

(Howard Brenton, 1975)[1]

When a director sets out to offer an audience a production of, say, Pinter's *The Caretaker*, s/he does so after collaboration with the stage designer and technical staff – all of them guided heavily by what the playwright has given them in the printed text towards an agreement on the nature of the space in which the dramatic events will be enacted. In this instance Pinter has given them very specific guidance, to the point effectively of direct instruction, about the nature of the room the audience will see as the play starts. Everything is carefully positioned, a map could almost be drawn.

The text tells us where the window and door are to be placed; it directs the placement of the smallest details of the cluttered set, including the statue of Buddha and the bucket that hangs from the ceiling to collect the drips. It thus to a large extent predetermines an audience response at the opening, even before the director, actors, & co. have had the opportunity to put their own brand on the play.

The room that greets the audience is loaded with clues which demand a response. What kind of world are we about to be shown in a play that is to be set in a room as cluttered, untidy and generally down-at-heel as this? Of course these clues, these signs may be misleading, deliberately or not. They may not signify a meeting between the kind of characters that Pinter is about to introduce us to at all. We may in fact be about to watch a performance of a contemporary equivalent of *The Importance of Being Earnest*. But this doesn't really matter. What is important is that the audience is being cued to expect a certain kind of social perspective on the evidence of what the room displays. If it is being tricked in some way, then that creation of expectancy will have its own part to play.

It was in this sense that Joe Orton relished the prospect of seeing his *What the Butler Saw* produced at London's Haymarket, 'the very bastion of escapist bourgeois entertainment' as John Lahr describes it when quoting Orton's diary in *Prick Up Your Ears*:

> 'That'd be wonderful,' I said. 'It'd be a sort of joke even putting *What the Butler Saw* in the West End at the Haymarket – Theatre of Perfection.' We [Orton and the impressario Oscar Lewenstein] discussed the set. 'It should be beautiful. Nothing extraordinary. When the curtain goes up one should feel that we're right back in the old theatre of reassurance – roses, french windows, middle-class characters.'[2]

In this instance the set, and indeed the very theatrical setting, was intended to mislead the audience, to cue an expectancy out of key with the events that would occur within Orton's room; a room that offered a set of theatrical and domestic signals with which the audience would be quite familiar, the action then working against, defamiliarizing, decoding even, those signals. Similarly, a piece about the harsh realities of life on the streets today enacted in a set for *The Importance of Being Earnest*, for instance, might quickly be understood to be making a rather obvious point about the gap between the lives of the rich and the poor in contemporary society.

That this kind of cuing of response is possible results directly from the physical realization of the room on stage. A room belongs to someone, is the disputed territory of someone or, at the very least, proclaims something about its social function (a doctor's waiting-room, for example). A regular theatre-goer presented with the detailed instructions provided by G. B. Shaw at the start of the printed text of *Heartbreak House*, for instance, would not need any prior knowledge of either play or writer to arrive at some quite sophisticated decisions about what the set was declaring.

That we are given a detailed description of a room fashioned as a ship with an exterior view of the Sussex hills and a garden with an observatory might well suggest a symbolic usage of the set. But at the very least the theatre-goer would be able to sketch out a plausible outline of its owner; even if they were not able to accurately predict the kind of play that was to follow.

In this second part of my book it will become rapidly apparent that just about all of the plays considered take place in a room or rooms. Very rarely do the playwrights take the action into the larger public arenas favoured by their declaredly politicized contemporaries; and so, very rarely, is there any *actual* meeting between anything but the most carefully delimited social representations. And always there is a very strong sense given of the way in which the possessors of the room not only see their possession as an integral part of their own social projection of themselves, but as a territorial statement of exclusion.

In Simon Gray's *Melon*, for example, we are shown one of the series of Tuesday evening 'music' sessions held at the house of Melon and his wife Kate. He talks of them early on as 'not just a part of our marriage, but a part – no, at the very centre – of *their* lives', but later admits to his psychiatrist that they were actually gatherings at which he could demonstrate his control over both wife and friends: 'Um, I led the band, orchestrated the – the essential sound, developed the counter-points and – and so forth'.

The room as set in *Melon* not only promises, and indeed delivers, an emphasis on the domestic but, by its additional inclusion of Melon's workplace and his psychiatrist's office, stresses the way in which this domesticity is male-dominated. The events are re-enacted through the consciousness of Melon, and again this will be typical. The earlier naturalistic tradition that had sought to look at life lower down the social ladder had perforce to consider the role of women, if only because they were always present as perpetuators of the domestic order. Elements of this survive in Bennett's television plays, for instance, where the mother figure is frequently depicted as trapped in the home, and it is very obviously a key to Wesker's achievement in *Roots* – a play that is most interesting when it concentrates on the relationship between mother and daughter. Interestingly, Wesker had to resist enormous pressure not to once introduce the absent boy-friend, Ronnie, thus allowing the play to foreground female experience in the domestic context.

This is rarely the case in the plays that I will be considering and, given the fact that most of these plays are set in middle-class domestic establishments it is worth thinking about a little. It is not necessary to embrace any considerable degree of feminist thought to realize that there is absolutely no reason at all why, by the date it was produced, the central figure in *Melon*, a successful publisher, should be a man. Or, indeed, why the equivalent figure in

Ayckbourn's *A Small Family Business*, for instance, should not be a woman. Whilst gender expectations in the kind of world depicted in *Roots* had changed little in the intervening years, in that of the middle classes depicted in the new mainstream they certainly had.

Given the increasing – if still minority – emergence of women as business entrepreneurs, bank managers, head teachers, publishing editors, and so on, it is revealing that in a drama so concerned with the activities of such people the women are never called upon to lead, but always to continue to play the supporting roles as wives, mothers and mistresses. It is left to men to emote and to intellectualize in a territory where women, if they are present at all, are often little more than cyphers – as referents for the social position of their men, or tedious reminders of the limitations of their social aspirations.

In a period dominated by the presence of a woman as British Prime Minister, a play such as Caryl Churchill's *Top Girls* (1982) – with its complex debate about the conflict between feminist struggle and female success in a male-dominated world – stands as a conscious affront to the combined efforts of the mainstream to ignore social change. A more sympathetic depiction of women is frequently to be found – increasingly so in Ayckbourn, and in a late work like *Passion Play* by Nichol, for example – but it leads only to an emphasis on their role as victims, never as active, let alone equal, protagonists in the action. Madness rather than individual assertion is presented as their only conceivable way out.

Most of the other plays I will be considering will be set entirely in a room or rooms of a house. But even a theoretically more neutral space, such as a hotel room, the setting for Michael Frayn's *Make and Break*, brings with it its own political rules. Before Garrard, the managing director, arrives, the temporary receptionist announces that she is going to take a shower. The consternation on the part of the long-serving secretary, Mrs Rogers, is not alleviated by five attempts on the part of the other characters to answer her objections: 'She shouldn't be using the shower . . . You know perfectly well she shouldn't . . . It's Mr Garrard's shower . . . This is Mr Garrard's suite. It's booked in his name. That's his bedroom and that's his bathroom . . . We have the use of the sitting-room. But the bedroom and the bathroom are his . . . We don't use the shower. You wouldn't use the shower. Mr Prosser wouldn't use the shower.' The realities of office hierarchy are here reflected almost satirically in the woman's concern for the invasion of her male boss's space, and the connected threat to his status.

Elsewhere, in plays located all or in part in the workplace, there is frequently evidence of a struggle to attain superiority, squabbles over the ownership of chairs or desks, for instance. When this territorial imperative is located solidly in the domestic heart of the family, then its articulation is all the stronger. An audience has no difficulty in sympathizing with the angry householder's attack on the intruder in Ayckbourn's *A Small Family Business*, even if by the end they may be less certain about the justification for killing him:

Jack: Why were you creeping round the back door?
Benedict: I wasn't sure if this was the right house.
Jack: (*Angrily*) What do you mean, the right house? Slinking about in the dark, terrifying the life out of my teenage daughter. What's your game then, sunshine?

The rooms proclaim the right of property ownership – and the struggle, whether domestic or extra-domestic about that right of possession, is a dominant theme in the narrative of the plays. But they proclaim more than the simple right of ownership. They define the terms of reference in which the struggle is to be considered by the audience. The room, like the language of the characters who will occupy it, declares itself in class terms. The fierce attempts to win possession of the room by Mick, Aston and Davies are dramatically exciting, but for the spectators they are largely voyeuristic. Theirs is not a room over which many members of the audience would wish to be engaged in battle. In terms of its iconography of class position and status it reflects nothing of the world they will return to once they have left the theatre. It was for this reason, amongst others, that Pinter found it necessary to be so specific about the construction of a set so unfamiliar in its social resonances to a 1960 audience at the Arts Theatre Club.

By the time Pinter came to write *Betrayal*, eighteen years later, the process of establishing the set is not done in the same kind of detail. The nine scenes are located more briefly: 'Pub. 1977. Spring'; 'Jerry's House. Study. 1977. Spring'; 'Flat. 1977. Winter'; 'Robert and Emma's House. Living room. 1974. Autumn'; 'Hotel Room. Venice. 1973. Summer'; 'Flat. 1973. Summer'; 'Restaurant. 1973. Summer'; 'Flat. 1971. Summer'; and 'Robert and Emma's

House. Bedroom. 1968. Winter'. Possibly the only clues towards
the depiction of a particular life-style here are that at least one
character has a house with a study, and that one or more of the
characters can afford to take a hotel room in Venice in the most
expensive season of the year.

But a reading of the play provides the necessary information:
not to depict the various locations in the meticulously described
way demanded by the text of *The Caretaker*, but with a due reflection of the way in which the registers of language and cultural
signification identify these characters as inhabitants of a world a
long way removed from that of Mick, Aston and Davies. And
again, after the comparative neutrality of the opening scene in a
pub – comparative because a decision will have to be taken about
what kind of pub is to be suggested – the audience will be presented with evidence of a physical confirmation of the characters'
social status. The room is always more than an adjunct to the
performance. It is an integral part of it, allowing an audience to
make decisions based solely on the particular fact of its existence.

Now, the most immediately apparent clues given to audiences
of contemporary mainstream theatre is that they are precisely not
about to be shown the kind of social world offered by Pinter in
The Caretaker in 1960. Through the 80s and into the 90s audiences
were presented with a series of well-furnished rooms – rooms that
defined the social parameters of theatre in a way that excluded all
but a social grouping that fell between the upper and lower
middle classes.

It was not impossible to locate a play, at least in part, at the
workplace, but it was always a workplace that stressed the professional or executive function of the characters in society; a very
high percentage of whom were not surprisingly found to be either
writers or cultural producers, or in some way (literary agents,
publishers, etc.) executives in the bureaucracy of cultural production and consumption. I say not surprisingly because it is evident
that frequently both plot and setting, if not necessarily the biographical details, came fairly directly from the lives of their
creators, creators who were, to anticipate the argument, always
male.

That this did not *automatically* result in an inward-looking
drama of personal reflection is because of the carefully realized
lives, and settings, of the characters. If the parameters were
narrow, then so were those of the audience. They may have been

as unreliable a gauge of the overall realities of British life as was *Dallas* for America, but they were located where their audiences located the areas of real debate in post-79 Britain. Their sets proclaimed the wealth of a Home Counties world that was doing more than alright economically, and are perhaps most significant for what they exclude.

Some obvious consequences follow. A play which is set in the house of a married couple is more than likely, any thematic or symbolic intents notwithstanding, to have at its narrative centre a concern with things domestic. This may well consist of an interest in the relationship with children – *A Day in the Death of Joe Egg*, for example – or the effect of outside pressures, of work for instance, on the economic and emotional fortunes of the family. But it will almost certainly include a consideration of the state of the relationship itself.

That, in contemporary mainstream theatre, this will almost always include the introduction of an adulterous relationship by one or both partners might be seen as one of the ways in which this theatre is taking on board the problems of modern marriage. Its effect in the plays is to suggest a strain between the success, and indeed the correctness of the model suggested by the succession of plush interiors with which an audience is presented – images of their own successfully modelled homes – and the desire on the part of some or all of the characters to find an emotional life which threatens the disruption of this model. But it is the model that survives, both in terms of the carefully designed set and of the narrative conclusion which normally finds some resolution, however personally unhappy, of that tension. The plots conclude with a perpetuation of domestic life in the set. The family model may be threatened by the necessities of plot but it is never seriously threatened.

Of course, this emphasis on domestic and extra-domestic relationships is not the only theme to be explored by the new mainstream, although it is the most important. At the more liberal end of the spectrum, the mainstream produced a stream of plays that concentrated on the articulation of individual struggle. Key plays in this tradition are *A Day in the Death of Joe Egg*, *Equus* and *Whose Life Is It Anyway?* But, whereas the first two of these plays enact the struggle precisely within the constraints of the domestic room, Brian Clark's play isolates the individual in a hospital ward, a victim wanting only to be allowed to die. In 'Theatre and Fiction',

David Edgar discusses the way in which this line has been developed in the mainstream, seeing the paradigm as 'the unexpected Broadway success of Lanford Wilson's *The Fifth of July*, in which the hero is a homosexual, legless Vietnam War veteran, who achieves personal growth through teaching dumb children to speak'. He cites in addition the *Elephant Man*, *Duet For One*, *Children of a Lesser God* and '(I regret to say) *Nicholas Nickelby* (the retarded)':

> What happened in general was an altogether more subtle privatisation of concern, which reflected the way in which the political and social obsessions of the 1960s had become personalised and thus rendered harmless in the 1970s, as the 'we' generation turned into the 'me' decade, the Pot Generation matured into the Perrier Generation, and the concern for the future of Planet Earth mutated into an obsession with the state of Planet Body, as the middle classes of Britain and America jogged slowly to the right. So by 1980, the demand was no longer for plays about the masses resisting the disablement of class or racial oppression, but for drama which dealt with individual cripples overcoming literal disabilities. In New York and then in London, the wheelchair, or at the very least the crutch, seemed to become a compulsory theatrical prop.[3]

It is perhaps dangerous to link together such disparate plays, and certainly a wider discussion would need to consider the significantly large number of plays on AIDS-related issues as in part a response to the concerns of large sections of the world of theatrical production with the implications of these issues – although, interestingly, they have not been subsumed into the mainstream repertoire. But it is in such ways that the dividing lines between the mainstream and alternative theatre traditions are drawn.

I want now to look in some detail at the significance of the model of the room in two plays of the 1980s – Tom Stoppard's *The Real Thing* of 1982 and Alan Ayckbourn's *A Small Family Business* of 1987. I have chosen these two plays because, although they by no means exhaust the potential usage of the room motif, they do suggest quite divergent strategies in its deployment.

An audience arriving at the Strand Theatre in November 1982 would almost certainly bring with it certain expectations about the kind of theatrical tricks that might be on offer in a new play by

Stoppard. What they were greeted with, once the concealing screen had been removed, was the sight of a living-room obviously the product of considerable wealth. There is evidence, by way of the architect's drawing-board, of the profession of the man inhabiting the room (evidence later confirmed in the dialogue of the first scene).

The man, Max, is alone, seated in a comfortable chair finishing a bottle of wine. He is building an elaborate pyramid out of a pack of playing-cards. Just as he is about to add a finishing touch, he senses that the door has been opened:

> *Max*: Don't slam – (*The front door slams, not violently. The viaduct of cards collapses. Superfluously, philosophically*) . . . the door.

This is the opening of the play. The man who, we either already realize or are about to be told, is an architect, sits in a beautifully designed room drinking alone and building a house of cards that collapses at the first intrusion from outside. Before we learn anything further, possible metaphorical significances of the man's activities in its physically realized setting intrude. We might be here faced with a critique of the state of modern architecture or perhaps with a portrait of an architect who can no longer function properly, either professionally or personally, or both.

The scene that follows is full of the kind of witty dialogue so familiar to Stoppard's audiences. During the course of it Max gets the house-of-cards wrecker, his wife Charlotte, to admit that she has not in fact been on a business trip to Geneva. His discovery of her passport left behind eventually leads her to confess – wrongly as we later discover, for she had taken out a temporary passport – that she has been away with what is the latest in a string of lovers. She leaves the room and him at the end of the scene. 'Max *remains seated. After a moment he reaches down for the airport bag, puts it back on his lap and looks inside it. He starts to laugh. He withdraws from the bag a miniature Alp in a glass bowl. He gives the bowl a shake and creates a snowstorm within it. Then the snowstorm envelops the stage.*'

The final effect is achieved by the lowering of the screen so that the entire stage-world reflects the microcosmic storm of the present from Switzerland. Pop music takes us into the next scene, which is set in the room of a house which it soon transpires is the property of Charlotte and her husband *Henry*.

The effect is to displace the certainty of the audience in their reading of the first scene. And soon it is discovered that it has been in fact simply a scene from a play written by Henry. The play is called *The House of Cards*, and in this second scene Charlotte uses the entrance of Max, her fellow actor, to disparage the play's construction: 'If he'd given her a lover instead of a temporary passport, we'd be in a play. But he could no more do that than he could architect a hotel.'

Now, that this first scene is revealed as being actually a scene from a play, allows Stoppard to introduce a number of key themes in a play which is going to be largely concerned with two things: the emotional, and adulterous, relationships between the characters; and a prolonged debate about the nature of playwriting and acting, and in particular Henry's emphasis on the craft of writing as all important (as epitomized by his long analogy with, almost inevitably, the construction of a cricket-bat in the first scene of the second act), set against an argument for a theatre that concentrates on political and social issues (where the style is conveniently demonstrated to be less important).

But this deception of the audience serves a greater purpose. If it can be brought to accept that this degree of articulated wit is appropriate for the discovery of adultery, and then be shown their mistake, it means that they will be lulled into accepting just about anything as a conceivable version of reality. It is a trick Stoppard repeats later in the play when we see a meeting between Annie, Max's wife at the outset but Henry's by the fourth scene, and a supposed prisoner of conscience being transposed into the play that the prisoner wishes to write.

In such a world what really is the 'real thing'? In this play Stoppard deploys the set in part to confuse expectation. Its naturalism may, as we have seen, be just the formulaic naturalism of the theatre, and it may easily be transposed – as it is, by being converted temporarily into a railway carriage, in a later scene. Its use creates something of a defence mechanism for the playwright. It scarcely needs the later revelation that the political prisoner, a young army lad who has staged a demonstration at the Cenotaph, was not motivated politically but simply acted to impress Annie. The possibility of anything being allowed to have a serious political import in this play is denied by its very structure, a structure which insists that if the theatre is a mirror of life, the only things it reflects are the ordering and shaping processes of the theatre.

The room in *The Real Thing* is thus realized as a naturalistic construct in which real emotional struggles might take place precisely in order to demonstrate the danger of taking anything at face value. The audience is shown dramatically that the set for the first scene is just that, a set, and this discovery hangs over the rest of the performance. The effect, in this instance, is to draw the audience into a world which is almost entirely self-referential. The attack on a politicized theatre is obvious enough – in the treatment of the prisoner's play, for instance, polished by a Henry who can earlier refer to having seen an actress 'in *Trotsky Playhouse* or whatever they call it' on television. But equally the defence of the kind of theatre that interests Stoppard can be made in ways which mockingly reflect the use of the set, allowing for an attack by Henry's daughter on his play, that might just as easily be on *The Real Thing* itself:

Henry: Didn't you like the last one?
Debbie: What, *House of Cards*? Well, it wasn't about anything, except did she have it off or didn't she? What a crisis. Infidelity amongst the architect class. Again.

Here, despite the important attempt made by Henry to argue that it really was 'about self-knowledge through pain', we are left with the abiding image of a 'house of cards' architect as both creator and subject of the play. That Stoppard is evidently trying to call into question such an analogy – creating a Henry who complains that he cannot write about love or jealousy, and then have him experience both – is ultimately irrelevant. Billington argued that a crucial difference between the first London production and the Broadway one was that whilst the former played the first scene 'with much the same cool artifice as the rest of the evening', the latter played it 'with a heightened Cowardesque camp so that even the slowest member of the audience would realise he was watching a play-within-a play'.[4]

However, this separation of styles is of more significance theoretically than actually in such a play. For there is really no way of reading the significance of such a distinction. The dialogue is consistently witty and artificial, and an audience is given no real reason for 'trusting' any one part of the text at the expense of any other.

We can see a slightly different but related use of the model in

Melon. Gray goes to great pains to distinguish the three acting areas inhabited by Melon in his prefatory directions to the text. There is to be a single set consisting of four rooms, thus allowing his protagonist to move smoothly, and without a break in the play's narrative, between locations. 'As this is a play about memory, there should be no scene breaks, each scene beginning almost before the previous scene has ended. It must be fluid, in other words.'

The instructions include a suggestion that the bedroom – 'where sex usually takes place' – should be on a higher level. It is obvious that, in constructing a set to be used in this manner, there will be a consciously created tension between the expectancies of a naturalistic plot development and an actual progression that frequently denies such expectation. The room offers an audience one group of conventions against which another group are to be played.

We could think of this another way. The set proclaims an ordered world, a model of the bourgeois family unit as represented by the home. The partial disruption of the conventions established by the set allows for some degree of questioning of that model. This is a very characteristic feature of the new mainstream, and represents fairly clearly the assimilation of theoretically *avant-garde* strategies back into the ultimate safety of the room. For any mainstream tradition can continue to develop only through the incorporation of oppositional strategies, which are then sanitized or moved to within the parameters of bourgeois liberalism.

The room in the new mainstream will very rarely be the simple inflexible location of the old well-made play tradition. The reanimation of the tradition comes in part, and is signalled by, the unreliability of the stage model as experienced by the audience. It will be entered by dream/nightmare sequences – as it is in *Melon* and *Make and Break* – and it will allow questions to be raised. But, ultimately the fact of the model will prevent any real disruption of the social order that it represents as a physical presence on stage.

To take a very different example of the model: in June 1987 an audience arriving at the National Theatre to see Ayckbourn's new play, *A Small Family Business*, would equally have very strong expectations of the kind of drama that might be on offer. Like Stoppard, Ayckbourn was a very successful and established writer with a strong sense of individual style. Audiences were accustomed to seeing plays by him that offered two dinner parties taking place simultaneously around the same table in two differ-ent houses (*How the Other Half Loves* of 1969); three plays that showed events in three different locations in and around the same house over the same period of time (*The Norman Conquests* of 1973); and a continuous and linking action in three different bedrooms (*Bedroom Farce* of 1975).

So, greeted as they entered the auditorium with the rear-view sight of a carefully created 'cross-section of a modern or recently modernized house, perhaps on an executive-type estate', his audience might already anticipate that things will not be as simple as they appear. With the audience I had to discover, what the director or any reader of the text is told from the outset, that this opened-up house will operate as the different residences of all the characters in the 'small family business' without any alterations being made to the rooms' contents.

A simple explanation of this device would be to say that it allows the playwright to move the action from house to house without either a great deal of effort and money being spent or by scaling down the complicatedly constructed set, allowing a more mobile form of particularization to signal the moves. And cer-tainly, on the Saturday afternoon matinee that I attended, the audience applauded politely every time the set shuddered slightly to indicate, with a change in the lighting state, that we had moved. But this is not the point.

Again the set will operate not simply as a naturalistically realized location for the prosperous lives of the play's characters. Its very adaptability, its anonymity, will become a central part of Ayckbourn's theme. The instructions on the set in the printed text make the point very clearly. Everything is modern and lacking in individuality. It has 'neutral carpeting'; the back kitchen is contemporary and 'sufficiently lacking in detail to be practically identical to a hundred other kitchens'; the bathroom has units 'all in a matching, unobtrusive pastel shade'; and the sitting-room is 'once again modern and nondescript, rather as if the owners had in all cases settled for a modern range of good, modern, mass-produced units to satisfy their needs throughout the house'.

The houses his characters possess are to be thought of as indis-tinguishable. He even allows for audience laughter when one or other complains that they cannot remember how to find their way around what is an identikit version of their own home. The con-tinual repetition of 'modern' in the instructions is significant. This house, which represents the trappings of success in the Thatcherite years, is tawdry, unimaginative and capable of endless reproduction.

The particular importance of this is that the small family business in which Ayckbourn's characters are involved is Ayres and Graces (the name coming from those of the original proprietors, the almost senile grandfather and his now dead wife), whose label proclaims its adherence to a world of graciously naff living. For it is a business that turns out the kind of modern furniture and fittings with which the house is indeed supplied. The metaphor of architecture and structure of Stoppard's play here gives way to the smaller achievement, that of the characters providing the furnishings for their own set.

The house is therefore both the locus of the series of inter-related domesticities of the play, and also the embodiment of the realities of the business that unites the family. It provides Ayckbourn with the opportunity to look critically at the ideology of the small family business that was at the heart of the Thatcher rhetoric.

It opens with Jack taking over the firm, a moral man determined to get rid of even the most petty of dishonesties in the running of the firm. Almost immediately blackmailed into hiring a private investigator to examine the corrupt practices of the firm – rather than allow the investigator to press for prosecution against his daughter for shop-lifting – he ends by conniving with the rest of the family in a systematic process of fraud; covering up the killing of the investigator, and planning a drug involvement with the business's Italian connection in a way which invites comparison of the running of this family with that of the Mafia.

The play is certainly not uncritical of the family's activities – activities which see the play ending with the daughter apparently dying from a drug overdose – but it is very hard for the text of the play to overcome the ideological weight of the endlessly flexible family home that dominates the stage. *A Small Family Business* ends as it had begun, with a surprise family celebration in Jack and Polly's home. The house remains at the end, as solid as the family that continues to inhabit it, leaving questions hovering of course but with no suggestion that the set might be demolished.

The difference between the two models provided by Stoppard and Ayckbourn is that the unreliability of the room in *The Real Thing* acts to prevent questions being asked; whereas in *A Small*

Family Business its solidity stands as a deliberate affront to the questions that Ayckbourn wishes to ask about the nature of the family unit in such a society. They represent the two polarities of the new mainstream ideologically – a theatre that insists that ultimately wit, play is all, and a theatre that at least attempts a liberal critique of the model.

What this suggests is the need for a relocation of, amongst other things, the way in which we define the notion of political in relation to theatre. Most of the debate on the matter – usually allowing the tag 'political' to be attached to writers who are left of centre, as opposed to those of the middle ground or right of centre who are deemed to be somehow non-political – has foundered on the insistence on arguing from the point of production. The plays are thus the products of individual writers who can be seen either to have a conscious political intent in writing, to be hostile to such an intent – as in Stoppard's early career – or to supposedly ignore the whole area in favour of an emphasis, impossibly, on domestic relationships outside any larger context. It is essential that the debate is moved from the point of production to that of reception. It is in the dialogue between performance and audience, or rather audiences, that the politics of a play is formed; and it is here that attention should be directed. A central part of my argument in the chapter on Ayckbourn's plays is a consideration of the difference between audiences at Scarborough and London's National Theatre and the resultant effects both on the playwright's own writing and on the way in which individual plays were read politically. For, to argue that a play can somehow maintain a political neutrality is as absurd as the opposing supposition that a play can only be deemed political if it proclaims itself so in crude *'agit-prop'* terms. In the post-modern world more than ever there are no neutrals – either side of the stage.

I want now to look directly at the most successful playwrights of the new mainstream. My choice is to a degree selective, but made with the intention of demonstrating the variety of stances available in post-1979 'serious' theatre – a theatre with many rooms, but with a distinctly limited social landscape discernible through their windows. But first a brief non-digression.

In a book that carries as part of its title the claim to be considering 'British contemporary mainstream theatre', a number of rather obvious omissions may seem apparent. For many readers the two most obvious will probably be that the playwrights are all male, and that they are all (Stoppard in an admittedly rather complex way) English. It is worth dwelling on this a little.

Some of the most important and exciting drama of the 1980s was produced by women writers; to cite the work of Caryl Churchill and Sarah Daniels alone, for instance, is to ignore a real body of new writing that sought to define the problems of contemporary society in ways that, directly or indirectly, related them to a specifically feminist analysis. It is indeed arguable that the major energy of the committed drama tradition post-1979 stemmed from those various feminist discourses that many analysts have seen as the most significant component of contemporary political debate on the largely ineffectual left. And it is true, of course, that Churchill's *Serious Money* was one of the more significant transfers from the Royal Court to London's West End in this period; a play that both acknowledged the continuing dominance of a male culture in the world of the new money markets, and sought with a disturbing honesty to consider the compromised position of women in that world.

But, although there have been a number of one-off mainstream successes for women writers in the contemporary theatre – Mary O'Malley's *Once a Catholic*, for instance – that mainstream continues, as always, to remain effectively the property of male writers. Just as I described the Hugh and Margaret Williams' plays of the 60s as incorporating watered-down versions of alternative themes, so the new mainstream has occasionally, and partially, at least responded to aspects of feminism; but, by its very nature, it has done so in ways that seek to strip it of any real degree of radical challenge.

To return to my earlier point, it has done so because the entire production side of the theatre, from the theatre impresarios and owners, to the directors, writers and stage staff, remain largely male; and it has done so because it is assumed that the audiences are similarly constituted. It is not that a mainstream audience actually consists entirely of – to synthesize this argument into a larger one – white, middle-class male heterosexuals; it is rather that it tacitly assumes this consensus, constructing, in effect, an 'ideal' audience for which plays will be produced. It does so precisely because this construction is an essential part of the marginalization of alternative perspectives that allows for the perpetuation of any mainstream culture – be it theatre, pop music, advertising, or whatever – drawing from, but diffusing the energy of, oppositional strategies. The consumer society has an active interest in the consumption of opposition, can indeed not continue to develop without it.

Thus, just as a woman writer wishing to introduce specifically feminist themes onto the stage is effectively denied access, so a potential member of an audience expecting an incorporation of such discourse will be quickly disappointed; and the wheel continues to turn. Jill Dolan put the point well in 1988, when she sought to deconstruct the idea of such an 'ideal' audience by a feminist spectator:

> The feminist spectator might find that her gender – and/or her race, class, or sexual preference – as well as her ideology and politics make the representation alien and even offensive. It seems that as a spectator she is far from ideal. Determined to draw larger conclusions from this experience, she leaves the theatre while the audience applauds at the curtain call and goes off to develop a theory of feminist performance criticism.[5]

Not allowed an acceptable place in the mainstream, feminist theatre is forced, has been forced, to develop in what remains of the alternative theatrical world. Susan Bennett made the point more generally in 1990:

> Not all challenges to the mainstream are, of course, accepted. Brecht suggested that innovations which require a repositioning of cultural markers will only be accepted if they rejuvenate rather than undermine existing society. Perhaps for the reason Brecht suggested, there has, for many workers in marginalised theatre, been neither the opportunity nor the desire to participate in the mainstream. Not all writers and performers have been content to challenge from within the mainstream cultural definition and location of theatre. In the political and/or performance aims of alternative theatres, the idea of theatre is generally repositioned and invariably expanded.[6]

And what venues then remain for (the resiliently deceased Agatha Christie notwithstanding) the woman writer who might seek to write on other than gender-specific issues – denied both the mainstream and its alternative?

In the final chapter I offer an analysis of the programmes of 164

British mainstream theatres in the 1992 autumn season. From the point of view of the second consideration raised, the 'Englishness' of my chosen writers, what is most striking is the degree of uniformity of the theatrical programmes. Of course there is Welsh language drama in Wales, as surely as Liverpool shows a distinct bias towards plays written by playwrights associated with that city; but in theatre after theatre, all over that uneasy conglomeration that is still described as mainland Britain, relatable patterns emerge. To ignore these patterns, to highlight the impressive amount and quality of work still being produced in Scotland's Traverse Theatre, for instance, would be to embark on a different kind of analysis. For magnificent though the efforts of the Traverse are, they are no more representative of the overall state of Scottish theatre than are the equally impressive efforts of the Theatre Royal, Stratford East, of the English.

For, if it is possible to talk of the mainstream as having a conscious, rather than a tacit, programme, then one of its central planks is a stress on the conformity, the exchangeability in commodity terms, of the theatrical product. The continuing use of the 'British' tag is an important part of that programme – a point made only too apparent in the recent and continuing obsession of the media with the role of the British monarchy, as with Thatcher's appeal to a jingoistic patriotism at the time of the Falklands conflict and the miners' strike. It is for this reason that I write of the British theatre – only too aware of the political problems involved in so doing. Thus, the fact that my choice of writers is all English is as much a part of those problems as that they are all, for instance, male.

6

Peter Nichols: All my Life in Tudor Manor

Hedley: What should they know of England who only know Heathrow?

Quennie: Knock it off, Hed. I know England. I lived all my life in Tudor Manor till I came to my senses. The irony, the privacy, the un-quote eccentricity. Over there you hear so often about the wonderful British theeyater you almost come to believe it so last night I went to a play. Irony. Sooner or later, no matter how the writer tries to slice it, the actors finish in a row delivering quote-unquote witty lines, and discussing the state of the nation. No conflict, no action, no resolution, no hope. Everybody goes home depressed out of their skulls.

Hedley: I'd have thought the West End theatre was the last place to look for an awareness of change.

(Peter Nichols, *Born in the Garden*, 1979)

There could be no more suitable writer with whom to start this section of the book than Peter Nichols. His dramatic roots lie in the first modern revival of the 50s, with television work dating from 1959; and he even received a passing mention in John Russell Taylor's *Anger and After* (1962). His first stage play, *A Day in the Death of Joe Egg*, was not produced until 1967, however, and in the years that followed his has proved to be one of the most important voices of the new mainstream.

His plays have been consistently successful and highly acclaimed critically. Both *Joe Egg* and its successor, *The National Health* (produced by the National Theatre at the Old Vic in 1969), were winners of the *Evening Standard* 'Best Play of the Year' award, and his work through the 70s was similarly honoured.

At the time of the May 1979 Conservative election victory he had a new play ready for production, a play that provides a perfect insight into the state of the new mainstream and its relationship to contemporary history. The play, *Born in the Gardens*, opened in Bristol in August of that year before transferring to the Globe in London in 1980. Its ostensible context, the events surrounding the funeral of a husband and father, places it securely in the world of domestic affairs and grief that has been the major preoccupation of his work, but it is undeniably a play that seeks to address the 'state of the nation' question.

The action takes place in a rambling and run-down mock-Tudor mansion. The house, whose neighbours are on one side squatters, and on the other Chinese, is now inhabited by the recently widowed Maud and her son Mo, a dealer in genteel nineteenth-century pornography and a lover of traditional jazz. They are both uneasy leftovers of a past world, attempting to deal without a great deal of success with a modern one of microwaves ('Michael waves', as Maud insists on calling them), deep-freezes, dishwashers, dimmer lights and colour television. Surrounded by all the apparent evidence of the supposed consumerist paradise, Mo mourns for the passing of the 78 rpm record (his traditional jazz is now stocked under 'Nostalgia' at the 'new Music Emporia': 'anything before last week is under Nostalgia'), and Maud abandons her colour television in favour of a black and white model (as Mo says, 'She never took to colour. The people didn't look natural') which she watches with the sound off so that she can address the faces on the screen.

The electronic goodies are provided by another son, Hedley, a backbench Labour MP, though Maud is unable to remember which party he represents, and hopes that now his Conservative Party has been elected he will be able to do something about the decline of the nation, a decline she attributes chiefly to the influx of foreigners, best represented for her by 'Sambo' at her local shop which she patronizes, along with the local hypermarkets, to buy mammoth supplies of packet soups and Tampax to stock her deep-freeze in an attempt to convince Hedley that she is really making use of her present.

The play's almost automatic cataloguing of a satirized world of consumerism is an insistent theme, and this alone makes connections with the earlier Absurdist tradition. But Nichols is more specific in his contextualization of the action. This is the England of the 1970s Labour administration as seen through a series of exceedingly unprogressive eyes. Not only is Hedley quickly revealed as totally unsympathetic to any real thoughts of socialist

change, but he is joined for the funeral at the house by his twin
sister Queenie, a born-again Californian, who has managed to
incorporate her visit, and its expenses, into a commission for an
American newspaper article on 'The Sick Men of Europe', with
visits to Ireland, Italy, Spain and Portugal to follow. Given her
views on her native land, her name is consciously ironic. Asked
how she has found things after a fourteen-month gap, she is quick
to respond:

> No, nothing's changed. Not the little gardens as you come in at
> Heathrow, nor the little garden sheds, nor the chimneys
> stacked on the little houses. And however homesick you may
> have felt out tnere in the real world, you could suddenly
> scream. The airport staff huddle in truculent groups like
> working men from a *Punch* cartoon debating the earliest
> moment they can decently take their tea-break. No one moves,
> except after reference to some petty set of ideological quibbles
> based on a Labour Party mythology about the bad old days.
> And everything's so small – it's Dinkytown . . . No, nothing's
> changed, there isn't room. And because of that it's all getting
> steadily worse.

Mo's ironic question, 'You discovered all that before you left the
airport?' does little to destroy the vigour of the critique. It simply
allows Queenie to identify irony as the other great awfulness of
contemporary Britain, launching her into the attack on the theatre
quoted at the outset.

Her twin brother's role as Labour MP should, of course, provide
a meaningful opposition to her attack, 'The net curtains are
coming down all over England,' he tells her, but his is a position
of both personal and public disillusion. He knows he will now
never rise to Cabinet office, and he concludes the play by essentially accepting his sister's pessimism:

> *Hedley*: I should be used to this by now. You bring them heaven
>   on earth and they throw it back in your face.
> *Mo*: Heaven's not on earth, is it? By definition.
> *Queenie*: It can be. But not for everyone. There's never enough to
>   go round. You let the mob into paradise, they come in
>   mobile-homes playing radios. They cage the gorillas and kill
>   the whales.

The reference to the 'gorillas' takes us into the symbolic heart of the play. We learn early on that the zoo at Bristol, the town where the play is set as well as originally produced, housed a gorilla that, it is claimed, was the oldest one in captivity. It is he, Albert (the name probably ironically recalling that of Queen Victoria's consort), who was 'born in the gardens' – a theoretically wild animal, opposing the world of civilization and the electronic gadgetry of the new Garden of Eden, but caged, as he has been from birth, and contained. Indeed, he is now dead, safely stuffed and on exhibition in a museum for tourists to gawp at, much as Hedley imagines could happen to England in a near future: 'Mock-ups of all the sights at the airport. A huge Disneyland with a monorail to take you straight from your plane to Buckingham Palace, the Tower, *The Mousetrap*, the Waxworks, a typical English pub, et cetera, finishing with the biggest Y-front shop in the world and this would lead you back to the departure lounge without having to go to London at all.' There is never any expression from any of the characters of the possibility of change, other than for the worst. The potential freedom of a world of socialism is reduced in this argument, as elsewhere in the play, into a diatribe against *demos*, the mob, that can only be expected to litter the garden.

Maud and Mo also see themselves as 'born in the garden', but it is an Eden of impossible nostalgia. In this sense the house, with pretensions to a Tudor antiquity which are actually mock, becomes the location for a debate about the state of the country – continually given modern additions by the interventions of the Labour MP, Hedley, which are always resisted by the ambivalently portrayed traditional inhabitants (for it is only in Mo and Maud that Nichols locates any real warmth, any real fervour, however absurd they may seem). As always, it is the convert to the ideology of the new world, Queenie, who brings the recurring imagery of 'heaven', 'garden' and 'paradise' into the sharpest focus:

Merrie England! A fake-Tudor mansion with a lot of modern equipment no one knows how to operate or repair. The telly is the best in the world – even if the sound doesn't work – the corner shop is run by an African Asian, the post office by a Sikh, the doctor's from Hong-Kong and the natives are all unemployed.

Hedley and Queenie plan to sell off Tudor Manor, which is already part of the family company's assets, at a profit (pragmatic English politician and American entrepreneur united in a deal to sell off the country for what it will yield), and rehouse Maud and Mo in a modern duplex – near to London rather than Bristol Zoo. They leave the action abruptly, Hedley to return to the twin demands of a shell-shocked wife and mistress, Queenie giving the outline of her account of 'The Sick Men of England' down a transatlantic telephone line to a lover who she becomes aware is already entertaining an alternative bed-mate.

The last scene returns us to Mo and Maud alone again, the guests departed and the coffin that had dominated the room at the outset finally removed. Nothing has changed, and in this account of the state of the nation nothing is ever going to change. A Conservative administration has taken over from a Labour one, but the pair's dialogue continues as before, two almost Beckett-like characters living in their mutually recreated pasts. Mo continues to play old jazz records, and instead of the fresh start wished upon them in a new house, Hedley has settled instead, and for once quite suitably, on the installation of a waste disposal unit. It was a bleak vision with which to welcome the brave new world of monetarism.

Now, it is possible to identify two quite distinct, though related, lines of development in the play; and these relate to comparable lines of development in Nichols' work as a whole. The first allies him strongly with the native Absurdist tradition discussed in Chapter 4. It posits an essentially nostalgic opposition against change, modernism, and the like, offering a satirical critique against a world of consumerism quite easily linkable to early efforts such as Cooper's *Everything in the Garden*. The second concentrates on the role of the family, always seen at moments of crisis (for in Nichols' world to be in a family is to be in a permanent state of crisis). The result is that, in the best of his work, the thematic concerns of the play are debated by characters given a solid social and domestic background. If they discuss the state of the world, they do so with a conscious attempt on the part of the playwright to engage the audience in the psychological reality of the characters.

The most extreme version of the first line of development is to be found in *The Freeway*, one of the last contemporary plays to be performed by the National Theatre at its Old Vic home in 1974 before it transferred to the South Bank. In this play Nichols invokes a slightly futuristic world in which all political parties are united in promising the freedom of all citizens to run a car, and in which all other social and caring services for those who cannot do so have been sacrificed in the cause of making the country a gigantic 'free' way.

The play opens, and is entirely set, in a traffic jam caused by the combined efforts of the Scrubbers – the 'anti-motor group whose avowed aim is to paralyse the Freeway' – and a strike by the Wreckers' and Breakers' Union. Thus Nichols is able to postulate an ultimate nightmare in which the newly appointed Minister for Movement is unable to do anything about moving the traffic in an England which has symbolically, and in reality, come to an absolute standstill; and at the same time to offer nothing other than, on one hand, the activities of a group of militants described in terms of mindless Luddites and, on the other, vestiges of the worst parodies of the trade union movement, as an opposition.

The historical context is important. In December 1973, the Conservative Prime Minister had declared a state of emergency, and introduced a 'three-day week' to conserve energy supplies as a result of the second miners' strike. The strike, and Heath's response to it, was to bring about the fall of the government (in itself accounting for the vehemency with which Margaret Thatcher sought to break the miners in the struggles of the 80s). The Labour Party were able to form a minority government after a General Election the following May, and in October of 1974 – the very month that *The Freeway* opened – Harold Wilson went to the polls again and returned with a working majority.

The play is unequivocal in its distaste for what is represented by the spread of the importance of the motor car – the despoilation of the countryside, the systematic vandalization of urban life, the lack of spending on public services. Indeed, the narrative setting allows Nichols many characteristic swipes at the absurdities and casual brutalities of the contemporary world. For instance, although the traffic is stalled in the middle of what is left of rural England, virtually no remnants of traditional rural life are left. There are no animals in the fields (only dairy complexes in distant sheds), and the only non-human sounds we hear are of the hungry guard dogs patrolling the wire fences to contain the would-be travellers within the bounds of the freeway and frighten potential thieves as the situation moves into a struggle for simple survival. Early on, an American describes how children are brought to see chickens ('the old-fashioned kind with the beaks left on') at the British Columbia county fairs and May, one of the inhabitants of the motor-home that dominates the set, is allowed to respond, 'That's nice, keeping up the old ways'. The world of factory-farming is well within reach of the play's satirical account of this 'brave new world'.

These kind of attacks link easily with those offered by the kind of bourgeois-consumerist satires thrown up by the Absurdist tradition. And Nichols provides a representative set of characters to engage in debate. But what they represent is limited and limiting. There is, sure enough, a Conservative lord, James, accompanied by his mother Nancy, and, Les, a union-supporting Ford worker who has risen to the rank of supervisor, but there is almost no one to develop the argument beyond an essential agreement on the awfulness of what is happening. The sole exception is Wally, who has left the car factory in protest at the inhumanity of the production line, a vaguely anarchic figure who is left alone at the end of the play once the 'Great Walk' off has started, a hunter armed with weapons in the jungle. A short example of the dialogue will demonstrate the problems of structural discourse. Les has been describing the factory policy of first attending to the production line before looking to the welfare of a man who has collapsed in action:

> *Les*: One night, I remember, just as a shift was starting, a fellow drops down right by the line. 'Course, all the lads crowd round but just then the buzzer goes and the line starts moving. I said 'All right, lads, get on with your work.' And being as they trusted me, see, James, they turned to it, sticking on the hub-caps while I got an operative to take the casualty's place, then called the ambulance men. D'you know, he was stone dead. Gone off the first instant, they reckoned, and been lying there ever since. So – as I said to the lads during tea-break – no purpose would have been served by disrupting the line, losing bonuses. No, that line never stopped.
>
> *Wally*: Nor did the men. That's why I quit.
>
> *Nancy*: It's been confirmed that the Scrubbers are the cause, James.
>
> *May*: Dirty little animals.

Nancy: They should be thrown into gaol along with the trades-
union leaders. Don't you agree, Mrs Lorimer?

James: Mother, you must learn to distinguish between a gang of
unwashed narcissists and a body of democratically elected
delegates. Mrs Lorimer, a brandy and soda?

The problem being that, in this play, it is effectively impossible
to make such distinctions. James may here appear to be making a
valid point; as the play develops it is increasingly clear that he is
simply rehearsing a useful line for his 'constituents'. The play
deploys the various contributors to the debate as, quite simply,
part of the satire. Even though several of them do behave
humanely in the emergency – Nancy even helping to deliver a
baby – there is no suggestion that this temporary social cohesion
can lead anywhere.

By the end James, his escape route assured, is able to talk to Les
of the Houses of Parliament as the place 'where we conduct the
friendly tug-of-war between the apparently different interests of
your faction and mine', and only Wally is allowed a dissenting
voice. Accused by Les of being a 'bleeding malcontent' he
responds:

Wally: I watched them greedy bastards run the world. And I
watched them turn the rest into greedy bastards too. Like a
plague it's been, except not with rats but money.

Evelyn: If it's a plague, there's nothing to be done then, is there?

Wally: Quit running. Make it work, wherever you happen to be.

That there is an oppositional voice to be heard at all in itself
singles out this play; but Nichols' characters are too wooden, too
obviously satirical tools to give much weight to such, anyway
minimal, opposition. Wally's is not a critique of labour, simply a
localized complaint about the treatment of labourers. Of all
Nichols' stage plays, it is the least naturalistic, the one where he
has leaned furthest away from the creation of rounded characters,
the one that perhaps most obviously relates him to the earlier
Absurdist roots.

For the most single significant fact about Nichols' writing career
is that he, more than anyone I will discuss in this book, was
entirely reliant on television as a medium for his early work; a
medium that both encouraged and nurtured a naturalism that is

almost inescapably associated with the writer. Brian Miller in 1981:

> His television plays are assumed to come straight and undis-
> tilled from his own life. Perhaps it is his concentration upon
> family and domestic subjects, the parallels to be drawn between
> characters in different plays, the high degree of naturalism in
> the dialogue and ease of characterization suggesting 'slice of life'
> that reinforce this view. Nichols isn't, some might say, a true
> dramatist at all, but a human tape-recorder, albeit a highly
> accurate and selective one.[1]

Although Miller goes on rightly to argue that, this impression notwithstanding, Nichols' television plays are actually very skil-fully constructed with a considerable emphasis on form, the general point remains. His television plays do place a heavy premium on naturalism, and they do involve a series of rework-ings of apparently biographical material. And it is this second line of development – opposed to the unusually skeletal discourse model of *The Freeway* – that really accounts for his success as a stage writer.

What Nichols offers his audience, above all, is a series of stock-takings of marriage and the family, by no means separated from wider social contexts but in which the personal and the domestic are always strongly foregrounded. When he did belatedly make his stage debut as a writer, with *A Day in the Death of Joe Egg* in 1967, he received immediate popular and critical acclaim. The play, which concerned the efforts of a young couple to deal with life with an unresponding 'human parsnip' child, was thought to breach new theatrical ground.

In many ways, its success could be paralleled with that of Brian Clark who, in 1978, struck what was obviously the correct audience nerve with *Whose Life Is It Anyway*, a play concerned with the efforts of a patient wanting to take responsibility for his own death rather than allow the hospital's insistence on perpetu-ating his existence on ethical grounds. Like Nichols, Clark had also served a long television apprenticeship; eleven years apart, both writers gained the biggest hits of their careers with works that seemed to depend more on the topicality of their themes than on any innate virtues in their plays.

However, the comparison should not be taken too far. Nichols used the break from television to experiment in a way that he had clearly found impossible before. From the start the piece insists that it is a stage play, with the man, Bri, addressing the audience direct, bawling them out for their lack of concentration and promising to keep them there all night. The technique of asides is used frequently throughout the play, giving the audience a privileged position as the couple attempt to enact and analyse both their own relationship and the 'umbilically' linked one with the unresponding child.

This willingness to experiment with the parameters of naturalism has characterized all Nichols' efforts for the stage. His *The National Health* of 1970, for instance, was given the sub-title *Nurse Norton's Affair*; the play moved between the main plot, which concerned the attempts of the inhabitants of a male hospital ward to create individual identities for themselves in a world of unifying institutionalization, and a parody of the sort of television 'soap' that sees hospitals primarily as locations for nurse and doctor romances.

But his supreme achievement on stage to date is *Forget-Me-Not-Lane* (first staged at the Greenwich Theatre in 1971, televised by the BBC in 1975, and revived at the same theatre in 1990). In it Nichols draws from his experience of television naturalism – he even took time out while writing it to provide the BBC with the related script of *Hearts and Flowers* – but uses the resources of a stage in a way that would make his a significant contribution to contemporary theatre if he had never written another word. Its lack of recognition is a disgrace; its deployment of stage space evidently an impetus to the writer to continue his attempt to infuse the mainstream with experiment, but he was never again to succeed so brilliantly.

Irving Wardle praised the play extravagantly on its revival in 1990, even though he was critical of the production. What he stressed, above all, was its originality in 1971 when, as he argues, it was pioneering techniques since copied by other writers:

Memory, as Nichols presents it, is Pandora's box. Open it, and you lose control of the contents. Novelists know all about this. To show it on stage required a new technique, which Nichols supplied by combining direct narration with remembered scenes, all located in a continuous psychological present. For audiences primed on the flashback, it came as a stunning insight when the remembered characters started talking back to the hero – 'I'm part of your mental landscape for ever, duckie,' – until he is left screaming at them to leave him alone.[2]

What this continual and fluid movement to and fro through history allowed was an intense analysis of the pull of family – both good and bad – over the life of the individual. It operates almost on the level of a publicly rehearsed drama-therapy project, though always with the knowing skills of a superb dramatic craftsman present not only to shape the piece, but to make clear to the audience that they are having that shaping displayed to them. For instance, in the second act, we see the father, Charles – who is actually dead and being recalled – playing his new set of mail-order records, much to the chagrin of his wife, Amy, who can think of other things to spend the money on. The son, Frank, tries to interpose, moves himself into another time and is immediately moved again by his wife, Ursula:

> *Amy*: Only last week I asked for the money for a spring outfit and he said we couldn't run to it. As though he hasn't got enough records banging away all day and night.
> *Frank*: Why don't you take some interest in his music? Isn't that one of your common interests?
> *Charles*: You hold your tongue, Sonny Jim.
> *Frank*: Sonny Jim? I'm nearly forty. A middle-aged man with three whopping kids.
> *Ursula*: No, at this time you were nearly thirty and Matthew hadn't been born.
> *Frank*: Oh, Christ!

Nichols' intricate tracing of the tangled relationship between father and son is unmatched on the modern stage. A comparison between the deployment of two similarly functioning scenes in *Forget-Me-Not-Lane* and Peter Shaffer's *Equus* will serve by way of illustration.

Towards the end of Shaffer's play the boy Alan – whose supposedly motiveless blinding of the horses provides both the starting-point and the focus of investigation – describes a visit to a soft-porn movie. The scene is acted out so that we discover the presence of the boy's father in the audience at the same moment as Alan. This scene and its aftermath provide what is in effect the final piece in a jig-saw, the sudden jolt of realization on the part of the boy of the double standards which have ruled his domestic life.

The scene functions much like that in a conventional stage thriller – when the audience suddenly learns that the nice Vicar is not so nice after all. It is, like all of the revelations in the play, clumsily inserted and dramatically too glib. Towards the end of Nichols' play, the son, Frank, asks his mother to recall a variety concert they attended in 1940. Instantly, as always, the scene moves smoothly into the dramatization of the event, but this time it has been carefully prepared for. The significance of the variety turns in the lives of mother, father and son has been an integral part not only in the remembered history of their relationship but in the very way in which the play is structured. We have already met these particular performers, Mr Magic and Miss 1940; Frank's father's noisy opposition to the man's smutty jokes is not intended to serve as a kind of instant explanation of anything – rather it comes as the culmination of a series of 'recalls' that stress the complexity and not the simplicity of the event's effect psychologically.

In his later plays, Nichols continued to plunder versions of his own life, but with a new element, the kind of self-reflecting irony that Queenie describes as being the peculiarly English disease in *Born in the Gardens*. Where *Forget-Me-Not-Lane* operated as a savagely comic examination of his own roots – a brilliant synthesis of all his work to that date – his subsequent work was forced to move on, to consider not where the playwright had come from, but where he had got to and, more disturbingly, where he was going to. For he was now a popular and successful playwright with access to worlds unknown by the characters of *Forget-Me-Not-Lane*.

In his diary account of that play's genesis Nichols starts off by informing us that it was written in a 'detached Victorian house beside Blackheath in South East London' bought with the royalties from the Broadway run of *Joe Egg;*[3] and from this point the lives of the characters in his domestic plays start to become increasingly upwardly mobile. By 1974, the action in *Chez Nous* has moved to a writer's rebuilt retreat in France, and the characters' speech has acquired a knowing wit not previously to be found. It could be said, with reference to Tynan's remarks earlier,[4] that as his own success as a writer has improved his financial lot and social status, so have the trappings of the characters he writes about improved; in this he has perhaps reflected most accurately the *angst* of the winners rather than the losers in the world of modern monetarist economics. But then, in the 80s, it was the winners who were mostly patronizing the British theatre.

No better example of the kind could be given than Nichols' first stage play of the 80s, *Passion Play*, which was performed by the RSC at the Aldwych, before being immediately revived in the West End, in 1981. The opening set description gives us a fair idea of what to expect. It 'resembles (and at times represents) a fashionable art gallery', and the characters we will see on stage are of the stuff of which the finances of a 'fashionable art gallery' are made.

The play is about adultery, about its passions and its deceits; and by the same token, it is about marriage and its passions and deceits. It was territory that had been handled memorably by Pinter in his only major stage play since *No Man's Land*, *Betrayal* (National Theatre, 1978), where the playwright had used the simple device of reversing time to show the affair as over before it had begun. But where Pinter ekes out the dialogue in characteristically economic style, Nichols' characters engage in the fully developed cut and thrust of witty repartee in a manner comparable to those of Stoppard's *The Real Thing*, to the extent that it would be entirely possible to imagine the two sets of characters meeting at events on the same social round.

I make these connections deliberately, for they are a measure not only of Nichols' assured status as a writer by the 80s but of the way in which *Passion Play* embraces the world of privilege of this then coming decade – a world of success far removed from the harsher economic realities of earlier work. The plot centres chiefly on James, a wealthy picture-dealer and restorer, his adulterous relationship with Kate, at twenty-five just half his age, and its effect on his previously unthreatened marriage with Eleanor, a woman it transpires he hardly knows. He spends much of the play restoring a classical painting of the 'passion' of Christ, and concludes it by repairing a blemish on an all-yellow modern acrylic; moving from the old to the new but, by implication, losing on the way the emotion of 'real' art (a point reinforced by the exhibition of Kate's photographs taken as she zooms across the world that James and Eleanor attend in the course of the play).

But the main force of the play does not come from this rather uneasy symbolism, for it is hard to see art in this world as anything other than money. It comes almost entirely from the interplay between the characters, interplay in which wit always threatens to give way to real emotion. It results in some wonderfully comic moments – perhaps the most successful being Eleanor and James' being brought to accept the idea of a *menage à trois* in bed by a Kate who, it emerges, has actually come to tell them about a new lover she has met on a plane. Theirs is an international world in which assignations can be planned on a global scale, and if the characters have worries – and they do aplenty – then lack of money is certainly not one of them.

The play depends heavily on the sheer cleverness of the dialogue to carry it through but, as always, Nichols has a theatrical device or two to spring on the audience. James' real problem is that, as the man said, he wants to have his cake and eat it too – to keep his happy marriage and at the same time maintain his relationship with his mistress. To this is added his sense that, somehow, he has lost out, that the lack of inhibition displayed by Kate is a continual reminder of all the things that he had never done, or been able to do, when young. To this end, Nichols introduces two alter-ego figures, Jim and Nell, who occupy the stage at the same time as James and Eleanor. Frequently debating with their 'real' counterparts, they become increasingly independent as the play develops. In Act II the four take part in a complicated argument:

> *Eleanor*: If you think it's only your poor old cock she's after, you're flattering yourself.
> (*Jim gives her a glass of water.*)
> *Nell*: She wants to take you away from me.
> *James*: I don't think we can ever know with her. She belongs to another generation – free of convention, independent –
> *Nell*: Hah!
> *James*: One of the people men of my age wanted to create.
> *Jim*: Yes, the freedom we advocated is the air they breathe.
> *Nell*: (*to Jim*) Her independence is based on daddy's tax-dodge trusts.
> *James*: She parks on double yellow lines, she walks straight to the head of queues, she grabs what's going –
> *Eleanor*: In other words, disregards the morality you've always lived by.

James: I've been very moral, yes.
Eleanor: So go to her. What's keeping you here?
Jim: You!
Nell: An old flavour?
Jim: *(indicating the room)* This!
Nell: A prison?
Jim: *(to* Nell) We need her, Eleanor. She can save us.
Nell: You can't have both.
Jim: Why not?

What is also very much of the 80s about the play, however, is that its preoccupation with a world of wealth and privilege notwithstanding, Nichols has responded to a decade or so of feminist critique of, amongst other things, the depiction of women on stage. The central figure may be a James who goes jogging with a pocketful of ten-pence pieces in his tracksuit pocket to phone his mistress; but as the play develops we are increasingly shown the other side of adultery, a side Eleanor had been told about at the beginning by Agnes – estranged wife of Kate's now dead lover.

It is Agnes who informs her of Kate's new liaison with James, and it is to her that Nell talks about the 'specialist' her husband has prescribed for her emotional problems after the revelation:

Nell: I thought I was going mad. They told me it was a symptom of the menopause.
Agnes: Who did?
Nell: The doctors.
Agnes: All men?
Nell: Yes.
Agnes: They're everywhere.

And a little later Agnes spells it out for her. The doctor she has been sent to is the same one her husband advised when she found out about his affair: 'Their old chum Michael at the Middlesex sends all the psychologically battered wives to him. It's part of the male conspiracy.'

The strength of this female perspective in the play is in part evidence of the way in which all mainstream traditions depend upon the incorporation of oppositional strategies for their continued survival. However, it is also a logical development to expect from a writer in whose work women have never played a

simply supporting role. But Queenie's almost incidental remark to
Mo about his pornographic books ('Why is it dirty books are
never to do with sex, only cruelty?') in *Born in the Gardens* pales
into insignificance when set against, for instance, Sarah Daniels'
radically feminist attack on pornography in *Masterpieces* (1983).
The degree to which feminist ideas are able to be incorporated
into *Passion Play*, a work aimed at a solidly mainstream audience,
results only in a further strand of a still open debate – and cannot
actually change the determining structure of the model.

And so the play finishes with two alternative endings played
simultaneously. A Christmas party is about to start at the house.
For the first time Eleanor and Nell separate, the wife to get ready
for the party, the alter-ego (now acting independently) to plan a
parting. James welcomes guests whilst, unseen by the others, Jim
and Kate embark on yet another sexual encounter. Meanwhile
Nell leaves by the front door, opting for her own life outside
marriage in a way that Eleanor still cannot – and the play's last
words are given to Eleanor, still keeping up appearances and
wishing everyone 'Happy Christmas'.

This move towards a redefinition of the drama of adultery
should have resulted in a fascinating series of plays as Nichols
sought to come to terms with the new world of the 80s. Sadly it
did not. His next effort was *Poppy* – which was accorded the
status of first new play at the RSC's new Barbican theatre in 1982.
It is a peculiar piece of lavishly produced knockabout pantomime
dealing with the opium trade between Britain and China. Using
many of the devices of the creakiest of early 1970s *agit-prop*
theatre, it concludes with a desperate attempt at contemporary
relevance as Queen Victoria is transformed into Elizabeth II and
Dick Whittington into a modern city gent for the final curtain call.
It is not difficult to see why Nichols should have been allowed to
indulge himself on such a scale by the RSC – no more than might
be thought his due by this date – but sad that he should have
moved so far, and so unsatisfactorily, out of his usual territory to
do so.

Despite the controversy surrounding the production, *Poppy* was
successfully transferred to the West End, even as *Passion Play* was
being revived. Dispirited by what he saw as the latest of a series
of struggles with theatrical managements and directors, Nichols
announced that he had retired from playwriting; whereupon he
retreated to the country and failed to write a novel. His dis-

illusionment with the theatre was, he announced, absolute: 'The theatre has lost her bloom, and her wizened features are raddled under the rouge'.[5] In 1984 he produced *Feeling You're Behind*, a biographical work in which he attempted to place the always obviously personal basis of his work.

And then surprisingly there was *A Piece of My Mind*, a strange comedy about a playwright who stops writing plays and retires to the country where he fails to write a novel. It toured the provinces before coming to the London Apollo in 1987. In it, the playwright considers the efforts of a playwright, Ted Forrest (in his 50s, as was Nichols, just) to act out a play in public about his early success and later decline into lack of popularity and silence.

It is a play that takes Nichols back into the heart of Absurdism, a point made sardonically by one of the actors, temporarily playing a critic and commenting on Forrest's unhappy relationship with his agent: 'The scene where he batters his agent to death in her office aims to be Absurdist but manages to be merely absurd.' It abounds with jokes borrowed from the likes of Pirandello, Wilde and Beckett and offers, amongst other things, a complete ironic history of modern British theatre – a history in which Nichols himself figures along with Alan Bennett, John Osborne, Robert Bolt, Michael Frayn, Julian Mitchell, Tom Stoppard, Christopher Hampton, John Mortimer, Simon Gray, Peter Shaffer and Charles Wood as examples of writers who can be seen as 'supporting the status quo' as opposed to 'advocating revolution'.

In its structure, though not in its development, it looks back to *Forget-Me-Not-Lane*, as the action wanders in and out of different 'real' and stage presents, with Forrest sometimes taking part in the action and sometimes commenting on it. It is a play that is completely impossible to pin down, as is clearly its intention, and one that comes not only from Nichols' own perceptions of his life but from his particular relationship, as a writer for the mainstream, with the institution of theatre:

> I've been asking myself the question: if I could write without thinking all the time about the potential effect and appeal of a play, without thinking about all the commercial aspects and all those things you have to think about as a pro, would that mean I could free myself to start thinking and writing in a new way? Could I retreat from being a very public sort of playwright into something more irresponsible?[6]

As far as the public were concerned, the retreat from the 'commercial aspects' was taken very seriously, the play coming off after a short London run. It remains to be seen how, or indeed if, Nichols proceeds in the future. But then, although the play was reviewed, this may just be part of the joke. The published text tells us that the first performance took place on April 1st. Or not at all?

7

Simon Gray: Bloody Finished at Last

Jeff: I'm English, yes, English to my marrow's marrow. After years of buggering about as a cosmopolitan litterateur, going to PEN conferences in Warsaw, hobnobbing with Frog poets and Eyetye essayists, German novelists and Greek composers, I suddenly realise I hate the lot of them. Furthermore I detest women, love men, loathe queers. D'you know when I'm really at peace with myself? When I'm caught in a traffic jam on an English road, under an English heaven – somewhere between London and Cambridge . . . Oh Christ – it's my bloody opinion that this sad little, bloody little country of ours is finished at last. Bloody finished at last.

(Simon Gray, *Otherwise Engaged*)

Despite his early plays' appropriation of many of the aspects of English Absurdism, Simon Gray's work is the nearest the contemporary mainstream comes to a reworking of the territory of the well-made drawing-room comedy supposedly killed off in the mid-1950s. His characters live on their wits, and by their wit, in a world of social privilege and ease; in a world that may on occasions be seen to be in a state of decline, but is still populated by characters who, however uneasy they may be about their own personal circumstances, are united in a last stand against the values of a modern world.

That on occasions they may have succeeded in this modern world does nothing to ease their distaste for its values. Beneath the witty dialogue there is always, at best, a cynicism and, at worst, a bitterness. Berated by his colleague Michael for the quality of the books they publish, the successful publisher Melon is easily able to answer the objection:

Michael: You know what I hate most about what you've done here, that for the most part we don't even put out honest-to-God crap, for people to read on trains or planes or in the lavatory. We just process commodities. That happen to come in book form.

Melon: Fortunately a lot of people seem to think our commodities useful. (*Working on his calculator.*)

Michael: What you mean by useful is that they make a profit.

Melon: I certainly mean that too, because if they didn't we wouldn't get our wages, would we. And I find mine bloody useful. Don't you?

Michael: Harkness and Gladstone had a great list once. And a tradition. A long tradition. Then you came.

Melon: It had a long overdraft too. It was just about to go under, tradition, list and all. Then I came.

The invocation of the 'tradition' is important, for it is by continual reference to what is understood to be the 'traditionally English' that Gray's characters define their own sense of discomfort or despair with the contemporary. It is a tradition that is, like the unwanted publisher's list, no longer required in a world of popular culture and product promotion; but it is a tradition that provides the ideological base of his characters' lives. That their degree of articulacy extends to an understanding of the irredeemably past nature of that tradition is what prevents his plays from being merely displays of witty dialogue. That the dream may always have been socially divisive is enthusiastically embraced by them; but that it may have been only a dream is the more frightening thought that lurks subversively in the wings for other, less seduced, writers to voice – David Hare in *Teeth 'n' Smiles* (1976), for instance, which presents a very different portrait of 'Cambridge culture' to that so frequently conjured with by Gray.

Ironically, for a man whose stage work proclaims a continual disdain for the workings of the popular media, Gray was more than usually reliant on television to initiate his writing career. His first real success as a writer for the stage did not come until 1971, when *Butley* was a major box-office hit at the Criterion. Like many of his subsequent plays, *Butley* was directed by Harold Pinter and starred Alan Bates. The play, which was dedicated to 'the staff and students, past, present and future of the English Department, Queen Mary College, London', was set in an office modelled on

Gray's own room in that College where for twenty years he was a lecturer.[1]

I start with these connections for two reasons. Firstly, because with all Gray's subsequent work for the stage, *The Rear Column* of 1978 excepted, there is the pervasive feeling given that the plays, whilst not exactly autobiographical, are effectively reworkings of how various parts of his life might have been had people had in real life the wit and precision of his stage characters. Gray has said that he was not Butley, but that he might for a while after have modelled himself on Bates' enactment of the role.[2]

Secondly, because to consider Gray's work in its entirety is to experience the sense of a Gentlemen's Club, a club from which large sections of his audience would be ejected whatever their own thoughts on their own suitability for membership. And like all traditional Gentlemen's Clubs it would clearly not help their cause if they should happen to be female or, the high incidence of homosexuality in his plays notwithstanding, gay.

The prevailing ethos of his plays is not simply masculine. It is a very particular kind of masculine. His male protagonists inhabit a world of privilege, the privilege of wealth usually but, if not, the privilege of education certainly. The twin poles of that world are London and the Home Counties, where the life of (preferably) leisured irony is to be led, and Cambridge, where the practice, if not already perfected, is to be learned.

In *Quartermaine's Terms* (1981) – drawn loosely from Gray's own experience as a teacher of English to foreign students in Cambridge – we are shown the staff-room lives of a disparate bunch of teachers in a declining language school in Cambridge. The school operates as a symbolic location for the ineffectual continuation of the colonial system. The students are spasmodic in their attendance, and the teachers lax in their attention to duties. Only the school's co-founder Eddie Loomis, who will retire before the play's end, can find an optimistic view of the students' involvement in the quintessentially 'English' game of croquet: 'you know, I always feel that if ever our little school had to justify itself, we could do it by showing the world the spectacle of an Italian, a Frenchman, a German, a Japanese, a Swedish girl and a Belgian girl, all gathered on an English lawn, under an English sky to play a game of croquet.'

Loomis is proud of the school's reputation as not the biggest but the best in Cambridge 'which, when it comes down to it, means in the country'. The theme is a recurrent one in Gray's work – as late as 1990 he has a distraught teenager bemoaning the fact that she has only got C grades in her A Levels: 'And that's fail in this family, fail is not getting As in everything you don't get scholarships in and then not going on to Cambridge to win prizes.'[3]

One of Loomis' proudly introduced new innovations in the school curriculum is a lecture course on 'British Life and Institutions'. In the second scene of the play, he meets Quartermaine who has, as always, left his class early, in the week that it had fallen to him to give the lecture. He excuses himself by saying that the new projector had broken – for he is a man completely incapable of handling a world of modern teaching aids – and that he had 'run out of steam a little' relying on his own anecdotes: 'I chose Oxford Colleges – to give them the other point of view, for once.'

Quartermaine is the centre of the play, a deeply unhappy man eager to baby-sit on demand to fill the gaps in his completely empty social calendar. As the play develops he is left sitting in a chair in the staff-room before each break and, discovered there each time on the school's reopening, he gives the impression of never having moved. His teaching, ineffectual at best, lapses into complete silence by the end, unable as ever to put a single name to any of his supposed students.

That he should think a lecture on Oxford Colleges might be the best way of talking about the other side of 'British Life and Institutions' is, of course, entirely characteristic of a man entirely cut off from a public or social world. But the course serves a no more efficiently colonial function when undertaken by Quartermaine's colleague, Windscape:

> Yes, I got into a bit . . . over our parliamentary system. Usually it's perfectly clear to me but this time it all came out rather oddly. Or it must have done, as I had the whole lot dismissing it with contempt – the three or four from the Eastern bloc, all the ones from Fascist countries – the French were the loudest, as always – but even the Japanese – normally such a polite, reticent man – and I don't see how it happened or what I said, but it was rather hard being lectured at on – on political decencies – and shouted at . . . After all, I was only explaining our constitution, not boasting about it.

The school's inculcation of the superiority of the British way of life is as problematic as its teaching methods are inadequate. The Cambridge perspective may be all there is for them, but it is seen to have no real function in a modern world – a fact underlined by Quartermaine's steady movement towards total inertia.

Into the lives of the language schoolteachers Gray introduces an outsider, Derek Meadle, who has, horror of horrors, obtained a degree at Hull University. The new part-timer arrives with trousers ripped, after a bike accident involving some Japanese students, is constantly injuring himself, and is generally apprehended as a kind of social no-go area. His return after the summer half-term one year later in Act II sees him no more integrated into their world. He has been to Sheffield, he tells them, for the funeral of his aunt; to which Windscape responds brightly: 'Sheffield, I know it well. Fanny and I went there the year before Susan was born, we were doing a tour of out-of-the-way urban domestic architecture.'

Meadle, who soon collects an unseen Librarian wife and a working honeymoon in Cleethorpes, is a character who, were this an Ayckbourn play, would end up running the place. As it is he spends most of the time being mocked by the others, increasingly desperate in his attempts to achieve the full-time status of his colleagues. Windscape tries to convince another teacher to be more gentle with him, even though he is not really 'one of us'. 'I do sometimes feel, strictly between ourselves, that it is hard on Meadle as the only part-time teacher – and we must be careful in the staff-room not to show any – any – well make more fun of him than is absolutely necessary.'

As it is, when Loomis retires, it is Windscape who will take over the running of the school. Meadle has by now been taken on full-time – a qualified intrusion of non-Cambridge values accepted by the plot but not by the ideology of the play, for Meadle is no less satirized a character by the end than he had been at the beginning. And it is left to Windscape, in the last moments of the play, to dismiss Quartermaine – even this sinking vessel of state being no longer capable of sustaining what he represents.

The effect is, however, to create what is clearly intended as a feeling of pathos towards the redundant man. Gray wrote later: 'I have to admit to a deep personal attachment to Quartermaine himself, who embodies for me aspects of a world that had vanished so poignantly before I'd even finished making fun of it.'[4] For if this is a world whose historical moment has passed – in which the inadequate teaching of the language and ideological assumptions of a bankrupt culture by the no longer needed educated elite is all that is left – Gray has nothing to put in its place. His satire is nostalgic and never, to use a word that would be ridiculed by his characters, progressive. It has nowhere to go.

I have concentrated exclusively on the male characters in this play because it is hard not to. There are in fact two female characters, but their roles are peripheral. Melanie Garth is presented as a neurotic mess and a convert to a jokily presented evangelism. For most of the play, her life is dominated by the off-stage spectre of another woman, her mother, who dies, probably killed by her daughter, in the course of the action after being ungratefully nursed by Melanie. Windscape too has an off-stage daughter, who is reported as going progressively mad and as in need of constant sedation. Indeed, it is worth noting how frequently Gray introduces such depictions of women into his plays – as burdensome to the men who run the world, neurotic and, above all, dominated by their supposed function as breeders and nurturers. By the end of the play Meadle's unseen wife is pregnant and the only other female character, Anita, has just given birth. Her response to the difficulties of teaching the 'British Life and Institutions' course reinforces the sense of gender distinction: 'I always make them explain our politics to me, and then just correct their English, whatever they say – one of the advantages of being female, I suppose.'

Anita's connection with the unseen and philandering husband Nigel provides a direct link with Gray's next significant stage play, *The Common Pursuit* of 1984 (but continually reworked throughout the decade for subsequent productions). For Nigel runs the kind of literary magazine the continuing survival of which provides the narrative thread of the play.

The Common Pursuit (the title coming from a work of the same name by the Cambridge literary guru F. R. Leavis) opens and concludes in the Cambridge of the 1960s. A group of undergraduates meet to plan a new literary publication. One of their number, Humphrey (who will be killed in the course of a homosexual encounter before the narrative concludes), has decided to withdraw his poems because 'I don't like them':

Humphrey: Besides I'm going to be a professional philosopher. So I'll have to concentrate on thinking until I've got my First and a job in a university.

Martin: That's what you want, is it?

Humphrey: I haven't any choice. As you can't be a professional philosopher except in a university.

Martin: Do you want to be in any particular university?

Humphrey: This one will do.

Martin: (*laughs slightly*). Any particular college?

Humphrey: This one will do.

Martin: Well – that's quite a prediction, really.

Humphrey: It wasn't meant to be. More like an obituary, in fact. But if I'm going to institutionalize myself, I suppose I might as well do it in one of the better institutions.

The audience response at such moments is, perforce, an uneasy one. If they identify with the world as it is portrayed on stage, then they must do so with a very strong sense that they are being sent-up. If they do not identify with it, then they are continually made aware of their exclusion from its brilliance. Gray is fond of playing tricks on his audiences in ways that emphasize this dilemma. In his review of the play's revival in 1988, Mark Steyn points to one such moment in performance. In the first scene, the culturally ignorant Martin is corrected on his musical taste by Humphrey: ' "Do you like Vivaldi?" asks Martin, a propos of the background music. "Yes," says Humphrey, "but not as much as Bach." Pause. Modest laugh from audience. "Which this is," he adds. Huge laugh from audience.'[5]

The question posed to the audience at such a point is whether they are a Martin or a Humphrey, not a particularly heartening choice but the only one on offer. And the only way of being allied with Humphrey is to possess the knowledge that it is Bach that is playing, and not Vivaldi, and so to be able to get the laugh in before being told to. The cultural references in Gray's plays are legion, and they are to a high culture whose inclusion is precisely a part of the process of exclusion with which so many of his characters are concerned.

The narrative of the play jumps through the inter-related history of the characters; the magazine being first threatened with closure on financial grounds, briefly rescued by the machinations of one of their number on the Arts Council panel, and finally subsumed into the publishing enterprises of Martin, who had expressed only an administrative interest in the venture at the outset. In the course of the play Marigold, who opens the action in a passionate embrace with the putative editor, changes ownership. After their long affair and subsequent marriage, Stuart – knowing that he is unable to provide her with a child – has her pregnancy and her affair with Martin discovered to him in a meeting between the three at the latter's office. Stuart responds as only a protagonist in one of Gray's plays can, with an instant piece of extemporary wit: ' "Well congratulations." (*Pause. He turns to* Marigold) "No, don't worry. You've managed the traditional thing. Which is to tell the husband and father in one breath, so to speak".'

It will be Martin's money that will take over the venture and their world, and not the literary pretensions of Stuart (in as much as we can take them seriously, even without the additional symbolic weight of his sexual sterility). And it is Martin's words that end the play when Gray returns us to the 60s Cambridge study we had seen at the opening; words that now look forward ironically to the success of the enterprise on which they are about to embark. Asked by Stuart what they were talking about, Martin replies, 'Um. What were we about to give the world. Wasn't it?'

The problem is that, as so often with Gray's work, we are both asked to respond to the characters as witty embodiments of a satirized landscape and at the same time somehow think that their efforts actually amount to something. Steve Grant reviewing the play in 1984:

> In Gray's plays, intelligence and wit are substitutes for vulner-ability and the rigours of time. Gray, as artist, stands aloof; while his plays have been accused of small-mindedness, aridity and arrogance, they are also painfully truthful in so far as obser-vation can be 'truthful' . . . In *The Common Pursuit* Gray has written an elegy for a generation not perhaps lost but whose achievements are not perhaps what they were. His characters are real: drinkers in the Spectator pubs of Soho, weekend scribblers of poetry, tele men, adulterous dons, stay-at-home publishers. They represent the soiled meritocracy of post-war Britain and the victory of grubby reality over the ideals of youth and art.[6]

For after all, what were they 'about to give the world'? The play's narrative loop reinforces a sense that it really wasn't very much.

And so we are left with a vacuum, a vacuum in which the willingness of the chain-smoking Nick to sell out to the highest bidder at any point does at least have the ring of plausibility. This, yet another missionary vision of failed post-Cambridge cultural colonization, has ultimately nothing much left to declare but its wit.

Cambridge was also the setting for *Close of Play*, in production at the National Theatre at the time of the 1979 General Election. It was directed by Harold Pinter, whose *Betrayal*, dedicated to Gray, was playing at the same time in the same complex. Indeed the play's title, with its association with the conclusion of the day's activities at a cricket-ground, provides further links between the two men – who were in the habit of looking in at events at the Oval ground during rehearsals for *Quartermaine's Terms*.[7]

The particular 'close of play' is that of Jasper, a classics Professor – played by Sir Michael Redgrave – living past his time with Daisy – played by Dame Peggy Ashcroft – his second wife, as it is revealed late in the play. The play opens in darkness. The faint sound of an organ is heard, gradually swelling, louder and louder, as the light picks up a man who 'appears to be asleep' in a chair. The play will close in a similar fashion after the man, Jasper, has uttered his only words of the night, the repeated 'the door is open' – a reference to the door at the end of the Crematorium conveyor-belt mentioned anecdotally in the course of the action. The fact of Jasper's death is, then, both the preface and the conclusion to the narrative.

Two brothers and their wives are assembled, ostensibly to communicate with Jasper, the father, but actually to use his never-communicating presence as a silent and therefore non-condemnatory prompt for a series of complaints and confessions about their lives. Benedict is a hopeless alcoholic working for the BBC, and his wife Margaret a successful novelist who has come with the express purpose of leaving her husband behind when she leaves. Henry is a malfunctioning doctor and his wife Marianne an obsessively nurturing mother figure.

The other visitor is Jenny, accompanied by a son boarded out at the same school as that of her dead husband Dick, the third brother, who has been killed in a motor-bike accident. And, indeed, most of the confessional material relates to a past of sibling rivalries and unhappiness. In this house the male present is only to be found in a world of lies and fantasies. Henry conjures up the vision of an unpleasant working-class woman with uncontrollable children – a virtual parody of social deprivation – to cover the fact of his affair with a patient. Benedict has invented a non-existent therapist who is helping him with his drink problem. Not content with the mere invention, Gray has him create a full-blown sado-masochistic relationship as a measure of the problems his character has with his own sexual identity:

> *Benedict*: Cheeks Prothero! Had a crush on Dick, didn't he Hen – and old Coote – Coote Wilson – and all of them come to think of it . . . God, I'm glad you sent us to one of the best schools in the country, Daddy, aren't you Hen?
> *Henry*: I certainly don't think it did us any harm.
> *Benedict*: (*pouring himself another drink*). Vintross is queer. Gay, I mean. Did I tell you? . . . He's got this Philippino house-boy. Opens the door, takes your coat. Got a pretty beaten look to him, so I expect there's a cupboard full of things, eh, hand-cuffs, leg-irons, whips, masks, S.S. uniforms – that sort of gay, you see. Ballsy-gay.

They are not attractive characters. As Frank Marcus noted when reviewing the play in 1979: 'Clearly it was not his intention that we should like his characters, but the sustained misanthropy unleashed upon them proved finally to be counter-productive.'[8]

This raises very real problems since, in a play which is less obviously a simple vehicle for the wit of its author, it is hard for an audience to accept the characters as nothing more than satir-ized beings caught in aspic. Despite Marcus' conclusion, an em-pathetic response appears to be being sought, but to what end? The play does not just conclude with Jasper's death, it proclaims the collapse of a whole way of life, but what is an audience to make of it? The bitterness is real enough, as is the bile against an outside world – for although the audience depends on the brothers' fictions to populate that outside world, the play offers no qualification of their disgust. The Cambridge house is caught in a psychologically haunted past that will not allow any real notion of a present to intrude. A funeral has been arranged, but to whom or about what should we express our regrets?

The theme of personal disintegration is one that pervades all Gray's plays, and is most clearly articulated in his final stage play of the 80s, *Melon* (1987). The play examines the mental breakdown of its eponymous hero, a successful head of a publishing house. As always, the fact of success is to be seen as a measure of failure. The Michael who will take over his job accuses him early in the play, 'At college you said you wanted to be a writer', to which Melon replies, 'I matured into wanting to be successful instead'.

Melon is Gray's supreme embodiment of the art of witty discourse, his verbal puncturing after his breakdown therefore the more effective dramatically; and the use of a direct address (validated by the non-appearing psychiatrist figure) that continually interrupts his displays of wit serves only to enhance the sense of a man once totally in control, now looking back in bewilderment at where it all went wrong.

In Act I, after a dazzling display of Melon's verbal manipulation of the other characters, Gray has him return to the psychiatrist's office to reflect:

> Of course I can see – in retrospect. Looking back, that is. I don't deny – can't deny – that I was somewhat lacking in – in – that I was sometimes rather over – um. But it was only – only – my manner. And also, don't forget, it's me – me myself is telling . . . Remorselessly. And in fact, also inaccurately. At my own expense. Because of course there wasn't any special evening, any particular evening, but a sort of flavour of an evening, and years ago . . . they didn't all happen together really. On the same evening.

These confessional intrusions not only serve to engage audience sympathy for the character, they act additionally as a kind of deconstruction of the way in which wit is deployed in Gray's plays. As Melon says, it did not really all happen quite as the script would have it; the character has been allowed to create his own dramatically condensed version of his past.

The degree to which the audience can engage with Melon is unusual in Gray's work, and helps make it his most interesting stage play to date. But it is an engagement that an audience makes at some cost, for it brings with it the invitation to complicity in the character's essentially unpleasant approach to his fellow beings. For instance, it is possible that an audience may respond to his agony at the discovery that he really cares about his wife's long-running adultery with Rupert, a BBC front-man who naturally he despises above all his acquaintances. But this must be measured against his own mechanical affair with a secretary whose A-level essays he corrects as a part of the ritual of coupling.

Or again, Melon is shown early in the play in a desperate attempt to communicate with his son (an unusual enough event in itself, for children are almost entirely excluded from any part of the dialogue in the other plays) but, as always, Gray cannot resist the temptation to use his protagonist as a mouthpiece for diatribes against all things progressive; diatribes which, of course, may or may not represent the author accurately. Learning that the son has formed a friendship with a Japanese boy gives Melon the opportunity to play the game of 'racial stereotyping' (as he does also with his Jewish acquaintance Jacob). And learning that the friend wants to be a policeman, Melon concludes with a characteristic catalogue of issues: 'Well, we'd better not get into that one, eh, or in no time we'd be into CND, the bomb, American air bases, setting a moral lead versus requiring a deterrent to negotiating, so forth.'

There are no such problems about Gray's most recent stage play, however. In *Hidden Laughter* (a Michael Codron production at the Vaudeville theatre in 1990), he considers the lives of a nouveau-riche family as they lay claim to the country cottage retreat that is theirs by right of their 80s success.

The husband, Harry, is a literary agent and his wife, Louise, a writer. In itself this would seem to take us into familiar territory in Gray's work, but now the play (whose title ironically invokes T. S. Eliot and a world of 'high' culture of which his characters have no understanding) treats them simply as objects of satire. They are the products of the modern world against which all Gray's other protagonists precisely define themselves. The tone is uncomplicatedly satirical and, for once, Gray steps completely away from any possibility of identification of the values and aspirations they espouse.

Many of the familiar components are in place. Harry's office-lover deceives her way into the cottage as a relief secretary, and there is even a doubting Vicar, Ronnie, who eventually does wonder whether 'young Nigel would care to have a peep at an odd – rather odd – charming little navel I stumbled across in St Turd's in Little Sodfuck'. Nigel, the son, is indeed the only one to escape from the bankruptcy of the rural retreat; but he does so permanently disabled after being gored by a bull. Returning from university he tells the Vicar that he had wanted to reply to his letter, and Ronnie asks what he would have written, 'Something smart and Cambridge?'

Louise has taken on a package of modern progressive ideas with the new money. Much given to agreement by family consensus, she is aggrieved when she discovers her daughter not only smoking but playing a transistor radio while she is trying to type:

> It was right underneath my concentration, you see. Banging away. Like a headache. And anyway, we come here to get away from all that – pop and London and fashionable noises – we all had an agreement that we wouldn't – but why are you smoking? . . . – you know that Daddy and I would never dream of issuing prohibitions and orders, there's just been an agreement between us all, that's how we work as a family, through agreements.

An audience has no difficulty in decoding the desired response to such characters. They are easy embodiments of an England that, in terms of the despairing nostalgia of Gray's other protagonists, is 'bloody finished at last'. They may have aspirations for their daughter to make it to Cambridge but they are now as cut off from all that is represented by Cambridge as they are from ever realizing their rural idyll.

And so, we the audience are left with a choice in Gray's work. Either we identify with the disillusioned, yet witty Cambridge elite no longer confident of the ideological dominance of its values, or perforce we are to be seen as the inhabitants of the new world – as objects of derision and satire. Gray leaves no other position. Other than, of course, dismissing the choice altogether which is, effectively, to leave before the interval.

His sense of despair is deep-rooted. He expressed the all-inclusive terms of reference that it implied in 1977, when his own sense of the division gave no grounds for optimism:

> I don't think there's anything you can do. Things will just get worse and worse. I think we're a less civilized country than we were. It seems to me that as the ostensible gaps between classes disappear, the gap between educated and uneducated people increases because of some fraudulent ideas of democratization.[9]

If there is a radical edge to be found in his work then, it is of a political position well to the right of the successive Conservative administrations of 1979 on. If his characters increasingly enjoy the fruits of their selectively created wealth, they do so with a total hostility to the new market forces that allowed it. The resultant air of cynicism is one that pervades his work, but it is clearly a cynicism that has found its own market.

Gray's success in the mainstream has been matched by a continuing demand for television scripts – another College drama, *After Pilkington*, was screened in 1987, and this has been followed by a television version of *The Common Pursuit*, his adaptation of J. L. Carr's *A Month in the Country* for the 'Screen on Four' series, and a regular flow of productions since. Never has his stock been higher, and never perhaps has his brand of disillusioned wit seemed more appropriate as the dreams of the new wealth of the first Thatcher years have turned increasingly bitter: even for native audiences keen to find an uneasy identification with the cleverness of his characters. It will be interesting to see how these characters brave the ever more troubled waters of the 90s.

8

Alan Ayckbourn: Very English, Very National

> Of course, everyone has politics and everyone has attitudes to
> politics. I'm certainly anti-extremist; I'm very English. But
> again, I sit, I suspect, in the middle of most English opinion.
> The Tory party right wing fills me with total despair, as
> indeed does the Labour party left wing. I suppose the nearest
> I get to being political is that I'm rather attracted to things
> like the Social Democrats. That's the sort of area I'm after.
>
> (Alan Ayckbourn, 1981)[1]

Alan Ayckbourn is not only by far the most popular contemporary British playwright; he is, after Shakespeare, the most
produced native playwright ever. A constant factor in London's
commercial theatre, and a frequent one at the National, his plays
enjoy continual revivals in the professional theatres around the
country and are regularly produced by the thousands of amateur
companies with which this country is peculiarly blessed.

It is not just the popularity of his work that needs stressing, but
its wide social base. During the course of a recent performance of
Ten Times Table given by the local Midland Bank Players I was,
however, struck with a strange conviction, later confirmed by
checking the records. I was watching the play in the Drama Studio
of the university where I work, a venue which has perhaps a 50
per cent student usage and is thus frequently hired out to such
amateur companies. Over the years there have been a great
number of productions of Ayckbourn's plays, but not a single one
by a university group.

It is a small but telling point. For all his popularity – some
critics, including Michael Billington, would say because of his
popularity – there remains a suspicion that somehow Ayckbourn
is not to be taken seriously as a playwright. He describes the circumstances under which Sir Peter Hall came to direct the first
Ayckbourn play put on at the National, *Bedroom Farce* in 1977.

137

Asked why he thought Hall might have wanted a play from him, 'the most commercial of commercial writers', Ayckbourn said that Sheila Hancock persuaded the director to see a performance of *Absurd Person Singular*: 'I don't think Peter had seen anything of mine – or anyway, he'd registered me as a boulevardier. But he went along to see this, and I think he was quite impressed: he found it quite dark, and more interesting than I think he suspected it would be.'[2]

In the event the piece he provided was, in the playwright's own words, 'a very jolly play', a farcical romp by outrageously conceived characters between the bedrooms of three different houses. The irony of the appearance of such a play at the National at the time when his other work was in fact beginning to acquire a more sombre tone was not lost on Ayckbourn:

> I didn't quite know why I'd written it. It was very strange. It cropped up in the middle of my serious phase: this rather jolly play suddenly arrived. And I think I was rather rude to it. I said to it: 'I'm an Absent Friends man now, a much more serious dramatist.'[3]

Bedroom Farce proved very successful, moving from the Lyttelton to the Prince of Wales to become the very first transfer from the National to the commercial theatre, the forerunner of a development that has become of major economic importance for the subsidized theatres of the National and RSC. Since then, four further Ayckbourn plays have had productions at the National; and although one of them, *Way Upstream*, was a financial disaster as a result of a build-up of complications involving an expensive set with a floating and fully operative boat, his work has been otherwise well received and well-receipted there. In 1985, Ayckbourn was not only appointed as a Company Director at the National, but was allowed to develop productions by other writers with his own company.

He is then, by any accounts, a force to be reckoned with. Possessed of a quite dazzling ability to present audiences with a steady progression of plays that they are only too anxious to pay to see – and able to produce them frequently to order at the very last minute, the plays' titles often announced before a line has been written – Ayckbourn's is a unique talent in the contemporary theatre. In what follows I will be less interested in questioning the undeniable fact of that talent, than with considering the social roots of his popularity and its significance. And to do this it is inevitable that the starting point should be Scarborough, a northern seaside town that had already moved somewhat down-market from its more fashionable beginnings by the time Ayck-bourn first made its acquaintance.

It was at Scarborough that that first play for the National started its stage life, and where all but *A Small Family Business* did too. It was at Scarborough that Ayckbourn effectively started his theatrical life; it is with Scarborough that Ayckbourn is irre-trievably linked – diversions to Stoke, BBC Radio and the National notwithstanding; and it is in Scarborough that virtually all of his work first sees the light of publicly performed day.

He first joined Stephen Joseph's Company at the Library Theatre there in 1957, and the great proponent of theatre in the round soon encouraged him to try his hand at writing for the stage. The first play to be performed under his own name, *Mr Whatnot*, was directed by Ayckbourn there in 1963 before it gave him his first London run the following year at the Arts Theatre. Everything about the play declares an indebtedness to an Absur-dist tradition, and its London production was reviewed by *The Times* on 7 October 1964 under the heading 'Theatre of Ridicu-lous'.

The Library Theatre gave James Saunders' *Alas Poor Fred* its first performance, and at the time Ayckbourn started to get plays produced David Campton was developing his 'comedy of menace' plays under Joseph's heavy guidance. From the outset Ayckbourn saw his role as dramatist in quite a different light, taking seriously his mentor's admonition to get holiday-makers' backsides on the seats:

> I think Stephen did recognize, if nothing else, that he'd found a writer who, nurtured a little, could possibly keep his box-office afloat, allowing David, who was running in parallel with me, a chance to develop his less commercial style – because he had distinctly two. Stephen was much more keen for David to get on with his Four Minute Warnings and his View from the Brinks, continuing with Lunatic Views, than his commercial stuff. I was left rather in the position of being encouraged to carry on writing, in the hope of bringing in an audience. Which I did . . .[4]

In his occasional comments on the function of theatre, Ayck-bourn has continued to stress his sense of himself as a popular writer working for a theatre that stresses the importance of 'fun' and 'entertainment'; and he has remained consistently opposed to the notion of a political theatre that, in his words, seeks audiences that 'want to be instructed.'[5]

Michael Billington has pointed to a possible link between Pam in Edward Bond's *Saved* and the young working-class mother, Evelyn, in *Absent Friends* (Scarborough 1974, Garrick, London, 1975). He talks of her 'totally expressionless, gum-chewing taciturnity . . . [as] she rocks her baby's pram with mechanical listlessness, takes no evident interest in what is being said to her and is only roused from her catatonic passivity when Marge asks her point-blank if she and Paul are having an *affaire*'.[6] It is an interesting possible connection, particularly in view of the totally unsympathetic characterization she is given; and a further connection may be made when it is realized that the name Colin, given to the guest who stays endlessly to mourn his drowned fiancee in Ayckbourn's play, is the same as that of the drowned man in Bond's *The Sea*.

However, whatever the validity of these links – and the possible oblique attack on Bond's theatre – what is most striking about Ayckbourn's writing in this respect is the way in which it has managed to develop effectively without reference to this kind of politicized drama. His work connects with, and develops from, a tradition totally hostile to that of the committed school of writers. Its roots are to be found generally in the kind of stock repertory plays experienced by the young theatre-writer, and specifically in that domestic brand of Absurdism that I considered earlier. Elements of the Absurdist tradition can be found in even his most recent work; in *Henceforward* (Scarborough 1987, Vaudeville, London, 1988), for instance, which is set in a futuristic London and concerns the efforts of a technologically obsessed man to convince his ex-wife and a social worker that he is about to be married to a mechanical robot, and can thus provide a suitable home for their child.

Ayckbourn is not a naturalistic playwright. His dialogue is infused with a sense of the absurd. But what distinguishes his work from its English Absurdist models is that his characters are not conceived from outside, as objects of convenient satire. His characters are rarely sufficiently in control to be witty; they become comic in as much as they articulate, or attempt to articulate, the domestic problems of modern life. Problems like trying to sell a second-hand car when a test drive proves out of the question, as is Dennis at the start of *Just Between Ourselves* (Scarborough 1976, Queen's, London, 1977), for example:

Dennis: I'll let you into a little secret. This car has barely been out of this garage in six months . . . As a matter of fact, frankly, the wife's had a few, what shall I say, health worries and she really hasn't been up to driving.

Neil: Oh, I'm sorry to . . .

Dennis: Oh, she's better now. She's very much better now. But she's gone off driving altogether. You can see, look – look at that clock there – I'll be surprised if it's done fifty thousand. (*Peering in*) Here we are. Fifty-five thousand two hundred and fifty-two miles . . . well, fifty-five, fifty thousand, round about that figure.

Neil: Amazing . . .

Dennis: I'd let you have a test drive in it now but – actually it's a bit embarrassing – the up and over door there, you see it's gone and jammed itself somehow, can't get it open at all. Still that's my next job . . . I'll tell you what I can do for you. I can turn it over for you. Then you can hear the sound . . . I can't run it for too long, not in an enclosed space, you understand, but . . . bit of choke . . . right, stand by for blast off. (*Engine turns over but fails to start.*) She'll be a little cold. (*Engine fails to start again.*) Come along, my beauty. She's been standing, you see . . . (*He tries again. It fails to start.*) Come on. Come on, you bastard. (*Engine turns and starts to fire.*) There we are. Listen to that. Purring like a kitten.

Neil: Beg your pardon?

Dennis: (*yelling above the din*) That's with the bonnet open, of course.

Neil: Yes.

(*They stand and survey the turning engine. After a moment, it starts to misfire and peters out. Silence.*)

Despite the deliberately predictable outcome of the exercise, Ayckbourn has already provided a number of clues to suggest that what an audience is faced with here goes beyond the simple boundaries of a joke about second-hand cars. We are told that the car actually belongs to Dennis' wife who has been ill. What we will discover is that she is in a progressively deteriorating mental state and will be helplessly catatonic by the play's end. We are told that the car cannot be taken out of the garage. What we will discover is that Dennis spends all his spare time in this garage, the door of which he cannot fix, working on ill-fated DIY projects, carefully cocooned from any real contact with his wife. The language in which Dennis allows such revelations to be made is both comic and disturbing. It is a 'secret' that the car has not been out of the garage for six months, but an openly known 'fact' that his wife has been ill during this period. The car's failure to function will presage the breakdown of his wife, and that we are left in no doubt as to which of the two's welfare has priority with the husband – and the attendant consequences of that prioritization – is what moves the play's narrative away from the merely absurd to the human.

This bleakness of tone was something which developed in Ayckbourn's work through the 70s, but his concern with humanizing the characters in his Absurdist landscape was to be found in his work at least as early as 1970, and *How the Other Half Loves*. In this year Ayckbourn was appointed Artistic Director of the Scarborough theatre, a position he has held, save for a two-year sabbatical at the National, to this day. Stephen Joseph had died in 1967, and Ayckbourn had divided his time between working for BBC Radio and directing and writing for the Scarborough summer seasons. In 1976 he supervised the move to a new venue, known as the Stephen Joseph Theatre, and Scarborough extended the scale of its operations, offering an all-year programme rather than one just for the summer tourist season as before. Any account of Ayckbourn's work has to take very seriously his almost unique position in British theatre – matched only by the second most popular contemporary writer for the stage, John Godber, at his Spring Street base in Hull – as a playwright with his own theatre to run.

From the outset Ayckbourn was interested, and involved, in all facets of theatrical production; and thinks of his primary employment as a director rather than as a writer – play-writing typically taking up only about a single month of each year. And his plays reflect this wide base of experience, written as they are with a real knowledge of the potential workings of the theatre, with a strong reliance on playing around with the conventions of the particular models deployed.

As his work developed this disturbance of the conventions of the domestic comedy play became his most famous trademark. Audiences for an Ayckbourn play were confronted with a seemingly straightforward set with the almost certain knowledge that it would be used to in some way defy its apparent limitations. By the end of the 70s he had seemingly tried every possible permutation; but in *Taking Steps* (Scarborough 1979, Lyric, London, 1980) he found yet another. The action takes place in a two-storied house which is created as a single storey on stage. The potential for farcical business is obvious, but this and the many other games that the playwright has played with the supposedly solid geography of the home means that the set is no longer defined simply as the locus and signifier of social positioning. It becomes a part of the action. Michael Billington in 1990:

> The house itself thus becomes a character in the farce: a gaunt, ghostly, doomy, looming Victorian pile in which two beds are better than one, in which the audience can see people trying to make their ineffectual escape down imaginary flights of stairs and in which separate crises can erupt a few feet away from each other.[7]

The house as a confirmation of domestic certainties, as a bolt-hole from the problems of an outside world of work and stress (at least for the men), becomes instead a part of the sad and disintegrating lives of the families that inhabit it. The single dramatic feature that has most appealed to theatre-goers about his early work serves then as a disruptive force, albeit comically so.

To take a classic earlier example: in *How the Other Half Loves* (Scarborough 1969, Lyric Theatre, London, 1970) Ayckbourn uses a single overlapping set as the simultaneous home of two different married couples. That of Frank and Fiona Foster has furniture that is 'smart modern reproduction', that of Bob and Teresa Phillips' is 'more modern, trendy and badly looked after'. From the outset the audience is thus confronted not just with the fact of a dually inhabited room, but with a deliberately conflicting sense of who occupies the space.

Frank is Bob's boss, and Fiona and Bob are having an affair, unbeknown to their respective partners. As a cover the lovers manage to involve Bill Featherstone, another employee, and his wife Mary, each of whom is supposedly having an affair which has necessitated a late night counselling session and thus an excuse for an otherwise unexplainable absence from home. It is therefore entirely inevitable that Bill and Mary will be invited to dinner at each of the two houses on subsequent evenings. At which point the fun really begins.

Ayckbourn has presented events happening simultaneously in the two houses from the outset, the two sets of characters passing without noticing each other – but there has always been a slight imbalance of timing between the two households. The scene is set then for the dinner parties to take place simultaneously in the two houses with the same guests but on subsequent evenings. The potential for comic business is apparent. Ayckbourn plays up to the audience's wildest expectations. He not only beautifully distinguishes between the social milieu of the employer and the employee, but between the behaviours thought appropriate by Bill when being entertained by a boss or by a colleague.

This observation of status and class distinctions does not simply add to the comic confusion of the two dinner parties, however. It is central to what Ayckbourn is considering in the entire play. That the two sets of characters should be occupying precisely the same stage space actually serves to reinforce the fact that they live in two totally different worlds. The social divide is indicated in terms of the cultural iconography of the shared set, with its opposing styles of interior decor, and is reinforced by everything we learn about their distinct life-styles and attitudes – right down to the very different ways in which Teresa and Frank each deal with the fact of their partner's infidelity.

And where better than a dinner party to display the class divide? In a short interlude the two wives plan their shopping for the events in a crossed dialogue that immediately precedes the chaos:

> *Fiona and Teresa cross to the coffee-table and pick up pads and pencils.*
> *Fiona*: (*thoughtfully*) Avocado.
> *Teresa*: Packet of chicken noodle soup.
> *Fiona*: Courgettes.
> *Teresa*: Sprouts.
> *Fiona*: Sour cream.
> *Teresa*: Spuds.
> *Fiona*: Pork.

Teresa: Chops.
Fiona: Marron glacé.
Teresa: Treacle pud.
Fiona: Kirsch.
Teresa: (*as an afterthought*) Booze!

This is a listing that would need some modification today, hypermarkets having changed the class parameters of food consumption quite remarkably; but it was offered by Ayckbourn in 1970 with the certain knowledge that it would serve, like the many class signifiers in the play, to identify the relative social status of each character. Furthermore, it was presented with a certainty of audience laughter. It has a satirical intent drawn like so much of Ayckbourn's dialogue, from the domestic Absurdist tradition. It invites laughter in the same way that the dreadful Bill Featherstone's simultaneous grovelling to his boss and his openly critical attitude to his colleague does at the dinner parties that follow.

But the comedic effect is a complicated one. When Cooper's *Everything in the Garden* satirized the consumerist dream and aspirations of upward mobility, it had done so from a single, even social base. In contrast here, as so frequently, Ayckbourn satirizes at the same time as he is making social distinctions. In one sense the satire works at all levels; in another it is left to individual members of the audience to locate the particular focus of the satire.

It is this clash of life-styles – a clash with its roots firmly in the English class system – that gives the play its real dynamism, moving it away from the simple farcical model – and not Ayckbourn's tricks with time and place. And it is a clash that is explored over and over again in Ayckbourn's work through to the late 70s.

To make the point rather graphically, it is not the kind of stage meeting that could ever occur in Simon Gray's plays. For the social perspective is not only different; it focuses on the very kind of characters who are dismissed scathingly, and without any actual first-hand knowledge, in his plays. Ayckbourn's characters do not inhabit a post-varsity world. Far from publishing books and producing poetry magazines, they scarcely seem to read books, let alone own them; save for the occasional car maintenance manual or DIY guide.

The figures at the top of Ayckbourn's social heap are small town business proprietors – actually involved in a world of manufacturing – and those at the bottom are upwardly-aspiring members of the petit bourgeoisie. The characters in his early plays live in a world in which village fêtes and the regular calendar of small community events publicly punctuate the steady unfolding of their domestic lives, as surely as the rituals of Christmas and birthdays do in private. This is theoretically a very narrow band of society but actually, in terms of overall population figures, a very wide one. It includes, for instance, virtually all the paying customers who would be likely to pay to see an Ayckbourn play at the Stephen Joseph Theatre, Scarborough.

And this is important. Ayckbourn became popular because he is an extremely talented writer who knows how to entertain an audience, but he became so popular because his plays successfully identify the activities on stage with the actual lives of his audiences. 'I'm very lucky,' he has said, 'that my particular level of writing, classwise, is slap-bang in the middle of the English theatre-going public.'[8] And it is here that the fact of the social divide assumes real significance. There is space in his plays for the very careful articulation of conflicting attitudes of class to be received in different ways by different members of his audience according to their own sense of where they locate themselves in society.

Appalling though Sidney Hopcroft's behaviour is in *Absurd Person Singular*, it is still possible for members of an audience to enjoy his triumph over his social betters; just as it is perfectly possible for a section of an audience more at home in the world of Simon Gray's characters to find a reading of Sidney that sees him as nothing more than a satirical embodiment of vulgar ambition. The Scarborough plays allowed a series of entry points for an audience. The characters looked familiar, as did the articulation of the carefully observed strata of middle-class life. The distinctions of class are all in Ayckbourn's plays; and they are distinctions the niceties and implications of which are far more likely to be accurately registered at Scarborough than they are at a National Theatre where a good percentage of the audience will experience the characters almost voyeuristically – as alien beings in an unfamiliarly provincial landscape. It is this sense of a solid but divided social base – to his work and for his Scarborough audience – that makes the resultant havoc so seductive.

For everything that could go wrong, does go wrong, as the characters in his plays stumble from an opening domestic crisis that leads inexorably to a related and worsening series of crises. And the plays' dialogue, from the outset only uneasily naturalistic, becomes ever more absurd as his characters move from an opening of blocked discourse to a full articulation of their particular problems. So, a Bill Featherstone, who is initially introduced into the plot of *How the Other Half Loves* as apparently no more than a necessary alibi in the adultery plot, quickly develops as a full-blown monster in his own right.

His relationship with his wife Mary becomes a third strand in a play which depends for its plot on the ways in which the three couples have created their particular sense of the married state. Bill is a careerist and a bully; uncertain of how to behave himself as he climbs the social ladder, he nags constantly at his wife to obey the rules of a social game he cannot yet properly grasp – slapping her hand when she nervously bites her nails, forcing her to drink sherry that he knows will disagree with her, and ordering her to remove her cardigan on arriving at the Foster's dinner party.

Forced eventually to apologize to Mary – for wrongly accusing her of having an affair with Bob – he finds he cannot utter the words; and his wife is left to explain: 'It's difficult for him. He's never been wrong before, you see.' This is as nothing, however, to Bill's uncharacteristically lengthy expression of disappointment about her to Frank and Fiona when the former has mistakenly put the suggestion of her adultery into his head:

Do you realize, Mrs Foster, the hours I've put into that woman? When I met her, you know, she was nothing. Nothing at all. With my own hands I have built her up. Encouraging her to join the public library and make use of her non-fiction tickets – I introduced her to the Concert Classics Club – I've coaxed her, encouraged her to think – even perhaps bullied her, some might say . . . Her dress sense was terrible, my own mother encouraged her towards adventurous cooking – everything. I've done everything.

Michael Billington (1990) has written of Bill's outburst that it 'is one of the most chilling and funny in all Ayckbourn: a terrifying lower-middle-class conception of a wife as some kind of vacuum one fills up with hobbies and leisure pursuits.'[9] And the conjunction seems right. It is chilling in terms of the way in which the wife is objectified by the husband; but it is comic in its listing of the kind of cultural manifestations of improvement offered. The Concert Classics Club, in particular, allows some sections of an audience a sense of social superiority in the way that I described working in earlier English Absurdism. However, it also excludes from the luxury of that feeling any members of the audience for whom joining such a 'middle-brow' club might still seem a cultural aspiration within or even beyond their reach. Without overstressing the point, it is again worth noting that the social parameters of the Scarborough audience would be more likely to contain elements for whom the latter responses were possible than would that at the National – where the evidences of cultural aspiration would seem more uncomplicatedly ridiculed.

This is particularly significant when considering the aspect of Ayckbourn's domestic 'comedies' that is most usually stressed thematically – his depiction of the women's role in the various menages. In *How the Other Half Love* Fiona and Frank are treated with approximately the same degree of disengagement by Ayckbourn. But an audience is left in no doubt that once it comes to the level of the employees it is the two wives, Teresa and Mary, who are seen as the real victims. Marriage in Ayckbourn's plays is always at least a problematic condition, and most usually a terrifying one. And in play after play, all the real sympathy is extended towards the women. Not that they are ever allowed to take their future into their own hands. They embody the sterility of human relations in the marriage bond, what individual aspirations they might have had thoroughly repressed by the self-centred and frequently weak men they have opted for.

So the plays, set as they nearly all are in domestic locations, contain a narrative that both reinforces the sense of the family unit as the centre of social organisation and also suggests, by the treatment of the female characters, the personal damage caused by that unit. That the women are essentially passive victims and not active opponents of the model prevents his plays from ever moving beyond the merely disturbing to the really subversive. This leads to a kind of fatalism, accompanied as it very frequently is with the suggestion that the women actually get the men they deserve.

The strongest example of this came in *Sisterly Feelings*, Ayckbourn's second play for the National – opening in Scarborough in 1979 before being performed at the Olivier the following year. Essentially the play is constructed on a simpler version of the dramatic device that was to be used in *Intimate Exchanges* in 1982.

Following a family funeral, two sisters find themselves attracted to the brother of their brother's girl-friend. According to the result of the toss of a coin, one or other goes off with him at the end of the first scene and embarks on a passionate liaison. Thereafter, further decisions have to be made by whichever of the sisters is having the affair; but whatever narrative route is taken the play concludes with the same scene in which we are shown the pair reunited or still with their original partners.

That one of the sisters, Abigail, is married to a typically uncaring Ayckbourn male figure makes her version of the story marginally more interesting; and clearly, as a woman who bemoans the fact that she has stopped working after getting married, she is intended to stand as a contrast to her sister Dorcas who has a successful career as a radio presenter and no plans to marry her partner – who is anyway presented as a parody of the sort of card-carrying veggie radical who is always given a hard time by the playwright:

> *Abigail*: My husband is at his worst today. It is my mother's funeral and all he can think about is his bloody meeting. I don't know how long I can cope. I honestly don't (*indicating her father*) It's all right for him and his 'what you put in into it'. I've flung the lot in and it's disappeared without trace.
> *Dorcas*: You shouldn't have given up your job.
> *Abigail*: We can't have Mrs Smythe working, can we? That won't do.

But Dorcas, who as a single working woman represents a new possibility in Ayckbourn's work, will prove no more able to carve out a fresh direction than the bored housewife who is allowed a more articulate awareness of her problems in his earlier work. Conveniently the lover turns out to be an enormous disappointment for both sisters as an avenue to change – not that this would anyway be a very liberationist way of considering such change – and the bourgeois model is put back neatly into place whatever series of moves the narrative makes. Heads or tails? the domestic unit, however miserable, survives, and the plays always swerve away from any ultimate disruption of the model. The games that Ayckbourn plays with the stage conventions of time, space and narrative are subsumed back into an ending which is one of conventional, if bitter, foreclosure.

As Ayckbourn said in 1981:

> Of course one can write a play about women's liberation – it's a very important topic – but I don't think it's very satisfying when they stand on a chair and tell the men in the audience that they're pigs. And that's where I differ from *agit-prop* theatre, in that I hate being told things.[10]

His plays derive from an empirical observation of things as they are, and things as they are furthermore in a world – Teresa's ridiculed clipping of ecological articles from the *Guardian* notwithstanding – that is far removed from any sense of a political or cultural *avant-garde*. It is a world more obviously that of Scarborough – and identified as such by its original audiences – than of, say, Michael Frayn's North London suburbs.

Now, this sense of a playwright essentially at one with his audience was increasingly threatened as Ayckbourn became a London box-office property – a move that starts with *Relatively Speaking* in 1967, but was really confirmed by *How the Other Half Loves* in 1970 and *Absurd Person Singular* in 1973. From this point a regular pattern was established, of initial Scarborough openings followed by London productions by which his real critical reputation would be created. Ayckbourn has always been acutely aware of the difference. Questioned by Ian Watson in 1981 about his interest in the internal hierarchies of middle-class life, he made an interesting distinction:

> I get about a bit, because I live in a small enough town to do it. In London I probably wouldn't. In London, one tends to go from box A to box B. In Scarborough one tends to go to intermediate boxes and, because I am willy-nilly drawn into some of the social life, because a lot of the people there know me by sight, a lot of chat goes on, a lot of socializing with audiences, a lot of opening of fêtes.[11]

As Ayckbourn came to be regarded as a property of the London commercial theatre, so a harder edge started to form. The sense of empathetic engagement with a limited social world that would have been familiar to his Scarborough audience was perhaps less easy to perpetuate with the nagging thought that the plays would all ultimately transfer to London. Although Ayckbourn has said that 'the suburbs are a state of mind not a geographical location', there is ample evidence that London audiences regarded his characters as socially indistinguishable – the niceties of class distinction unobservable – and therefore as all equally satirized.

A typical London audience response to the characters of his early plays was thus one of social patronage, allowing a separation of the social worlds of the plays and the audience, in a way that threatened to trivialize them. Through the 80s the social locations of Ayckbourn's plays moved up the social ladder, nearer to those of a Home Counties professional world understood to be surviving well in the Thatcherite years. There is a lower-middle-class character in *Man of the Moment* (Scarborough 1988, Globe, London, 1990) – a man from a world of non-privilege brought to an expensive Spanish holiday villa to be confronted with the modern success story of the man whom he once tackled in a bank raid and who has since become a media celebrity. But there is no doubt where the social animus of the play is located – against the values of this new money.

The Revengers' Comedies (Scarborough 1989, Strand, London 1990) also takes a 'lesser being' into a world of privilege and power-broking in a comic reworking of a plot that started life with Patricia Highsmith's *Strangers on a Train*. And if such characters bring with them a sense of morality and decency, as representatives of Ayckbourn's earlier dramatic world, they have been progressively weeded out of an action which centres more and more exclusively on the wealthy lives of the financially successful upper middle classes. A sense of bitterness, of anger even, has taken over from the ambivalently expressed empathy.

Ayckbourn is well aware of the significance of being regarded as the property of a national – by which inevitably we mean London – rather than a provincial theatre. He expresses regret, but also an understanding of the reality of hard economics in the need to tailor his coat to the market:

The joy of having a theatre here [in Scarborough] is having the right to fail. If you're working in the West End you've got a quarter of a million pounds of people and materials and other people's money floating on it. It's not quite so easy to take that attitude, not if you want to do another one.[12]

But if the plays moved up the social scale, they retained the central concern with the family unit. The news simply got worse. The depiction of domestic misery was transposed into a harsher drama in which the role of the women as victims of a patriarchal society was increasingly foregrounded. By 1985, when *Woman in Mind* was produced at Scarborough (followed by a London run at the Vaudeville the following year), the action is seen entirely through the perspective of an unhappily married woman.

Susan looks after, and is neglected by, an incompetent Vicar, a kind of latter-day Casaubon who spends all his time working on a small pamphlet on the history of his parish. As the play opens Susan is recovering from concussion after stepping on a garden rake. In the scenes that follow, the familiar and awful figures of her own domestic life first parallel, and then interact with, a fantasy family she has created in her head as she progresses towards madness. Ayckbourn has talked of the response of one female member of the audience – 'I came out determined to assert myself as a woman much more'[13] – and certainly *Woman in Mind* is one of the most powerful pieces he has written. But again, strong though the depiction of the hell that her life literally becomes in this play is, the narrative suggests no way out – other, that is, than madness.

In itself, this would be a clumsy response to a play that so evidently breaks new ground both for Ayckbourn and for the mainstream generally. But when the play is put into the context of other political changes in Ayckbourn's work, it does leave awkward questions unresolved. For if the playwright's acceptance as a West End commodity has created a greater seriousness in his comic tone, then his appropriation by the National Theatre has caused him to turn the thoughts of the characters in his plays subsequently – both for the National and for the commercial theatre – to more overtly political themes.

Two years after the formation of the first Thatcher administration, Ayckbourn directed his own *Way Upstream* at Scarborough. The following year, with a different cast but again directed by him, it became his third play for the National Theatre, opening in the Lyttelton on 4 October. *Way Upstream* offers nothing less than a full-blown allegorical account of the state of modern Britain.

Two couples start out on a holiday cruise on a river that is identified in the stage directions as the Thames, a journey that will take them to Armageddon Bridge. The two husbands are partners in a business that produces, suitably enough in Ayckbourn's view of the contemporary world, novelty goods and souvenirs. Keith, whose marriage to June is disintegrating and will collapse before the end of the cruise, is the self-appointed captain, arguing that 'boats are a society in miniature' and that there can only be one leader. Alistair, who will end the play trying a new start with his wife Emma by swimming off with her to the other side of Armageddon Bridge, allows Keith to assume control of their holiday as he has of their partnership.

As the boat journey proceeds we learn that a strike is brewing at their works, a strike fomented by a never seen Ray Duffy. Were he to appear he would doubtless speak the old-fashioned trade union version of the kind of dialogue used to parody the new-age revolutionary Stafford in *Sisterly Feelings*: 'It's the whole repressive attitude of the entire organization wherein they are preconditioned into thinking along establishment lines that have been laid down by a privileged class which has had no contact or serious regard for the working person.'

At first operating through the daily visits of his secretary, Keith finally feels it necessary to go and sort out the matter for himself, thus ensuring of course that the strike does actually occur. Authoritarian management and intransigent trade unionism meet head on, whilst Alistair – 'The trouble is I can see both points of view' – feels helpless to intervene.

Alistair's position is that of the irredeemable liberal: 'They wouldn't listen to me, anyway. The only people who get heard in this world are the extremists. They're the only ones with the energy to shout loud enough.' And sure enough, with the full force of Ayckbourn's version of historical inevitability, the three remaining crew, now leaderless, invite onto the boat a pirate, Vincent, who we soon learn is being supported by a decadent and idle representative daughter of an earl, his girl-friend Fleur – 'My father's incredibly rich. He's the richest person I know' – who lives off the income from her substantial property holdings. Management and workers at war, the failure of liberalism to act allows fascism to emerge aided by a sympathetic aristocracy. Vincent soon has himself elected skipper and he and Fleur indulge themselves in S & M games with June, force Alistair off the boat, and make Emma walk the plank before she is rescued by the forces of liberalism – in the shape of a newly heroic Alistair.

The resultant play is a crudely political piece in a manner quite uncharacteristic of Ayckbourn. Labelled by one reviewer his SDP play, it was unmistakably an attempt to come to terms with both the old political agenda and the new. He wrote it, as he told Ian Watson, to investigate the nature of leadership; but also as an attempt to answer 'that question which every comfortable middle-class person asks himself at some stage, when he sees the news and reads the papers: "If danger threatens, how will I react?"' [14]

Way Upstream is his clumsiest play to date, but this self-conscious introduction of public and political themes is no isolated instance, however extreme it may be in this case. *Henceforward* is set in a nightmare version of London. The city is a dangerous jungle in which children are moved around in armoured vehicles under heavy escort; a city of no-go areas inhabited by rival gangs of dangerous and blackmailing thugs. As always the action of the play takes place in a room – the awfulness of the urban world only being monitored by what we are told by the characters – and it is a room in a state of literal siege, inhabited by a composer. The connections between the situation of the isolated artist – in this instance entirely wrapped up in his obsessive pursuit of computer music – and the bourgeois fears of an intrusive mob fuelled by the urban riots of the 80s are not hard to make, as Ayckbourn was only too aware:

> I don't think anybody who's lived in any urban society isn't convinced that at least it could happen – and, of course, the term 'inner cities' has been very much on everyone's lips since the 1987 General Election. [15]

This play is set a very long way from that mysteriously shifting Pendon of his earlier work. This is a London as imagined in terms of the wildest liberal nightmare. As such it is, however, but a stronger realization of the intrusion of contemporary reality that has characterized all his work in the 80s.

I have already considered *A Small Family Business*, the only play Ayckbourn has written specifically for the National Theatre. Here, we can see that not only has the social locus of events moved into the territory of Thatcher's newly enriched Home Counties, but again there is a conscious attempt to present an almost allegorical account of the state of the nation. A play that opens with a small business-man bemoaning the theft of paperclips from work and ends with him covering up murder and organizing a mafia drug contract is clearly straining the bounds of literalism a great deal. But that it is set firmly in the heart of the bourgeois family unit – here transposed into an at least dramatically logical extension of Thatcher's emphasis on the related values of the family, self-help and small businesses – returns us to the starting-point. His representation of the family unit may have moved from comic enactments of the banal and the pathetic towards real personal disintegration and madness. But when he is at his most incisive the focus remains firmly on the family. His attempts to provide a larger social context – one defined by reference to a brand of individualist liberal ideology – seem doomed, causing him to fall between the two camps: of a mainstream tradition which is unable to consider misfortune in other than personal terms; and a politicized theatre that sees such liberal posturing as irrelevant. Ayckbourn's real talent lies in the analysis of claustrophobia, in the damage done to the individual in the home. In attempting to open the debate into a larger political arena, he reveals only the limitations of debate imposed by the mainstream tradition.

9
Michael Frayn: Dust and Scaffolding

I've seen the plans. I've talked to planners. I tell you Owen, I know this town as well as I know the town I was born in. Two years from now there's going to be fountains splashing here, and bands playing under the trees . . . When you look you see only dust and scaffolding? . . . Let me tell you something, Owen. Those holes no longer exist. That dust is no longer there.

(Michael Frayn, *Clouds*, 1976)

The start of Michael Frayn's theatrical career did not coincide with the election of the first Thatcher administration of 1979, but the years that followed were to see him develop from a minor stage writer to a figure of immense importance. At the time of the electoral victory, his first properly successful stage play, *Clouds*, continued its London run, and the 80s were to be very much his decade. In that decade he twice won the 'Comedy of the Year' award, and in an article written in 1985, following the news that *Benefactors* had won the 'Play of the Year' title awarded by the same body, the Society of West End Theatres, he reflected on some of the moments that had given him most pleasure in the theatre. It is an interesting selection, placing him securely in a mainstream comic tradition. Included, amongst others, is the end of the first scene of Hampton's *The Philanthropist*, and the moment when the child unexpectedly gets out of her wheelchair in Nichols' *A Day in the Death of Joe Egg*. 'If I had sat in a box at the "Norman Conquests" or "Absurd Person Singular" I should certainly have fallen out of it.'[1]

Given that Frayn is, more than any other of the playwrights I have considered, a writer for whom ideas are central to the thematic structure of his work, it is particularly interesting to see how his work post-79 has reflected the values of the Thatcher

156

years. The recurrent theme in all his work is the conflict between the chaos and individuality of personal life and the various attempts of systematizers, planners, and the like, to create and maintain patterns of order. It is a theme that he has recently extended to his first film, *Clockwise*, in which John Cleese memorably plays a secondary school Headmaster trying vainly to keep to the schedules of his time-dominated day in the face of increasingly farcical disorder. In a period in which successive attempts at centrally organized bouts of supposedly organized planning have actually resulted in progressively worsening social chaos, it will be instructive to see how a writer of Frayn's skill and intellect has responded.

It was television, the medium that was to prove of vital importance in the formation of a new mainstream, that first allowed him to try out his dramatic skills. In 1968 *Jamie on a Flying Visit* was screened, a farcical comedy about the collision between the tired inhabitants of a post-war housing estate semi-detached (the action of the play 'to a considerable extent depends upon the house's character', according to a later note by Frayn) and a casually selfish rich visitor from an undergraduate past. This was a 'Wednesday Play' as was *Birthday* the following year, a story of family confusion. The first, in particular, is far more interested in portraying the absurdities of semi-detached life – with much of the comic business consisting of a progressive wrecking of the house as unsuccessful attempts are made to move uncontainable objects around its constricting confines – than it is in giving any serious consideration to the relationships between what are anyway a series of largely stereotyped figures.

They are slight pieces but it is important to note that the 'Wednesday Play' format and others were there to offer encouragement to new writers, something that is certainly not the case today. Frayn was sufficiently encouraged by the experience to write two more television plays; both of them were rejected and later reworked for the stage as *Alphabetical Order* (1975) and *Clouds* (1976), by which time the playwright had moved firmly away from the small screen, with only one subsequent TV production, *First and Last* for the BBC in 1989.

Although he had had a production, *Zounds!*, staged as an undergraduate at Cambridge in 1957, his first professional theatrical production came in 1970 with four one-act two-handers collectively entitled *The Two of Us*, at the Garrick. As so often, it was the encouragement of the impresario Michael Codron (to date responsible for staging six of Frayn's plays, as well as producing his only film, *Clockwise*, in 1985) that prompted the writer who until then had concentrated his energies on his work as a journalist – experiences of which are found in transmuted form in *Alphabetical Order* – and as a novelist – having published four novels before *The Two of Us* was first staged.

Frayn's first stage effort was a modest affair, mainly allowing the two actors, Lynn Redgrave and Richard Briers, the opportunity to move from one character to another between and, in the case of 'Chinamen', within the individual acts. The four pieces are unlinked in narrative terms, and seem more like revue sketches than sustained dramatic wholes, but together offer a series of limited perspectives on the mores of the suburban middle classes in a way that would become increasingly familiar both on stage and subsequently on television. The kind of characters played by Richard Briers, in particular – husband/parent figures trying desperately to establish a control over a world of petty but baffling complexity – now look indeed like almost a dry run for Briers' subsequent work in Ayckbourn's plays, and his parallel and related establishment of himself as the foremost practitioner of the art of the confused male lead in television domestic situation comedy.

The most interesting pieces are the last two: 'Mr Foot' where Frayn successfully provides a vehicle for the pent-up frustrations of the wife of a successful business-man with whom she communicates through the foot that has jiggled disapprovingly at her efforts through their married life ('Mr Foot doesn't want me to be *the little woman!* The medium-sized woman, yes; but not the little one'); and 'Chinamen' where the comic force derives from the complexities attendant on running two dinner parties simultaneously in different rooms in order to keep the newly separated partners in ignorance of each other's presence. This is a use of farce that looks forward to Frayn's own later efforts, and was to become very much the territory of Ayckbourn's early work.

Its comic investigation of suburban domesticity has its roots in the English Absurdist tradition, as is made quite clear in the opening lines of 'Chinamen' (a title derived from the fact that the husband cannot distinguish between any of the married couples that make up their list of dinner-party acquaintanceships). Stephen and Jo end the piece congratulating themselves 'that it all went off reasonably well', this despite the total havoc the couple have managed to create; they start it, as so often in this dramatic kind, preparing a dinner table, the husband trying frantically to remember the names of their indistinguishable friends:

> *Stephen*: David and *Laura*! David and *Laura*! David and Laura . . . ! (*He goes out into the living-room as* Jo *returns from the kitchen.*)
>
> *Jo*: *John* and Laura! *John* and Laura! For heaven's sake get it straight, Stephen. We've known them for ten years! (*She starts hurriedly distributing soup spoons, as* Stephen *hurries back in with another chair.*)
>
> *Stephen*: I can't really tell our friends apart, that's the trouble. John and Laura, John and Laura, John and Laura . . . They're all exactly the same – same age, same number of children, same sort of job, same income, same opinions . . . They even look alike! It's like looking at Chinamen. Nicholas and Jay – Simon and Kay – Freddie and Di . . .

What distinguishes 'Mr Foot' from the other sketches is the extent to which Frayn is here able to move his concerns away from the comically satirical, to create in the wife – appallingly nicknamed 'Nibs' by her husband – a brief sketch of the real human misery that lies behind the convenient stereotypes of the kind. Her worries about whether she had properly prepared him for his most recent trip to Belfast, for instance, certainly reinforce the line of satire:

> I did put the flask of coffee in his brief-case, didn't I? If he has to drink BEA coffee there and back he'll come back this evening in a great state of moral outrage. He'll sit there reading 'Coins of the Greek Colonies in Italy' and Mr Foot will go jig-jig-jig . . . (*Mr Foot does so, but* Geoffrey *seizes it and holds it.*) ' What's the matter?' 'What?' 'Nothing's the matter.' But Mr Foot thinks something's the matter. Disagrees with some statement in the book, perhaps. No, something I've done. I haven't wound the hall clock again . . . I've forgotten to put my stockings on . . . I've put the newspapers under the cushions . . . I've left the lavatory light on all day . . . (*She sits down again, watching* Geoffrey *apprehensively.*) 'Had a good day?' – No, no, no, that's wrong! Strike that out of the record! He thinks that's suburban

– something we certainly can't afford to be, living as we do in the suburbs.

But the satire is not mutually deployed. The husband is enshrined as the upholder of a set of suburban values that could have come from any of the plays of the English Absurdist tradition, and the wife, who is the mouthpiece of the satire, is thus separated from those values. She turns first away from and then on the husband by means of a dialogue with an imaginary third person, a man who has come to 'take a squint' at the wife to assess her suitability as prop for the husband who is, he assures her, definitely 'in line' for a new job. The hints of her involvement with the Women's Liberation movement are no more convincing than the fantasy she conjures with of running away with the non-existent investigator, but what Frayn does do is to identify her as a woman frustrated with the role of wife and second fiddle. Here, and less frequently elsewhere, there are hints of a world of tragic waste beneath the comic veneer.

This sense of waste is one that continually resurfaces in Frayn's plays – and is certainly something that might be expected from a writer who has become effectively the channel through which Chekhov has been displayed on the English stage in the last fifteen years, having followed the first translation of *The Cherry Orchard* in 1978 with what now amounts to the complete canon. But it is a theme that is always at war with a larger structural obsession with the mechanics of theatre in a way that looks back as much to Pirandello as it does to the great farceurs. The resultant tension can be seen well in *Alphabetical Order* and *Donkey's Years* (1977), the two plays which really established him as a stage writer, after the rather poorly received follow-up to *The Two of Us*, *The Sandboy* of 1971.

Alphabetical Order gives us a collection of sad individuals, all working with greater or lesser enthusiasm on a small provincial newspaper that will go bust as the play ends. The action takes place in the library of the newspaper, where the new employee, Leslie, sets out to create a carefully indexed order from the chaos that surrounds her on her arrival. The metaphorical transfer of the order/chaos model both to world events and to individual lives works neatly rather than convincingly, and as a result the play pulls in two not entirely reconcilable directions.

The wonderful near-ending, where the now unemployed staff

vent their feelings by destroying the neatness and precision imposed by Leslie on the cuttings library, littering the stage with the rejumbled contents of the files, is inevitably undercut by Frayn's attempt to draw the thematic threads together for his characters. Leslie, whose attempts to bring order have extended to the troubled lives of her colleagues, is given a final entrance. She is greeted with the hysterical antics of the staff, happier with confusion than with her efforts to alleviate it; given the bad news, her response is immediate and more dependent on the thematic balance of the play than on any possible psychological or industrial reality:

Nora: We shan't need any of it any more.
Leslie: But we shall! Shan't we?
Geoffrey: Need this? What for?
John: The paper's closed!
Leslie: The management's closed it. But we shan't accept that, shall we?
Nora: Shan't accept it?
Geoffrey: What do you mean, shan't accept it. We've got to accept it!
Leslie: Well, we'll take over the plant. Shan't we? We'll go on bringing the paper out ourselves.

The intrusion of the possibility of real political action is as misplaced – we have been watching the construction of a metaphor and not a workplace, after all – as is the likelihood of Nibs' genuine participation in the Women's Liberation movement in 'Mr Foot'.

But the problem is as nothing to that created in the next play, the action of which is concerned with a weekend of a college reunion. Frayn later talked of the play in almost Chekhovian terms, and certainly it would be entirely possible to think of such a play being constructed in a way that allowed the comparison:

In *Donkey's Years* middle-aged men find themselves confronted by the perceptions they formed of each other – and of themselves – when they were young, and by the styles of being they adopted then to give themselves shape in each other's eyes, and in their own. In the ensuing years they have all, consciously or unconsciously, slipped out of these shells, and when for one night they try to reinhabit them the effect is as absurd as wearing outgrown clothes would be.

It is a line of argument that he attempted to extend to *Noises Off* (1982), which according to Frayn is about 'the fear that haunts [the actors] . . . that the unlearned and unrehearsed – the great dark chaos behind the set, inside the heart and brain – will seep back on to the stage.'[2] It is easy to see how the order/chaos motif can be traced throughout his plays; less obvious is the degree to which such a seriousness can be accorded it. For the chaos in both *Noises Off* and in *Donkey's Years* is that of the stage business of farce. An audience may be entertained by the dexterity with which the farcical tricks are effected, amused by the wit with which the confusion is recorded in the dialogue; but, by the same token, it is hard to expect any level of real engagement at either the philosophical or the psychological level.

But this is not the real problem about the play. A piece which brings together a collection of people united only in the fact of their having received their higher education at an Oxbridge college is, perforce, building an audience expectation that in some way, personal or public or indeed both, the event will involve some kind of reckoning, some kind of re-evaluation. That it is set in an Oxbridge college will clearly be a major defining factor; we will be considering the 'state of the nation' from a ruling-class, or at worst management, perspective. However, not only does any sort of re-evaluation fail to take place, but Frayn's choice of characters ensures that the debate can never be extended beyond the narrowest of confines. The audience observes the characters' lack of development in the intervening years – the status games still being played between Headingley, now an Under-Secretary at the Department of Education and Science, and Quine, now a civil servant in his Department, for instance, and the perpetuation of the undergraduate pranks by supposedly grown men – but there is no analysis, no connection with anything outside these pathetic games.

Peter Ansorge made the point well. 'These characters, reverting to type, can't sustain more than a bright anecdote. They are not representative of a generation other than having been at the same college. As Simon Gray in *Otherwise Engaged*, Frayn seems to have nothing but contempt for the new generation – here represented by John Harding's politicized young English don. He can't, as

David Hare achieved in *Teeth 'N' Smiles*, open up the play to make a real comment on English educational scars – or even hint at the need to evade Oxbridge's snobbish brand of shrapnel.'[3]

Ansorge's mention of the leftish don, Taylor, helps to pinpoint the political weighting of the piece. It is not that he is alone in being ridiculed. The programme note that lists his published oeuvre as *Mythopoeic Structures in the Metonymy of Two Jacobean Children's Rhymes*, published by the *Revue des Etudes Semiologiques*, Toulouse, is evidently meant to be greeted with knowing smiles from a Shaftsbury Avenue audience not exactly versed in semiotics, but recognizing a modernist imbalance between children's rhymes and theory when it is handed to them in a note. It is, of course, actually less comic than the more traditional publications attributed to the visiting Tate, a *Complete Home Encyclopaedia of Japanese Flower Arranging* and *A Boy's and Girl's Guide to Overseas Development*, but then Tate, like his companions, is seen as a part of a past and unthreatening world; as characters to be savoured in their antics, rather than analysed in their meditations.

The programme note for Taylor acts as a cue, a call to the audience to dismiss from their minds the meaningful possibility of any real critique of what is represented by the world of the visitors. Indeed, Taylor's very first words in the play are to Birkett, the Head Porter in his fiftieth year of service with the college, reminding him that industrial action is to take place in a language that is not that of this workplace: 'You won't forget that the Joint Action Committee has banned overtime working as of midnight tonight?' And as the play proceeds so, surely enough, the leftist pretensions of Taylor are neatly, too neatly, punctured one by one.

Birkett's final words in the play – 'See you again in another twenty years, Mr Tate, sir' – leave us with nothing altered, the hierarchical structure in place, and the promise of a continuing perpetuation of its absurdities. That the major thrust of the play is towards the farcical should not blind us to the insularity of a world that may be being briefly mocked but which is never seriously threatened – the one outsider of the party, Snell, is indeed sedated and institutionalized by the end of the play, as is only appropriate for him in his role as spectre at an exceedingly grubby feast.

The most interesting character potentially in *Donkey's Years* is, as often in Frayn's work, a woman; indeed the only woman, the

Master's wife, Lady Driver (Penelope Keith in the original production), well known to most of the revisiting men in their undergraduate days, and now set in the role of supporting wife to a Master who never appears, and in search of a fresh liaison with an old lover that is always farcically prevented. In another sort of play it is conceivable that she could have been developed beyond the merest sketch that is demanded of her as the necessary prop in a farcical world – the only woman to be present overnight in an all-male environment, and therefore to be hidden, disguised, have attempts made upon her person, be described in their old-fashioned argot as a 'Popsy', and finally to be allowed to escape over the college roofs.

Frayn's interest in the mechanics of plot contrivance, not as brilliantly developed as they will be in his later work but still effective enough, prevents an audience from forming any real relationship with the characters. They simply will not take on the kind of empathetic role Frayn appears to want. In *Donkey's Years* the confusion of different rooms, different doors and different clothes is all, and the mad excesses of Mr Snell – crazily aware of all that he had been excluded from as an undergraduate, lodged the other side of the railway station instead of having rooms in college, and subsequently – do nothing to create a bleaker aspect to the piece. He is used simply to add to and confirm the essentially farcical base of the play.

The two other plays Frayn had staged prior to the 1979 Election interestingly push the tension between theme and stage business in the opposite direction. Both *Clouds* (1976) and *Balmoral* (1978, and subsequently reworked as *Liberty Hall* in 1980) appear to push a political context to the fore. The weaker of the two, *Balmoral*, posits a change in world history. The Communist Revolution having taken place in Britain rather than Russia, Frayn's play converts the royal residence into a state-run community for writers, offering an austere 1937 home for Enid Blyton, Hugh Walpole, Warwick Deeping and Godfrey Winn as they are visited by a journalist from the capitalist Russian press.

The choice of writers is not very promising, in itself pointing to the inevitability of a merely comic resolution of affairs, and what could have been an interesting approach to the relationship of writer to a world of public issues – something continually brushed against by Frayn – soon descends into a particularly dreary farcical romp. There is much talk about hardship before Frayn moves into the main action of the play. The Russian journalist has come to interview Walpole, who has first disappeared – into an overnight shopping queue in pursuit of ladies underwear, it transpires – and then dies. His body is crammed into a trunk and the dissident servant McNab is called upon to play a double-part – much of the humour dependent on the fact that the same actor has anyway been playing both parts – in order that the interview can proceed.

Harmony between the characters re-established, the long-awaited arrival of the Government Inspector, with the oft-rehearsed possibility of death or imprisonment in his pocket, is announced; and the play ends with the journalist finally discovering what is in the trunk, as he puts another 'dead body', an empty whisky bottle, in.

Clouds is altogether more interesting. Far more simply staged than his later works, which frequently need complicated diagrams for a potential director, the play is set in post-revolutionary Cuba; an island suggested simply by an empty blue sky, and to be created according to the varied imaginations of the three visitors. The three vie against each other to produce a more convincing portrait of life on the island: a traditional journalist obsessed with facts, and a woman novelist concerned with feelings and impressions have commissions from rival Sunday newspapers; the third, a fluent Spanish-speaking American with a book in mind, is convinced that he can get nearer to the real Cuba. In reality, each sees what they want to see, and any proper concern with the political dimensions of the plot quickly gives way to an interest in the manipulation by the novelist, Mara – again a lone woman – of the collection of men, Cuban and non-Cuban, all united across the political divide in frustrated dreams of what might be.

What separates this play from the other early works is that it is the first sustained attempt by Frayn to allow any real development of insight into character, even if what we mostly learn is that the characters do not understand themselves, let alone each other. It continues Frayn's fascination with the role of the writer (by *Noises Off* and *Look Look*, 1990, it will have become, significantly, the role of the playwright); but again, the actual connection with its setting in post-revolutionary Cuba is increasingly lost sight of. A comparison with, for instance, David Hare's *A Map of the World* of 1982 is telling. Set in the context of a UNESCO Conference on World Poverty, where the emotional tensions between two writers, an Indian novelist and an English journalist, both competing for the favours of an American visitor, are not separable from the main thematic concerns of the plot. 'Through this tangled maze of relationships, Hare offers a critique both of easy Western solutions to the problems of the Third World – suggesting in particular that no formal separation of worlds is possible – and of the reliable objectivity of this, or any other, analysis.'[4] There is nothing in *Clouds* that allows for such lines of analysis to be drawn.

What is nonetheless significant about Frayn's work is that, after the plays of the late 60s and early 70s, he has shown a willingness to move the action out from the limits of the domestic locale; a willingness to consider relationships between characters that stress their larger societal function. Even in *Benefactors* (1984), the third of his post-79 plays, where the action does take place within a domestic environment it does so with reason, the plot being concerned with housing. But in *Make and Break*, the play which really established his theatrical reputation, Frayn takes the action directly into the workplace, or at least into a very particular part of that workplace.

Like so many plays of the modern period, *Make and Break* opened – in a Michael Codron production – as a try-out at the Lyric, Hammersmith, before moving to the Theatre Royal, Haymarket, in April 1980. With *Benefactors*, it represents a real attempt to come to some kind of terms with the emerging world of monetarism, and for this reason – not accidentally allied to the fact that the two plays represent Frayn's best work for the stage to date – they demand a more detailed consideration.

Make and Break is set in 1980, and the action takes place on an exhibition stand set up in a hotel suite at an international trade fair in Frankfurt. As the play opens we hear three salesmen going through a series of well-rehearsed selling lines to three potential customers. The first, Tom Olley, is all prices and currency conversion tables, the third, Colin Hewlett, finishings and availability. It is left to the other man, Frank Prosser, to stress the adaptability of the product:

Now you want full demountability and you want full recoverability. But you don't want to end up with some kind of temporary accommodation for homeless families. Because you've looked at some of those demountable partitions on the floor down there, and you think a demountable partition's going to look and feel demountable . . . Well, just forget partitions. Partitions are things that rattle when you slam the door. These are walls. This is a wall system. Fully demountable, fully adjustable walls combined with a range of fully uniform finishes for your load-bearing elements. Movable solid walls.

And indeed, the set is just this, a display of 'movable solid walls' ('a complete internal environment' as Hewlett later describes it). Not only does the actualization of the product as set reinforce the duality of the product being sold, both solid and endlessly adaptable to the needs of the individual customer, but it presents the audience with a strikingly realized metaphor of Frayn's thematic concern with building and destruction. Furthermore, the farcical potential of a set that will allow walls to be turned round on their axes was not lost on Frayn, allowing for the unexpected intrusion of two 'nightmare' sequences into the action and giving the audience a wonderfully macabre shock towards the end, when a wall is turned to reveal the dead body of Olley.

The opening dialogue sets the action carefully. It is comic only to an outsider (the audience), its language a part of a recognizable business discourse. The salesman's distaste for a product that might look like 'temporary accommodation for homeless people' touches upon a theme that would assume major significance as homelessness steadily increased in the major cities of Britain throughout the 80s and 90s. And clearly Frayn's casual intrusion of it is intended to be received ironically in the context of a trade fair where the leading character will later formulate plans for the production of portable exhibition stands at £20,000 a time – roughly the price of an average semi-detached house in a provincial British city at the time.

Indeed, we will learn shortly that Anni, the temporary assistant they have employed, a German student, might well be able to formulate plans for such temporary accommodation:

Prosser: Nice girl, though. Real plus on the stand.
Garrard: Workers' rights.
Olley: Oh. Believes in them, does she?
Garrard: Organizes all the guest-workers in the big hotels. Turks, Greeks. All her spare time. She and her boy-friend. Tells them their legal rights. Stirs them up.

But Anni's role is never allowed to develop in ways that might threaten the political assumptions that underpin the salesmen's world. She will later bring news of a night on the town that had involved running away from the police in the course of a demonstration, but her interventions are peripheral. Like the only other woman in the play, the faithful secretary Mrs Rogers, she operates as little more than a foil for the characters in this, a man's, world. The opening dialogue that establishes the terms of reference for what debate the play offers is initiated and received by men. If there is implicit criticism of aspects of this male commercial ideology, there is no space in the play for the expression of any desirable alternative.

However, Frayn does almost immediately offer a very different opposition to the wall-building activities. The opening dialogue is twice briefly interrupted by the sound of an explosion, virtually ignored by the characters each time. It is only when Anni enters that an explanation is offered: 'Some people, I suppose, were exploding some things. Some shops, some U-Bahn station, I don't know.'

The image of destruction plays an important part in the play. The activities of the terrorists, continually and jokily related to Anni's political activities by the salesmen unable to distinguish between oppositional strategies, stand as a counter to what can then be seen as, ultimately, the worthy enterprise of building. Olley is later reminded that he too has been an agent of destruction, as an RAF navigator in the bomb raids on German cities in the Second World War, and he is quick to make the connection: 'It looked like the end of the world down there some nights. I thought that was that . . . Like woodland. Burn it back, and up it comes green next season. Like our walls – it's all demountable. As long as people have still got the ideas in their heads. As long as they've got the skills in their hands.'

There are then only two real alternatives offered in the debate: the world of work, and the activities of the terrorist – the one building (if only movable walls) and the other destroying. Frayn's choice of the particular version of construction – as opposed to, say, actual house-building – brings with it a deliberately problematic aspect, but its juxtaposition with the world of the bomber gives even this marginalized aspect of construction a credibility that is central to the playwright's intent.

The trade stand is not just a microcosm of the world, however;

it is to these men effectively their entire world. Even when the born-again Hewlett is prevailed upon to talk about an evangelical meeting he had attended, his colleagues translate the account comically into the terms of their own discourse.

> *Prosser*: They've just had some big do in tents down in Exeter. How many souls did you save down there, Colin?
> *Hewlett*: I mean we had over a thousand people coming forward.
> *Prosser*: That firm orders, though, or just enquiries?

Although given outside interests – Prosser, for instance knows all the opus numbers and keys of Beethoven's entire output, but cannot tell which is which – their lives are entirely taken up with the need to sell, and with the need to survive in the commercial jungle. From the start they are preoccupied with the imminent arrival of the 'new whizz-kid' Managing Director of the entire group of companies, who may well be about to sell the company off in a financial game; his casual interventions in the plot create a prevailing mood of worry and uncertainty, bringing into conflict as they do the twin activities of trading in products and trading in money.

However, Frayn carefully delays the entrance of the man who will stand as the ultimate epitome of the conflicting demands of this world, the Managing Director of the company, John Garrard. Played memorably by Leonard Rossiter, Garrard is Frayn's most magnificent creation, a frightening figure fuelled by the need to sell, unable to rest, constantly planning and scheming – he had hired Prosser, we learn, in the waiting-room at Golder's Green Crematorium:

> *Prosser*: Ted Shaw's old pal – Pat McGuire – it was his funeral. They were running ten minutes late.
> *Olley*: So naturally, John wondered how to fill in the time.

Earlier, Prosser has anticipated his arrival: 'I'll tell you the first thing he'll do when he walks in here. He'll rearrange that display. Fiddle, fiddle, fiddle, while he goes on about the emptiness of the order book and the price of paper-clips.' And when he does arrive, a day earlier than announced, the audience is not disappointed. Ignoring the salesmen, he carefully opens and shuts the

room door through which he has appeared, before calling for a
chair on which he stands to confirm that the hotel has indeed con-
tracted out to a rival firm. In the brisk conversation that follows
Garrard moves from the local annoyance with the door, through
the (empty) order book, his thoughts on the rival trade-stands, his
plans for expansion into Eastern Europe, and a scheme to market
permanent display stands to their competitors. He is only briefly
halted by discovering the naked Anni taking a shower in his suite.

From his first entrance, Garrard dominates the entire play. He is
one of the great creations of contemporary theatre, a monster for
whom the other characters feel immense affection, a nightmare
embodiment of the world of commerce, a monomaniac whose
energy carries an audience along. The secretary complains protec-
tively that they encourage him:

> *Mrs Rogers*: So he knows you're not going to let him go too far.
> You make him behave like a spoilt child.
> *Olley*: My sweet precious, he's the same with everyone! He's
> driven his wife into a home – his daughter's in Canada, never
> writes – his son no-one knows where he is – on a building-
> site when last heard of. This is his life! And it'll be the death
> of him. (*Pause*) At least he knows what he wants. That's his
> great strength. That's why he's got us all dancing through the
> streets behind him.

It is one of the play's more carefully placed ironies that it is
Olley and not Garrard who is found dead towards the end. The
likelihood of a heart attack is planted from early in the play and
reinforced by the calling of a doctor after he has collapsed in pain
with what, it transpires, is a slipped disc after making love to the
long-besotted Mrs Rogers. This, like everything Garrard does, is
driven by curiosity and he is as interested in questioning her on
the Buddhism course she has been taking as in actually getting her
into bed.

Garrard's hi-jacking of the play is vital. It turns it from a gentle
comedy into a savage if ambivalent celebration of the world of
trade. Garrard is not all-powerful, and much of his demonic
energy is given to plans to head off the possible disasters in store,
not knowing whether he will be promoted or chopped by the
overall Director. But he is powerful as a stage character in his
unswerving certainty that nothing else matters outside his world,

and that its values transcend everything. Recovered from what he had thought was a heart attack, he immediately sets about trying to put a deal together with the ex-East German doctor who has treated him, easily persuading him to use his contacts back in the East to get a contract for hospital doors. Presented with the possibility that he might be given control of three more companies, he protests that he could not possibly handle it all, and immediately sets about planning a managerial shuffle. He says he could not live if he could not work, and for once we believe him.

The sheer size of Garrard as a character gives the play its real strength. He is the model, the other salesmen but pale imitations. This intense concentration on the values and uncertainties of their world is vital to Frayn's intent and helps to demonstrate what he is precisely not trying to do. The characters are victims certainly, but the playwright is not attempting any kind of radical critique of the overall world in which they live, a point he makes strongly:

> I think *Make and Break* is about how we all compulsively exploit the possibilities of the world around us – about how we eat it – how we have to eat it – how we transform it into food and clothes and housing, and of course lay it waste in the process. Is Garrard more monstrous than the rest of us? If he seems so, isn't it because he lacks our saving hypocrisy – because he fails to dissemble the activities that we all have, that we all must have if we are to survive? I can't help feeling, too, that if the play is seen as some kind of attack upon business, or industrialism, this is assumed that no one would ever write about these subjects without moral condescension of one sort or another. I don't understand why this should be so; it seems to me unbecoming for writers and critics to condescend towards the people who feed and clothe them. It is true that some of the things industry produces are harmful or unnecessary. But Garrard makes walls and doors. Could anyone really think I am advocating a world without walls and doors? All I am trying to show is what they cost.[5]

Make and Break is then a somewhat unusual play to find in the new mainstream, but Frayn is surely correct in stressing the essentially non-radical nature of the enterprise. The argument is stacked too carefully, and if it raises larger questions than those posited by the playwright, it does so not by what is included but by what is rigorously not. Its novelty comes rather from its consideration of such matters at all in a contemporary theatre increasingly committed to the domestic and the personal.

All we learn of Garrard's son in the play is that he had been last spotted working on a building-site (a man who is actually building, we might note, rather than selling, as his father, the product of such labour). It is a small but characteristic irony of the play, but in *Benefactors* (1984) Frayn turned almost directly to the activity itself.

Four years on, the mood of the play is totally different. It is more sombre and less certain about its terms of reference, more deeply questioning than anything else Frayn has written to date. Although its terms of reference are very much those of the mid-80s, its narrative starting-point is, significantly enough, 1968; but it is a very different 1968 from that perceived by the playwrights considered in *New British Political Dramatists*.

The action of the play moves smoothly and without jumps from 1968 to the then present. Where time leaps need explanation, Frayn provides asides by the characters to the audience, one of a number of 'experimental' aspects of the play. *Benefactors* is populated by two pairs of married couples whose personal and public lives become progressively entangled in the fifteen years narrative span of the play.

David is an architect, commissioned by the local Council to design new housing for what his wife Jane and he dispute is either a 'slum-clearance' area or a 'twilight-zone'. Early in the play, the context is set by Sheila, wife of David's friend from undergraduate days, Colin:

> Sixty-eight. That was the year. He started on Basuto Road in April, just after Lizzie's birthday. They were such good friends, it was lovely. You felt you could always pop over the road for a chat. I used to go flying over there at all hours. I'd just slip a coat round my shoulders and push the front door open, and – Hoo-hoo! And Jane would be rushing around, doing fifteen things at once, and I'd sit in the kitchen and watch her and I'd think, Oh if only I could be like that! If only I'd got her energy! And the colours of everything in the kitchen were so warm and friendly. And David would come popping in for a moment on the way to one of his sites, and the children were lovely, and they'd all make you feel you belonged there.

Sheila starts the play as the most marginalized character. During her first scene she does not speak at all and these, her very first words in the play, are followed by Jane's 'Poor old Sheila'. In her first speech she is used to fill in the narrative detail about David's plans, and her jealousy of the order and energy of her friends' lives – in contrast to the chaos and uncertainty of her own – but Frayn uses such intrusions for a further reason. In this play, unlike his others, the characters are allowed to meditate in public on their own changing relationship to events public and private, a public and private which become increasingly indistinguishable.

Thus, Sheila's attraction to the friends' house stems in part from its superiority as a model of organization and effort, but increasingly, as the work that it produces, David's plans for the new development, assumes greater and greater significance, her interest is transferred directly to the rehousing scheme itself. She starts the play infatuated with Jane, and increasingly helping her with the running of the household, and then falls in love with David, becoming his secretary and working from his office-home.

The relationships between the two couples are totally inter-crossed in this way. Jane, who starts the play by telling the audience that she always opposed her husband's plans (even though she agreed with them), but acts as a domestic life-support system, ends it as the breadwinner and in direct opposition. She initially expresses a hatred for Colin but once he moves directly in opposition to the redevelopment plans, it is she who acts as the go-between once Sheila has left Colin and moved in with her work, and she who arranges funding for the opposition to be organized.

It is important to stress the complicated nature of these inter-relationships since they are absolutely central to Frayn's thematic concerns; concerns which lay heavy stress, as always, on the significance, and the cost, of planning in human terms.

David plans to redevelop a huge public site ('But that's where the work is, Jane, in local authority housing. That's where the real architecture's being done'). He starts opposing the notion of high-rise building on human grounds and, as the conflict between the increasing restrictions of the site and the need to house an optimum number of people builds over the years, he ends with planning that which he had opposed but which had always been predicted by Colin. Humanity gives way to an inexorable logic:

Skyscrapers, Sheila. That's the answer. That's the only answer.
I've tried every other solution, and it doesn't work ... The
highest residential buildings in Europe ... Because in the end
it's not art – it's mathematics. A simple equation. You collect up
the terms, you get rid of the brackets, you replace all the as and
bs with the number of three-person households and the length
of a coffin and the turning-circle of a corporation refuse vehicle
– and there at the bottom of the page on the righthand side is
the answer.

The interplay between the characters, and the skilful use of the
passing of time, allow Frayn a framework in which to air a series
of arguments about the function of public housing, redevelopment
against rebuilding, and so on. But always the debate has wider
resonances than this.

At the beginning of the play Colin refers to the proposed site as
Basutoland, and we learn that as well as Basuto Road, there is
Bechuana Road, Matabele Road, Machona Road and Barotse
Street. 'But when you think how fresh and hopeful that must have
sounded once, back in 1890!' David declares. His words recall a
British colonial past, as surely as do the names of the streets. What
is being redefined is more than a collection of houses, but it is a
proposed redefinition that has a more immediately colonial significance.

Despite her misgivings Jane is prevailed upon to do a door-to-
door survey of the streets, in an attempt to find out what the
people actually want in their new housing. She protests that she is
a social anthropologist and not a social worker, interested in
studying people and not in helping them, a model that comple-
ments perfectly that of the bureaucratic planner that David eventually becomes. But she discovers that people expect her to help,
and she ends the play working as a community planner. The
door-to-door survey is not a success, however. There is nobody in
or they refuse to answer; when she does find a door opening in
Basutoland 'a black face looks round the door' or a woman indicates that 'she can't understand my dialect'.

The remnants of Britain's colonial past are actually in the next
street; their further redevelopment is necessary as Colin sardonically points out, 'Otherwise the areas where architects and demolition contractors live will start to look a little grey and exhausted
again'. Jane's inability to locate David's supposed clients is telling.

Despite all the talk and *angst*, the most significant fact about the play is the absence of any actual members of the affected neighbourhood with whom the protagonists might actually engage.

Of course, this lack of human contact is part of the point of Frayn's theme, but the problem is exacerbated when the opposition to the scheme is taken up by Colin, who moves out of his house – his wife having decamped to that of Ibsen's 'Master Builder' as he has earlier characterized David – and into a squat in the proposed site. For, as Felix Barker noted, if Colin is the play's catalyst, he is also 'a sneering figure of frightening unpleasantness.'[6]

And it is on Colin's shoulders alone that any real opposition to the scheme will fall. He is not only its declared organizer – going so far as to stand, unsuccessfully, for Parliament – but he is the only oppositional figure we are ever allowed to see. The result is that what degree of radical opposition the play allows is expressed by a man whose sincerity is always in question, whose commitment to the cause of the people always to be doubted, and whose prime motivation is probably personal hatred.

What all this means is that the debate is never allowed to open up in a way that it would in a properly 'political' play. The redevelopment scheme is abandoned and, although Colin claims the credit, Frayn makes it perfectly clear that the scheme was dropped by the Council on simple grounds of economics. The play concludes with summaries of the lives of the four protagonists after the scheme's demise, and we are left with no political conclusion, save Jane's final realization that it is a waste of time asking people what they want: 'I suppose I've changed. I've learnt one thing from working with people anyway: they want to be told what to do'. It is not only a non-radical conclusion, it is not even a liberal democratic one.

What Frayn has written about his earlier work is still relevant here: 'So far as I can see, all of these plays are attempts to show something about the world, not to change it, or to promote any particular idea of it. That is not to say there are no ideas in them. In fact what they are all about in one way or another (it seems to me) is the way we impose our ideas upon the world around us.'[7] But his refusal to push *Benefactors* beyond these parameters means that in the end, all the thematic strands notwithstanding, what we are left with is a somewhat bleak study of the lives of some carefully located new Englanders and not the more searching exam-

ination of the state of the nation that appeared to be on offer. It is
as if the playwright had looked out from the mainstream, not
liked overmuch what he saw, and made his retreat.

In the event, *Benefactors* became the second of his plays to open
on Broadway. Although it met with a generally good critical
reception, W. J. Weatherby's remarks on the event are not without
point:

> Michael Frayn was first introduced to Broadway audiences
> through his backstage farce, *Noises Off*, and much of the audi-
> ence at *Benefactors* expected another farce . . . But when *Bene-
> factors* turned serious and remained so, a man behind me
> protested the play was not at all funny.[8]

For one major point about the play has been omitted. Although
it has its comic moments, and certainly three of the characters are
capable of wittily acerbic remarks, *Benefactors* is not a comedy. As
such it is virtually unique amongst the plays discussed in this
book. Shortly before *Benefactors* was first produced John Russell
Taylor published an interesting essay about Mainstream Theatre.
He concluded with the following question:

> Significantly, it seems that commercial and comic have to be
> synonymous: we are still waiting to see whether such a thing as
> a tragedy or even a strong drama can belong just as unmistak-
> ably to our own time and still achieve just as indisputable a
> broad-based popular success. Maybe *Equus* has done it: at any
> rate it stands out as the only play of the 1970s which can put in
> a serious claim. But otherwise, funny can find the middle-brow
> public, while serious has to be either safely classic or danger-
> ously contemporary.[9]

Taylor's wonder at whether the 80s might provide serious plays
within the repertoire of the mainstream is quickly answered.
Shaffer has certainly continued to do so, and to him could be
added the work of writers such as Julian Mitchell with *Another
Country* (1981) and *After Aida* (1985), or Hugh Whitemore with
Pack of Lies (1983) and *Breaking the Code* (1986), for instance – all
four plays with an impeccably mainstream pedigree. But the
implications of the question reverberate.

The predominant urge to comedy in the new mainstream is

both about an awareness of West End audience demand – above all to be entertained, to be sent home with a smile – and about a fear of exposure. To retreat from the classic guise of self-mockery and irony means that the playwright must actually find something to say that is in the end not simply self-referential. Interestingly, all four of the examples I gave above (plus *Amadeus*, 1979, Shaffer's most notable success since *Equus*) moved away from the contemporary in their narratives, drawing their source material from past history – even if that past history is on occasions allowed to raise more immediate questions. A mainstream theatre that is exceedingly reluctant to declare itself in overtly ideological terms will clearly have trouble in moving away from the safety of the comic mode – be it the comedy of wit, or the comedy of farce – when dealing with the contentiously contemporary.

It looks as though it has been a lesson well learnt by Frayn. His real box-office hit of the 80s was not *Make and Break* or *Benefactors*, but *Noises Off* (1982), a brilliantly clever, and totally empty, farce about theatre as theatre. Highly successful on its first production, it continues to appear frequently in professional and amateur theatres across the land. After *Benefactors* Frayn returned to the same well, producing *Look Look* (1990), another theatre as theatre comedy, in which the audience became the cast. It remains to be seen whether he will finally do what he more than anyone has threatened, and strain the limited and limiting confines of the new mainstream with what John Russell Taylor craved in 1981, a play about the contemporary world that dares consistently to take itself seriously.

10

Alan Bennett: The Leftovers

George: Will you hear my words?
Polly: What for?
George: That television. Here . . . Skip the first bit, I'm going
to rewrite that . . . burble, burble, burble . . . ours is still a
society in which we throw people into the dustbin, some
sooner, some later. We chuck some people in at fifteen, we
chuck others in at sixty-five. Our society is one that produces a colossal amount of rubbish. Litter, junk, waste. Yes?
Polly: The leftovers.
George: The leftovers. And in among the leftovers are people.
We waste people. The best society – I think a socialist
society – is one in which fewest people are wasted.

(Alan Bennett, *Getting On*, 1971)

The speakers in the above dialogue are George Oliver, a Labour
MP, and his second wife. The play went into rehearsal in August
1971, a little over a year after Edward Heath formed a Conservative administration, having ousted the Labour Party under
Harold Wilson. It is a context continually stressed in the text,
which refers to the paraphernalia of the election campaign – a red
rosette, cartoons from the satirical magazine, *Private Eye*, and so
on – as part of the casual decoration of the ground-floor of the
converted Edwardian house in which the play is set.

The play is in great part concerned with the efforts of George to
come to terms with, to examine the implications of, in his thinking
about socialism, that never actually mentioned defeat. Indeed, so
insistently articulate is he about his rethinking of socialism in a
modern world, that he fails to observe his wife's affair with the
handyman and the imminent death of his much-loved mother-in-
law, a resilient figure of an older left generation.

Although *Getting On* is not very obviously alliable with the kind
of contemporary political theatre that I discussed in *New British
Political Dramatists*, it is perhaps surprising to find it included in a
consideration of the development of a new mainstream. The

simple fact is that it highlights the rather different position that Bennett has come to occupy in this tradition. That the playwright should choose to centre his considerations of the state of contemporary Britain on the thoughts of a man who has tried throughout his life to represent a socialist perspective could, for instance, allow the play to stand alongside David Hare's *The Great Exhibition* (first produced a few months later in exactly the same historical context) – another play about a disillusioned Labour MP.

However, the possibility of making such a connection would have seemed somewhat implausible to any member of the audience of the version of *Getting On* that actually reached London after a series of provincial try-outs that started at Brighton. After a great deal of agonizing the part of the MP was taken by Kenneth More – whose most famous role had been that of Douglas Bader in *Reach for the Sky*, an uncomplicatedly heroic Second World War movie ridiculed in passing by Bennett himself in 'The Aftermath of War' sketch in *Beyond the Fringe*.

By the time the play got to the West End, More had so altered the character of George – in an effort to make him attractive to audiences – that, to Bennett's astonishment, a play that he had thought of as a serious piece was declared the *Evening Standard* 'Best Comedy of the Year' for 1971. Accepting the award, the playwright said 'it was like entering a marrow for the show and being given the cucumber prize'.[1]

Bennett stresses the point in his note to the republished text of the play; where he talks of its clumsy and unsanctioned cutting – 'the jokes were largely left intact while the serious content of the play suffered'. He had attempted to use the play as a vehicle for a debate that was centred considerably to the left of the concerns of contemporary mainstream theatre, and the concerted efforts of that mainstream had quietly sanitized its contents. And generally, Bennett's political perspective on the world he surveys has remained off-centre in mainstream terms. His hostility to Thatcher's successive administrations has been a matter of public utterance on a number of occasions; a major theme of all his work until about 1986, and his re-embracement by the stage, has been his depiction of characters who are precisely the 'leftovers' described by his 1971 MP.

His first stage play, *Forty Years On*, was an adaptation of a radio script in which the loose format of review sketches, parodies and pastiches was given a shape by the creation of a school play at a

symbolically realized Albion House. Like *Habeas Corpus* (1973), the
play that followed *Getting On*, it was highly indebted to the
English Absurdist tradition. *Habeas Corpus* is a fast-moving farce in
which deliberately caricatured figures address each other in terms
of an almost surrealistically constructed social world. It is a world
in which the cub-leader's ordering of an appliance to enhance the
size and shape of her breasts sets off a chain of mistaken connections, discoveries of long-past adulteries, and the like. Superficially, its dialogue is reminiscent of Orton's careful mixing of the
inappropriate. In the first act Mrs Wickstead talks with Mrs
Swabb, the char, and her son and daughter. She wants to empty
the house in readiness for the hoped-for visit of a lover; her
daughter is waiting to unwrap her parcel:

Mrs Wickstead: Mrs Swabb, you may take the afternoon off.
Mrs Swabb: But I have an enormous backlog of dusting.
Mrs Wickstead: I insist . . . all work and no play makes Jack a
  dull boy. And talking of dull boys, what are your plans?
Dennis: A long walk in the fresh air.
Mrs Wickstead: Splendid. And you?
Connie: Cubs. Why?
Mrs Wickstead: Just asking. I'm going to my cake-decorating
  class. I don't really want to, but we're electing a new secre-
  tary and it's like anything else: if the rank and file don't go
  the militants take over. (*Exits. They open the parcel.*)
Mrs Swabb: 'I was a spinster for fifteen years', writes Miss P. D.
  of Carshalton. 'Three years ago I invested in your appliance,
  and since then I have been engaged four times.'
Dennis: 'The Rubens, in sensitized Fablon, as used on Apollo
  space missions.' Try it on.
Connie: No. It's too late.
Mrs Swabb: It's never too late. Listen. 'In reply to yours . . . Etc.,
  etc. . . . They are easily fitted without assistance but to fore-
  stall any difficulties our fitter Mr Shanks will call on Thursday
  May 29th.'
Dennis: That's today.
Connie: But he can't. I'm not here. I'm at cubs.

This confusion of language styles was never to be deployed
again by Bennett in such a non-naturalistic way. Its effect here is
to create a stage world that can only be considered in comic terms.

Its characters are deliberately unreal and if occasionally they do touch upon matters of greater moment, the rapid action of the play does not allow the audience to dwell on the significance overlong. The humour derives essentially from the attempts of a very suburban non-permissive group to take on the challenge of a 60s' vision of the 'permissive society'.

What *Habeas Corpus* did, above all, was to confirm an audience expectation of Bennett as a comic writer of an essentially Absurdist mode. This has had undesired consequences. For although he remains one of the most gifted comic writers of his generation – unable, as he confesses, to resist the temptation of a 'bad joke' – his use of comedy has frequently masked his attempts to introduce some thought into the laughter.

The problems he had encountered with *Getting On* at the start of the 1970s were not repeated with the play that greeted the new decade, *Enjoy* (1980). But there is still an unresolved tension between the attempt to offer a critique of a changing Britain in the first months of the Thatcherite 'revolution', and the insistence on the use of a comic model that again harks back to Absurdist roots.

Enjoy could quite easily have been one of those 'gritty Northern realism' pieces much favoured by 1960s British film and television – it was, after all, the first time that Bennett had considered his own relationship with his Northern origins on stage. But a play that opens with Mam and Dad awaiting their imminent rehousing as their Leeds back-to-back terrace is about to be demolished, soon takes us into familiarly Absurdist territory.

They fantasize about their daughter's employment as an internationally jet-setting secretary; a fantasy that the audience has punctured on her first entrance, when it is revealed that she is a prostitute. Throughout, they are used primarily as characters in a satirically realized landscape, and the effect is often uncertain. The father, who has been immobilized by a hit-and-run accident, engages in a dialogue of disagreement and bitterness with his wife throughout the play. They receive a letter from the Council informing them that all the residents will be visited by an observer as part of a 'social study of selected families in this area'. When their observer, Ms Craig, arrives, it is immediately apparent that she is actually a man. Subsequently, we discover that she is actually their son in drag. Mam and Dad attempt to act naturally, Ms Craig resolutely taking notes and never speaking throughout.

The inevitable result is a confirmation of the worst stereotyping

of such an existence, as they argue in front of the visitor about the
way in which they are acting, and about their suitability as case-
studies:

> *Mam*: If you wanted to go two doors down there's one of these
> single-parent families. And he's a problem child. That's quite
> typical of round here too. We're not typical.
> *Dad*: We're not typical because of you. I'm the typical one.
> *Mam*: You're depressed. You're on tablets. That's not typical.
> There's none of that on our side of the family.
> *Dad*: I may be depressed, only I've still got hopes. This house
> depresses me. You say I don't help. I've given up trying.
> Because when I do it's 'Don't use that bucket, that's the
> outside bucket. Don't use that cloth, I use that to do under
> the sink.' It's a minefield this house. She's got it all mapped
> out. The dirty bits and the clean bits. Bits you have to wash
> your hands after, bits you wash your hands before. And
> aught that comes into contact with me is dirty. I dirty it.
> *Mam*: Well you do. You don't take care.
> *Dad*: I pollute my own house. Me, I'm the shit on the doorstep.
> *Mam*: That's a word he's heard other people say. He only says it
> to impress you.

The dialogue develops into virtually a parody of that offered by
the kind of drama of Northern realism mentioned above. It is
given an additional bite by the non-intervening presence of a
figure straight out of those Absurdist satires of bureaucracy. By
the end of the play Bennett introduces four more observers – thus
stressing that the only value of the proletarian life lived by Mam,
Dad and their neighbours is as material for the study of historical
and sociological anthropology – and their supervisor, a Mr
Harman, who walks round the room with his clipboard itemizing
the contents.

In the first act, Ms Craig had belatedly broken her silence to list
the clutter of useless detritus of objects stored on the mantelpiece:
'a shrine laden with the relics of the recent past and a testimonial
to the faith that one day the world will turn and the past come
back into its own.' Mam and Dad's is not just a sad life in its
domestic disappointments. Its time has gone. And so, at the end of
the play they discover that their house is to be carefully dis-
mantled and rebuilt as a part of a museum where they will

continue to live out their lives for the benefit of the nostalgic voyeurism of visitors.

However, an interesting parallel emerges between Dad's account of Mam's obsessively organized cleaning, and that remembered by the playwright in his own youth. Writing in his diary, Bennett recalls:

> My mother maintained an intricate hierarchy of cloths, buckets and dusters, to the Byzantine differentiations of which she alone was privy. Some cloths were dish cloths but not sink cloths; some were for the sink but not for the floor. There were dirty buckets and clean buckets, brushes for indoors, brushes for the flags. One mop had a universal function and had to be kept outside, hung on the wall. And however rinsed and clean these utensils were they remained tainted by their awful function. Left to himself my father would violate these taboos, using the first thing that came to hand to clean the hearth or wash the floor.[2]

Bennett has used his memory of his own childhood in Leeds, and transposed it into the satirical framework of the play. But that he has used it so directly – has indeed allowed its use to be so noted – should alert us to other readings of both *Enjoy* and his other work. It is a sad rather than bitter memory, one tinged with regret as well as humour. Had the connection then been apparent it would have further encouraged the identification of the playwright and Ms Craig made by one contemporary critic: James Fenton, whose 'subsequent abandonment of dramatic criticism to become *The Independent*'s correspondent in the Philippines was one of the more cheering developments in the theatre in the eighties', according to Bennett.[3] But although such an attempt at identification seems ridiculous in view of the satirical deployment of the role, that a connection can be made does suggest that the playwright is standing less securely outside the action of the play than its comic format alone might suggest.

The diary accounts of work on his plays provide frequent evidence of such connections, both in his own past and in the contemporary (and overheard) lives of others. For Bennett relies considerably on the recycling of the minutiae of the conversations that casually pass him in the streets, on buses, and so on. But their use also suggests a very particular relationship with the providers of such dialogue sources. Bennett is neither a social anthropologist nor a revolutionary. He chronicles the despair, the irrecoverability of a past world that may anyway be largely a construct of mythologizing memory. That his chronicling should frequently touch upon his own world and its memories – as well as on the gap between the world of his youth and his post-Cambridge success – makes the humour the more poignant, the more pointed.

It was then hardly surprising that it would be on television rather than on the stage that Bennett should reveal his real talent as a writer. Where the theatre virtually forced his work into an Absurdist tradition – turning accounts of individual failure and despair into symbolic enactments of the absurdity of domestic life – the intimacy of television allowed Bennett to focus intensely on the individuals as individuals. It did so, furthermore, with a ready-made tradition – by way of 'Play for Today' and the like – that encouraged unpatronizing accounts of the lives of ordinary people. Uninhibited by the actual presence of a stage audience that felt itself socially superior to, for instance, Mam and Dad in *Enjoy*, it could create for a writer the sense of an audience on a social parity with his characters.

His first television play was *A Day Out*, shot in and about Halifax for a BBC2 screening in 1972. Since then, there has been a considerable body of work, sufficient to now rank Bennett amongst the most important writers for television. He produced six plays for a London Weekend series in 1978/9; five for a BBC2 series in 1982; and, most famously, the six monologues collectively known as *Talking Heads* for the BBC in 1987. In addition there have been many other single plays, including the two published as *Office Suite*, of 1978/9. That he quickly realized the peculiar suitability of the medium for his work is evident from his words of 1985:

> The difference between writing for stage and for television is almost an optical one. Language on the stage has to be slightly larger than life because it is being heard in a much larger space. Plot counts for less on the television screen because one is seeing the characters at closer quarters than in the theatre. The shape and plot of a stage play count far more in consequence of the distance between the audience and the action. A theatre audience has a perspective on a play as a television audience does not. On television the playwright is conversing.[4]

The difference between the two mediums is well illustrated by
A Cream Cracker Under the Settee, one of the *Talking Heads* series.
The play is set in the living-room and hallway of a semi-detached
house inhabited by Doris, a lonely pensioner in her seventies. For
most of the piece Doris, memorably portrayed by Thora Hird, is
the only person present. Bennett allows his character to talk
straight at the camera, and thus at the audience, in a way that
would be impossible on stage. She does so, furthermore, in a carefully enclosed space which stresses the limitations of her social
world, and of her own perspectives on that world.

Doris is sitting awkwardly at the outset, having fallen whilst
attempting to dust a wedding photograph. In the fall she has
broken both her hip and the photograph of her and her dead
husband – a dead husband who, Bennett suggests in his 'Introduction', she has tidied into the grave. The focus of the monologue that
follows is defined as a chain of reminiscences and worries by these
connections. She has been told by her home-help that she is too old
to dust, and that she will end up in an institution if she persists – a
fear that becomes a reality in *A Lady of Letters*. But tidying up has
become her lifetime obsession and in this, her last attempt to create
order before her death, she tries to put together all the broken
pieces of her past – her unhappy marriage, memories of the child
that miscarried and those of the happy child she once was. On
stage, such a cataloguing would too easily tend to satire; here the
prevailing mood is of pathos, as the audience is pulled into an
understanding of the loneliness of her life. This sense of alienation
– both of theme and of technique – is heightened at the end of *A
Cream Cracker Under the Settee* when a policeman calls through the
door. Having received the reassuring answers to his questions that,
yes, she is alright, he leaves her alone again.

Before his arrival she has pondered on her and her husband's
names, Doris and Wilfred, 'Museum, names like that', seeing that
she is unrescuably a part of a past existence with no connection to
the present. In all these monologues Bennett creates a sense of
emptiness – an emptiness in the lives of the characters as they
seek to define themselves, to justify their own inadequacies; and
an emptiness in that the medium of television encourages the
deployment of a confessional mode which effectively absents the
fact of an audience at all. It is as if his characters can only now
talk because they know that no one is listening – a major problem
in all their lives.

His characters are all in some way – often in great part by their own acts – victims of a modern society which offers social workers and old people's homes in place of the certainties of family life on which their entire worlds had been constructed. For Doris, there has never been anything outside; for others, such as Muriel in *Soldiering On*, there is a real sense of loss at no longer having any larger social function:

> I had a word with a young woman at the Town Hall. Blue fingernails but civil enough otherwise. Said was I interested in Meals on Wheels. I said, 'Rather. I was 2i/c Meals on Wheels for the whole of Sudbury,' a fund of experience. Brawn not too good but brains available to be picked at any time. She looked a bit blank. Turns out she meant did I want to be on the receiving end. I said, 'Not on your life'. But message received and understood. The old girl's past it.

In such a passage Bennett uses the precise locaters of a vocabulary and syntax that proclaim a life lived amongst the military, and at the centre of good works, to suggest a desperation. His are marginalized beings, cut off from contact from any outside reality as surely as they are from doing anything about what they passively accept as their fate. At the end of *Soldiering On*, Muriel, having been tricked into selling her house by her son, is living in an unfurnished bed-sit far away from her friends. She concludes the play, still trying to keep up appearances in a world in which she now has no visitors at all, talking directly to the camera: 'I wouldn't want you to think this was a tragic story. I'm not a tragic woman. I'm not that type.'

Reading Bennett's 'Introduction' to the published text confirms what is anyway apparent: that these monologues are not only drawing heavily from memories of his own past, but that they operate almost as attempts at exorcisms of that past. The world of Northern England, only once considered on stage by Bennett, figures largely in his television work. Where the monologue form of *Talking Heads* had allowed a confessional voice to communicate with the audience, the dialogue of his longer pieces reveals the day-to-day reality of experience which the monologues recall and summarize. Three of the television plays are set in a hospital, and one in a cemetery: 'it's hardly surprising that several of the characters end up dead.'[5] Although the potential for comedy is always realized, it is a humour in which nostalgia is more than balanced by bitterness – a bitterness of regret for what has past, but a bitterness at the waste as well.

Bennett had looked back to 1911 in the first television play, *A Day Out*, which was concerned with a Sunday bike trip. He was to do so again in the screenplay for *A Private Function* (1984), a film about the preparations in a Northern town for a celebration of the 1947 Royal Wedding of the future Queen Elizabeth II. And if there is humour to be derived from the antics of a group of citizens arranging a feast in the context of post-war austerity and the black market, there is no doubting the expression of a real nostalgia for a past world of more certain values.

It is a nostalgia for a world that, as Bennett well knows, is only recoverable by the processes of selective memory. The museum view of the past offered to Mam and Dad at the end of *Enjoy* is to be regarded as a part of that process of selection. His inclusion of a socialist amongst the 1911 cyclists in *A Day Out* is in itself a pointed reminder. It is a view only available to an historical tourist – able to see the vista of a 'green and pleasant' England without the sight of the 'dark satanic mills' and all that they entail that greets his cyclists when they reach the brow of the hill.

Or rather, it is only available to an historical tourist and to a defector, one who has left that world behind, has effectively frozen it in time. In a sense this is Bennett's own position: that of a man looking back with mixed feelings at a culture that offers both nostalgic memories and despair, a culture from which he is now anyway excluded.

That this is arguable in general cultural terms makes Bennett's stage use of three examples of directly political defection the more interesting. He had first explored the theme in *The Old Country* in 1977. Hilary, a Communist defector from the 30s, lives out his life in exile in Russia. He and his wife so successfully perpetuate the sense of life in the England that they have left that the audience takes time to discover that they are in Russia at all. Hilary's has been a genteel defection – a part of the Cambridge generation and not of the proletariat as represented by the figure of Eric in the play. As the plot develops he learns that he is to be returned to England in an exchange and he wonders at the changes he will find, bemoaning the loss of Lyons Teashops in a sardonic manner:

Do I want the old place to change? I don't think so. I have left it. It must stay the same or there is no point in having come away. I certainly don't want things to improve. Though I remain, of course, firmly in two minds. Whereas ideologically I must count every sign of decay as an improvement, so my personal inclination is to think of every improvement as decay. Certainly where the end of Lyons is concerned. Was that presented as an improvement? I imagine so.

As a traitor, Hilary has a very clear sense of the 'old country' he would wish to have betrayed. In 1988 Bennett's *An Englishman Abroad* was produced at the National Theatre (having originally been written for television). The play, which is concerned with the actress Coral Browne's meeting with Guy Burgess in Moscow in 1958, was presented in a double-bill with *A Question of Attribution*, a play about Anthony Blunt, the 'fourth man' in the Philby/Burgess/Maclean affair, and his attempts to investigate one of the paintings in the Queen's collection in Buckingham Palace.

In the first play, Burgess is presented as desperate for the creature comforts of an England that again only exists in his memory. He has asked the actress to call that she might take his measurements back to his Savile Row tailor with an order for a new suit. In the second, Bennett makes great play with the fact that the man in charge of the royal collection – an epitome of aristocratic privilege, and a supremely undemocratic register of a national culture – should be going to be exposed as a Communist spy. One of the play's most memorable moments comes when Blunt finds himself conducting the Queen round her own collection. Her questions satisfactorily answered she delivers her exit lines, totally unaware of their ironic overtones:

Oh. Well, I must be on my way. Not, I think, a wasted afternoon. One has touched upon art, learned a little iconography, and something of fakes and forgery. Facts not chat. Of course, had I been opening the swimming bath I would have picked up one or two facts there: the pumping system; the filter process; the precautions against infectious diseases of the feet. All facts. One never knows when they might come in handy. Be careful how you go up the ladder, Sir Anthony. One could have a nasty fall.

Blunt's attempts to make an attribution, to prove an authenticity in a painting, are made in the context of an audience awareness that he is himself a 'forgery', and that he is about to fall off the social ladder that he has carefully built for himself – a ladder that has taken him away from any connections with notions of Communist egalitarianism and into a world of 'high' culture far removed from the concerns of the characters in Bennett's earlier television plays. The England that these defectors wish to hang onto, even as they betray it, is one that is a part of the machinery that helps create the despair and the bitterness so accurately articulated by the marginalized and unpoliticized characters in the earlier plays.

In 1986, Bennett confirmed the growing sense of his status when he accepted a commission from the Royal Court Theatre, after which his stage work all premièred at the National. The commissioned play was *Kafka's Dick*, in which Bennett brings back the dead writer to argue with his family, his biographer/friend Max Prod, and his supposedly unwanted posthumous fame; all of which occurs in the house of a contemporary Kafka enthusiast, Sydney (an insurance man as Kafka had been), his wife Linda and a father they are attempting to institutionalize.

A play that ends in heaven is set largely in a middle-class room that Bennett agonizes over in the stage directions – unable to decide whether it should be 'representational' or 'unreal' in the context of the unreality that will take place in it. Onto the satirized family life of the contemporary inhabitants – employing a use of dialogue that is more reminiscent of the Tom Stoppard of the 70s than anything else – Bennett adds a further layer of confusion with the surreal intrusion of Kafka and his companions. It is a fusion of two branches of Absurdism: the domestic and the political. That the two groups will be able to communicate, that the connection between past and present will be makable, is evident from the opening scene set in Kafka's actual lifetime. When his friend extracts a promise that he will burn all his writings after his death, Brod eventually responds in terms which would seem more a part of Sydney and Linda's world than Kafka's: 'Why not juice up the occasion? Ask one or two people over, split a bottle of vino, barbecue the odd steak then as a climax to the proceedings flambé the Collected Works?'

Brod's subsequent suggestion that he could arrange to have an odd work or two added to the 1933 Nazi 'burning of the books' is a reminder of the way in which Kafka's work has been read post-historically as a prophecy of the nightmare of modern totalitarianism. The link between Kafka's vision of his own time and the terrifying footnotes provided by events after his death makes a connection between past and present that is central to the play. It is a present not simply located in an ordinary house in England, of course. It had direct resonances for author and audiences with the rapid changes taking place in Eastern Europe. Fascism and state communism are the spectres haunting this feast.

Bennett had first invoked the figure of Kafka in his television play *The Insurance Man*, screened earlier the same year. Here, we see the writer in his professional capacity, making decisions on insurance claims for industrial injuries in the midst of a vast and impenetrable bureaucracy that recalls *The Trial* directly. The effect of these works is to move Bennett's concern away from the largely domestic – focusing on a Britain that has seen better days that were not perhaps really that much better – and to open it to a wider international context. What Kafka represents dwarfs the merely local concerns of a declining nation, invoking a European history that has tried what seem to the playwright to have been the obvious and unsatisfactory alternatives. As Bennett said of the *Single Spies* plays, 'The trouble with treachery nowadays is that if one does want to betray one's country there is no one satisfactory to betray it to.'[6]

At first then it might seem strange that Bennett should have turned to English history with *The Madness of George III* (1991), his most recent stage play. For not only is it a play about a period of constitutional crisis, but it depends for much of its humour on the casually made contemporary parallels. Whilst the King is enduring the anguish of treatment for his illness, a son, the Prince of Wales then as now, waits to take over the throne. Fearing that he may lose his power base, the Prime Minister Pitt appeals for 'five more years', as Margaret Thatcher had done – though the play came too early to allow the expression of Bennett's delight that she had finally been removed.

These and other parallels are discussed by Bennett in his long 'Introduction' to the published text, but they are not the real explanations for the play's success – and certainly do not amount to a consistent paralleling of themes. *The Madness of George III* is in essence a costume drama, and was received as such by enthusiastic audiences both at the National and when it subsequently toured nationally. It offers a jokey relationship between past and present – linguistically as well as thematically – in ways which place it in a line that would include plays as superficially distinct as *Beckett*, *A Man for all Seasons* and *Amadeus*.

That, its casual reference to things contemporary notwithstanding, it should find a home in the National Theatre is indicative of its status as a marketable product, offering a little history and a little contemporary revision of that history; plus a comforting placement of such figures as the playwright Sheridan, and of such events as the creation of Fortnum and Mason. The loss of the American colonies is presented simply as an affront to the King's dignity, and the French Revolution receives a dialogue that lasts for all of seven lines: concluding with Pitt's 'I do not think we have very much to fear from France this decade'. Of equal interest in such a context is the news that the courtier Fortnum has left in despair – 'Gone to start a provision merchant's in Picadilly, sir'.

Its undoubted success – recorded both in the box-office and in the critical columns of the reviewers – has established Bennett as a major force in contemporary theatre, and doubtless further National plays will follow. But that this play – ambitious and clever though it is – should serve as a representation of history at the National Theatre is perhaps more a reflection on the willingness of patrons in London and in the provinces to part with large sums of money for an evening of only slightly barbed cosiness, than it is an overdue tribute to Bennett's talents as a writer. For whatever else the play is about, it is evidently not about that nation of 'leftovers' whose lives have been so painstakingly chronicled by Bennett throughout most of his writing career.

11

Tom Stoppard: Open to the Public

Hostess: I'm afraid the performance is not open to the public.
Insepector: I should hope not indeed. That would be acting
without authority – acting without authority! – you'd never
believe I make it up as I go along . . . Now listen, you
stupid bastard, you'd better get rid of the idea that there's a
special *Macbeth* which you do when I'm not around, and
some other *Macbeth* for when I am around. Because I'm
giving the party and there ain't no other. It's what we call a
one-party system . . . So let's have a little of the old trouper
spirit, because if I walk out of this show I take it with me.
(Cahoot's Macbeth, 1979)

At first sight the above could come from an early Tom Stoppard
play – *The Real Inspector Hound* perhaps – with its familiar introduction of a pompous official mouthing the language of his trade.
It is only as we read on, or as we have the extract in its proper
context, that the comic inspector turns into a truly menacing figure
– able not only to stop the show, but to imprison the actors. The
familiar Stoppardian interrogation of a settled text (for *Hamlet* read
Macbeth) is no longer a part of an elaborate, if serious, joke.

Cahoot's Macbeth was dedicated to the Czechoslovakian playwright Pavel Kohout: a man who shares Stoppard's place of birth,
his profession, but not his working conditions. Stoppard's play
deliberately echoes the private performances given in people's
homes after Kohout had been denied the stage following the fall
of Dubceck – performances by, amongst others, the Czech actor
Pavel Lanovsky, who had been driving the car when the first
known copies of the Charter 77 documents were seized by the
police.

Stoppard's play was performed in a double-bill with *Dogg's
Hamlet*, a free-wheeling product of his Absurdist past that had
existed in its earliest form as *Dogg's Our Pet* in 1971. The sense of

conflict between the two is important for, however much Stoppard may wish to argue for the interconnections, they are the product of two quite distinct periods in his writing career.

In this chapter I will concentrate on his work from the late 70s on. In practice this cannot be done in isolation, and we shall find evidence of Stoppard's continuing indebtedness to an Absurdist tradition. But what interests me here is what happens to his work once he starts to move quite consciously towards the idea of a theatre that is 'open to the public', by which I mean open to the debate of public issues – and thus for Stoppard inevitably concerned with the definition of the role of the writer in the discussion about such issues.

Frequently criticized for his defiant adoption of a non-political stance in his earlier work – and able to write in the stage directions for *Travesties* (1974) that the lecture given by Cecily on the history of the Bolshevik revolution need not be included in performance ('is not a requirement, but is an option') – Stoppard has undergone something of a sea change. A man who in 1968 opposed the then current mood with a credo of non-involvement ('I burn with no causes. I cannot say I write with any social objective'[1]) now has causes and objectives aplenty. This has involved not so much a political rethinking, for his political position remains essentially unaltered, but a radical reassessment of his own responsibilities as a writer – a reassessment that has seen him not only alter his dramatic strategies, but emerge as a public spokesman on political issues.

Now, given the fact that the playwright actually started his own writing life as a journalist, it is perhaps hardly surprising that the change of direction should be heralded in a play about journalists and journalism, *Night and Day*, in 1978. He had already, somewhat playfully, explored the subject in *Dirty Linen* – the play that, like *Night and Day*, continued in performance as Margaret Thatcher formed her first administration. But in his new play he was to use it in an attempt to deal with issues more seriously. The printed stage directions are introduced with a sardonic remark that shows clearly Stoppard's awareness of the possible implications of such a change: 'Herewith, a few dogmatic statements tentatively offered.'

The play is set in an African country, formerly a British colony, somewhere to the south of Eritrea. English journalists gather in the hopes that a rebel skirmish might develop into something like a full-scale war. They have no real idea of where they are, of what is happening, or of what the fighting is about, not even an agreement on the pronunciation of the place names. Since it is to be via their reports that the events will be screened by the Western world, the unreliability of the news sources is more than simply comic. Adoma and its problems will be turned into just another fiction to be manipulated at will ideologically – a point made jokily by the *Daily Globe* reporter Richard Wagner. After ridiculing the accounts of the struggle as presented in the *New York Times* ('All writing and no facts') and *The Sunday Times* ('All facts and no news'), he considers the other newspapers that his camera-man, Guthrie, has brought with him from the plane:

> (*He looks briefly through the* Mirror.) Nothing. Well, that's honest anyway. (*The* Observer.) 'Sources close to President Mageeba are conceding that the peasant army of the ALF has the tacit support of the indigenous population of the interior and is able to move unhindered through the Adoma hills.' (*Considers this, nods sagely.*) True. (Sunday Telegraph.) 'Evidence is emerging that the civilian population of the Adoma region has been intimidated into supporting the Russian-equipped rural guerillas of the ALF, but according to army sources, the self-styled Liberation Front is penned up in the Adoma hills.' (*Considers this, nods sagely*) True.

What concerns him chiefly, however, is that he has been scooped on his own paper by an unnamed correspondent, and most of the narrative will be concerned not with the conflict in Adoma but with their struggles for supremacy. Ruth, the wife of their mine-owning host Carson, has slept with Wagner on a recent visit to London, and immediately fancies Milne, the unnamed correspondent who we are shortly to meet.

Much of the psychological interest of the play comes from Stoppard's creation of an alter-ego for 'Ruth', who is able to speak openly and unheard, letting the audience know what she really thinks about the other characters and her own situation. In a play about adultery it would be – and has been – an interesting device; but in a play that at least purports to be about the depiction of political events, it has the effect of foregrounding the personal at the expense of the political. And this is the real problem about the play. In moving towards a more naturalistic framework, Stoppard turns the play into a conflict about visiting Europeans (colonialists and journalists alike), and in as much as it possesses a political dimension its terms of reference, like its news reports, are European and not African.

So Wagner discovers that the reason why his rival has not been given a by-line is because he had worked through an official union strike on a Grimsby paper. Naturally, Wagner is a hard-line union man, and their personal rivalry can be expounded in crude political terms. The strike had been called because a new deal had been struck with the printers (as at the *Mirror*, Stoppard's text informs us, thus making a direct connection between stage fiction and contemporary reality). Wagner points out that this had meant that there were printers making more money than journalists, and Milne responds with a speech that comes direct from Stoppard, summarizing as it does the trivialization of the news that was touched upon at the outset. He reads from the *News of the World*:

'Exposed! The Ouija Board Widow Who's Writing Hitler's Memoirs' . . . 'It Was Frying Tonight And Every Night In The Back Of The Chip Shop!' . . . (*and the* Mirror) 'Some Like It Hot And Sweet – Sally Smith is a tea lady in a Blackpool engineering works, but it was the way she filled those C-cups which got our camera-man all stirred up!' It's *crap*. And it's written by grown men earning maybe ten thousand a year. If I was a printer, I'd look at some of the stuff I'm given to print, and I'd ask myself what is supposed to be so special about the people who write it – is that radical enough for you – Dick?

Wagner is able to trick Milne into going off to meet the rebel leader, while he waits at Carson's house for the expected visit of the country's President. The experienced journalist is forced to eat dirt but gets his story, whilst Milne is killed by the rebels. Ironically, Wagner is unable to get his story published because his telexed message about the black-leg Milne being employed by the *Globe* has brought about the shutdown of the paper through industrial action. Wagner ends the play heading for Ruth's bedroom; he has got the girl, but not the scoop. David Edgar pointedly stressed the way in which Stoppard used the leftish characters in both *Night and Day* and *Professional Foul*: 'Tom Stoppard stacked the cards so grossly against his left-wing villains – a drunken, boorish journalist and an insensitive lecherous sociologist – that if any of us [writers of the committed tradition] had tried the same gambit the other way round, we would have been howled off the stage.'

That the play should fail to address the larger issues that it appears to proclaim a concern with at the outset is not too surprising. What it does do is to bring Stoppard's obsessive concern with the importance of language into a directly political arena for the first time. Events elsewhere than in this fictional African country were to provide the cutting-edge for Stoppard. They were occurring in places perhaps equally unknown to Wagner and his journalistic colleagues – but not to the playwright.

In 1974 André Previn, then conductor with the London Symphony Orchestra, suggested that Stoppard write a play that incorporated a real orchestra. It was a suggestion embraced enthusiastically by the playwright. He worked on the idea of a millionaire who owned an orchestra, on the idea of a millionaire who played the triangle and owned an orchestra, and finally on the idea of a mad triangle-player who thought he had an orchestra.[2] The play itself stubbornly refused to be formed.

In April 1976, Stoppard met Victor Fainburg, a Czech dissident who had been arrested, imprisoned in a hospital-prison for five years having been adjudged insane, and then exiled. His actual crime had been to protest against the Russian invasion of his country following the 'Prague Spring' of 1968. In August of 1976 Stoppard addressed a London rally organized by the Committee Against Psychiatric Abuse, and tried unsuccessfully to deliver a petition to the Russian Embassy. His play at last began to take shape, *Every Good Boy Deserves Favour* duly being produced at the Royal Festival Hall in July 1977 with Previn conducting the London Symphony Orchestra. Six months earlier the Czech playwright Vaclav Havel had been arrested for his participation in the Charter 77 movement. Stoppard wrote in direct response to this imprisonment a month after it took place:

> Connoisseurs of totalitarian double-think will have noted Charter 77, the Czechoslovakian document which calls attention to the absence in that country of various human rights beginning with the right of free expression, has been refused publication inside Czechoslovakia on the grounds that it is a wicked slander.[3]

The play that was eventually performed at the Festival Hall centred on the related fates of two prisoners in Czechoslovakia.

Ivanov is mad, and believes that he has a full orchestra to accompany his triangle. His cell-mate Alexander is a dissident, imprisoned and declared insane after his involvement with the kind of political activities outlined above. Throughout the play Ivanov labours to persuade his fellow of the reality of his orchestra, a madness that extends to his insistence that Alexander must also be a musician.

His attempts to persuade him are grotesquely comic in themselves, but become increasingly threatening. The demand that Alexander declare which instrument he plays, for instance, being delivered in an imagery of the potential violence that will be meted out to the dissident should he not provide the correct answers:

Ivanov: Reed? Keyboard?
Alexander: I'm afraid not.
Ivanov: I'm amazed. Not keyboard. Wait a minute – flute.
Alexander: No. Really.
Ivanov: Extraordinary. Give me a clue. If I beat you to a pulp would you try to protect your face or your hands? Which would be the more serious – if you couldn't sit down for a week or couldn't stand up? I'm trying to narrow it down, you see. Can I take it you don't stick this instrument up your arse in a kneeling position?

The irony of Ivanov's delusion is stressed by the orchestral accompaniment to Alexander's long account of the activities that have led to him being incarcerated. It echoes the punishment that the teacher tells his son, Sacha, is even now being imposed on his father – that he write out 1 million times, 'I am a member of an orchestra and we must play together'. The state imposes a harmony that denies the efforts of such as Alexander to question, and the lunatic's view of reality in this world is seen as more desirable than that of the honest dissident.

The play's narrative is neatly concluded by asking the right questions of the wrong prisoners. Ivanov is able to deny that 'sane people are put in mental hospitals' and Alexander that he believes he has an orchestra – and the Colonel is able to order their release: 'There's absolutely nothing wrong with these men.'

The technical fusion between the orchestral format and the political theme is handled adroitly by Stoppard: its title refers to the well-known mnemonic for the notes in the treble clef, but also suggests that if the boy is good (toes the required line) he will find favour with the state; a sense that is reinforced by the notes that fill the bars between those of the play's title – F, A, C, E, or a human identity.

The play's ending was frequently misunderstood at the time of that first performance. It suggests simply a logical way out of the state's illogical algebraic problem – to pursue another of the inter-linking motifs of the piece – and is not to be regarded as a triumph of the individual against that state. But what is perhaps most significant about the work is that Stoppard should use the metaphor of orchestral creation at all.

For the play seeks to do more than register a simple protest against the use of asylums for political prisoners in Czecho-slovakia. It is concerned with the way in which the artist (the composer/conductor) might take on a political role, and also with the way in which such creations as the music that accompanies the dialogue might be produced under such a system of illogic and persecution.

As he was slowly shaping the play, Stoppard was becoming increasingly drawn into a direct consideration of the treatment of dissidents – and particularly dissident writers – in the Eastern bloc. He had agreed to write a television play about Russia for Amnesty International's Prisoner of Conscience Year, and had travelled to Moscow in February 1977. There he met a number of dissidents, and returned to write about his visit in *The Sunday Times* on 27 February. In May, Havel was released from prison, and the month before *Every Good Boy* received its first perfor-mance, Stoppard returned to his native Czechoslovakia for the first time since leaving it with his family at the age of two. There he met Havel at last – the two playwrights having had their first plays produced in the same year, 1963. In a sense, the two strands of the Absurdist theatre, the domestic English and the politicized Eastern European, were united at the very point at which the move towards the disintegration of the Russian Empire began to gather real momentum. Stoppard would provide an 'Introduction' for the republished English version of *The Memorandum*, and in 1986 his version of Havel's *Largo Desolato* would be performed by the Bristol Old Vic.

Stoppard not only focused his attention increasingly on the East, but did so in ways which called directly into question his own earlier stance as a non-political writer – a stance which was, however, never unproblematic. In doing this, the dramatic tension in his subsequent plays becomes centred on the role of the playwright as mouthpiece for the ideas that the plays embrace, or at the least seek to discuss. It is a vital change of direction in the work of a man who had always sought to swerve away from supplying a reliable perspective, and for whom the flow of wit, the clashing of ideas and styles had been all.

The television play that he eventually produced for Amnesty International's Year was *Professional Foul*. It concerns the visit of three English dons to Czechoslovakia for an Academic Conference. We are first shown them on the plane to Prague: Chetwyn who has become known for writing letters to *The Times* protesting about the treatment of 'persecuted professors with unpronounceable names', according to the second, McKendrick, a moral pragmatist from Stoke University, who is attracted to the idea that the third, Anderson, might be going to get directly involved in dissident politics on his arrival.

It is on Anderson, and what happens to him, that the play centres. He is invited to read a paper on 'Ethical Fictions as Ethical Foundations' but his planned truancy is not, as McKendrick thinks, political but with the intention of watching a football match, a World Cup qualifier between Czechoslovakia and England – he will use fiction to watch a game. He is asked by Hollar, an ex-student who had returned optimistically to his homeland in 1968 and is now employed as a lavatory cleaner, to take a copy of his thesis back for publication in England. The terms of Anderson's refusal to comply are perfectly in keeping with the safe world of Oxbridge ethics from which he has been briefly transported: 'Perhaps the correct thing for me to have done is not to have accepted their invitation to speak here. But I did accept it. It is a contract, as it were, freely entered into. And having accepted their hospitality I cannot in all conscience start smuggling . . . It's just not ethical.'

But the security of the theoretical position is about to be removed. Stopping at Hollar's flat on his way to the football to hand back the manuscript, he becomes involved in the police search of the rooms after the man's arrest. Released, he returns to the Conference and gives an impromptu paper on the rights of the individual and the rights of the state. The football match that he missed has been won by Czechoslovakia as a result of a successful penalty after a 'professional foul'. The Conference Chairman commits another such foul, declaring a fire alarm and clearing the Conference room (as the secret police had also done so in planting foreign currency in Hollar's flat). But Anderson eventually commits the most professional of all fouls. Knowing that he will be searched at the airport, he plants the thesis in McKendrick's suitcase, and moral expediency literally carries the day.

There is no doubting Stoppard's desire to bring the fate of East European dissidents to the fore, but the central thrust of the play remains with the resolution of the moral dilemma for the Oxbridge don. The English football team had lost as a result of foul play – foul play that the drunken McKendrick argues allies them with the ungentlemanly yobs on the terraces – but the English gentleman will achieve a small victory by his 'professional foul'. As always, the game is fixed, as the consummate stylist – admittedly more alert to the realities of the outside world – weaves his way past an unthinking, uneducated defence. The ball is a thesis on the importance of the individual, and the goal will be credited to the English liberal tradition.

Stoppard's fusion of themes remains resolutely Absurdist – we have earlier seen extracts from a Conference paper on the meaninglessness of language being simultaneously translated into three other languages – although the narrative resolution afforded by the more than usually naturalistic format of the television play allows a conclusion of sorts. Confronted with a world in which the domestic Absurdism of his early plays unexpectedly gives way to the more frightening Absurdism of the bureaucracy of totalitarianism, his characters have nowhere to retreat to – no comforting word games or philosophical conundrums left – and the plays cry out for a reliable mouthpiece.

The resultant problems are most easily seen in the television play about the Solidarity movement, *Squaring the Circle*, jointly commissioned by an English company, Television South, and an American one, Metromedia. The play was eventually screened in 1984, two years after the imposition of martial law in Poland – the point at which he had started work on the screenplay. Stoppard provides a lively account of the production difficulties in his 'Introduction' to the published text; difficulties that arose largely from the clash between what Stoppard wanted to do and what Metromedia, in particular, thought would be commercially viable.

But the main problem was concerned with the way in which

Stoppard wanted to present the narrative, using a narrator clearly identified as the author who would stress the dangers of taking on trust any material presented in the form of a drama-documentary. The narrator was to present what Stoppard saw as the inevitability of the failure of Solidarity to operate quite early within the continuing structure of a Communist state: 'Between August 1980 and December 1981 an attempt was made to put together two ideas which wouldn't fit, the idea of freedom as it is understood in the West, and the idea of socialism as it is understood in the Soviet empire. The attempt failed because it was impossible, in the same sense as it is impossible in geometry to turn a circle into a square with the same area – not because no one has found out how to do it, but because there is no way in which it can be done.'

Thus, although the play follows events from the formation of the union through until its official disbanding in December 1981, Stoppard is less interested in the chronicling of the history as such, than with questioning the way in which that chronicling is presented. The role of the narrator is foregrounded, just as the reliability of the accounts is deliberately and continually problematized. Thus, the play opens, for instance, with two different enactments of Brezhnev's meeting with Gierek in July 1980; enactments which are interrupted by the narrator's insistence that the audience is simply watching a fiction – 'That isn't them, of course – and this isn't the Black Sea. Everything is true except the words and the pictures' – and concluded by his aside to the camera, 'Who knows?'

Stoppard was eventually forced to accept a compromise, and the American actor Richard Crenna played the narrator in a way never satisfactorily explained by the screened play, and against the wishes of Stoppard himself to be identified as the story-teller. The wish to ally himself with a narrator uncertain of the exact components of the story he is telling is indicative of Stoppard's own uncertainty about his newly adopted role as political spokesman; but it also accurately reflects his sense of being a part of two cultures simultaneously. This was a theme he was to explore most memorably in his 1991 radio play, *In the Native State*, where – in what is one of his most impressive works to date, and one that moves him further than ever before from his Absurdist roots – the action moves between India in 1930 and the English Home Counties in the present, forging links that are both psychological and political.

But ultimately the sense of living in two separate cultures must lead to a choice; and with Stoppard the need to choose one necessitates the possibility of betrayal of the other. Alan Bennett was not alone in his fascination with the theme of treachery. It is a subject that has come to haunt the British mainstream, as well as providing source material for a host of novelists led by John Le Carré. What has proved most fascinating for such writers is that the defectors came from a Cambridge educated elite who not only apparently had most to gain by remaining loyal to the system but were seemingly representative of the most traditional vision of, to use Bennett's own phrase, the 'Old Country'. Their language as deployed on stage and in novels is completely at one with the witty, ironic discourse that characterizes almost all new mainstream theatre. Their disguise was, in that sense, quite perfect; and their betrayal, in the eyes of the establishment, that much more heinous.

In 1982, Julian Mitchell's *Another Country* transferred from the Greenwich Theatre to the West End (before being reworked for the screen). It is a thinly disguised account of Guy Burgess's life at public school, the place where Mitchell suggests he learnt, as a homosexual 'outsider' figure, to perfect the art of the double-life. The following year a stage version of Hugh Whitemore's 1971 television play, *Act of Betrayal* – renamed *Pack of Lies* – was produced in the West End. Its revival was symptomatic of public interest in the world of espionage and treachery, and was succeeded by his 1984 television play, *Concealed Enemies*, about Alger Hiss.

Given Tom Stoppard's fascination with the use and abuse of pre-existent dramatic forms, it is not too surprising that he too should have turned to his own version of the spy-story: in *Hapgood* (a Michael Codron production at the Aldwych in 1988). The play, which concerns the efforts to unmask a traitor in the midst of the British Intelligence network, owes much to the assimilation of Le Carré's register of technical jargon; although the labyrinthine twists of the plot leave the novelist's deployment of narrative surprises in *Tinker Tailor Soldier Spy* far behind.

The central protagonist is Elizabeth Hapgood, an agent compromised by her relationship with Kerner, a Russian double-agent: a relationship that has produced a son, now at public school. The plot is concerned at a narrative level with her attempts to trap her assistant, Ridley, a double-agent, and his twin brother; but the uncoincidental placement of all these, and more, doubles and twins – including the audience's acceptance that Hapgood herself may have a twin sister, and is thus also a double-agent – indicates that, in characteristic fashion, Stoppard has other things on his mind.

The opening scene, in which the audience is tricked into a mis-reading of a complicated series of switches in the cubicles of a swimming-pool, is a working example of Heisenberg's uncertainty principle later referred to explicitly in the play. In the world of espionage there are no certainties, visual or moral. The act of perception, by an audience or by a physicist, affects what is being observed.

However, the play does not proceed to the narrative inconclusion suggested by the deployment of such a thesis. Stoppard does provide, as the dramatic model demands, a satisfactory conclusion, and the audience is left, if confused, at least with the material to work out exactly what has been happening at every stage in the deception. The apparent uncertainty is thus carefully orchestrated by a dramatist who is always securely in control of the theatrical tricks and sleights of hand.

That this is so is important thematically because there is a line of argument rigorously pursued in the play that claims the irrelevance of the distinction between the interests of the British and the Russian agents. Having falsely promised Hapgood that he would not involve her son Joe – a 'joe' being also an agent, one of the many political/personal puns used in the play – her boss, Blair, defends himself to her, saying that in the end 'It's them or us, isn't it?' Hapgood's angry response, 'Us and the KGB? The opposition! We're just keeping each other in business, we should send each other Christmas cards', is a perfect formulation of the sense that all we have been watching is a game, a game apparently without rules, though actually very much with them.

It is a theme that Stoppard had already developed in the 1982 radio play, *The Dog it Was that Died*, where the practice of espionage is revealed at its most game-like. Here, an English double-agent, Purvis, has become so confused by his lives of parallel deception that he no longer knows who he is, and he ends up in an asylum. The long explanation offered by his chief does little to ease the confusion, leaving the audience as securely in a world built on Absurdist foundations as in his earlier work:

In other words, Purvis was acting, in effect, as a genuine Russian spy in order to maintain his usefulness as a bogus Russian spy ... The only reason why this wasn't entirely disastrous for us was that, of course, during the whole of this time, the Russians, believing us to believe that Purvis was in their confidence, had been giving Purvis information designed to mislead *us* ... and in order to maintain Purvis's credibility they have been forced to do some of the things which they told Purvis they *would* do, although their first reason for telling him was that they didn't wish to do them. (*Pause.*) In other words, if Purvis's mother had got kicked by a horse things would be more or less exactly as they are now.

The play's final words are provided by Purvis who says his doctor is of the opinion that the Chief too should be in the asylum. But in *Hapgood*, six vital years of change in Eastern Europe later, the conclusion takes us firmly away from the Absurdist framework of the espionage games. Hapgood ends the play watching encouragingly as her son plays Rugby at school. We have already seen her similarly engaged in scene three, but now she is accompanied by her Russian lover, Kerner, who as the play ends seems incapable of moving away from this quintessentially English scene: a scene in which the Anglo-Russian child is being initiated into the rituals of the English male establishment. She had already spelt out its significance in conversation with Blair after they have watched the first Rugby game:

Anyway, there's the male society thing, they're supposed to need that when they haven't got fathers ... I like all that manners maketh man stuff, and competition and talking properly and being magnanimous in victory and defeat – middle-class values, I'm in favour and I'm not going to chuck them because they happen to be shared by a fair number of people you wouldn't want to be seen dead with, they always were.

Joe, like Stoppard himself, has had his side chosen for him – a move away from Russia for Hapgood's son, and from Czechoslovakia for the playwright, and towards an enthusiastic embracement of middle-class English values. As Stoppard's work has developed away from its early insistence that style is all, and come to terms with the significance of its inherently political ideology, so his refusal to adopt a stance has become less absolute. The fact that the above credo in *Hapgood* is voiced by a female protagonist may still imply a defensiveness, but the need to take a stand has come to preoccupy the playwright increasingly. In a domestic context we can see evidence of it in *The Real Thing* (1982) with Henry's careful articulation of the importance of crafted language – as opposed to the efforts of the outrageously parodied figure of the would-be political writer, Brodie – but it is most evident when Stoppard has turned away from England and to events in Eastern Europe.

He has not been alone in responding to the events in the changing Eastern European world. In 1990, Howard Brenton and Tariq Ali's *Moscow Gold* was produced at the Barbican – a rapidly written piece about Russian perestroika – and David Edgar's *The Shape of the Table* was staged at the National, one year after the Berlin Wall had been demolished. Their political perspective on events is importantly different, however, and not based on the acceptance of the model of bourgeois conformity for its context. Stoppard, more than any writer of his generation, has brought the values of this world of English middle-class decencies into conflict with events in the disintegrating Russian Empire. For at base, however much and however wittily his characters may agonize about the details, this is how Stoppard defines his ideological position as a 'public' writer.

In April 1993, his *Arcadia* opened at the National Theatre. In it, Stoppard turned back to reconsider the world ultimately embraced by Hapgood and Kerner. The play shuttles between action in a Derbyshire stately home in the early nineteenth century and the present day, as the various characters seek to reconcile their notions of the pursuit of 'truth' with the changes in a surrounding but never seen landscaped garden that mirrors the changes in British society.

More immediately accessible than, for instance, *Jumpers*, it nonetheless returns the playwright to the world of wit and irony more in the spirit of the plays of Oscar Wilde than anything he has yet produced. For all its brilliant ingenuity – or perhaps because of its brilliant ingenuity – it fails to satisfy. The waywardness of sexual attraction which is seen to be the factor that will always defeat attempts to create a model of determining order on the world, return us to a drama in which the witty articulation of interpersonal relationships is all we are left with. The country house is a logical setting for Stoppard to arrive at; but it operates here less as a symbol of the changing state of the nation than as a hiding-place from the larger political problems of that changing world, both exclusive in its intellectual pursuits, and excluding.

12

Into the Nineties

Ted: All I had when I was your age went into a suitcase. I only wanted the use of a hall. I wanted to change the view from the French windows.

Tom: That's about all you will change through plays because 99 out of 100 people never go near a live theatre and when they do they want girls got up as cats or trains.

(Peter Nichols, *A Piece of My Mind*, 1987)

In February 1993 a new musical, *The Invisible Man*, transferred from the Theatre Royal, Stratford East, to the Vaudeville in London's West End. It joined the seventeen other musicals already to be found there, and is the second recent transfer from Stratford. But it differs from the other, *Five Guys Named Moe*, in one way. *Five Guys* had been backed by Cameron Mackintosh, the resultant income having been largely responsible for keeping the Theatre Royal in existence for the last two years; the new musical has relied entirely on backing from local supporters of the theatre. Either way, however, the fact of these two musicals points to the central dilemma confronting all non-commercial theatre today.

Without successful transfers to the West End, or for regional theatres a tie-up with a tour of other regional theatres, such as that of the autumn 1992 touring production of Coward's *Fallen Angels* that originated at the Thorndike Theatre, Leatherhead, there is no longer the funding available to allow such theatres to survive. In the case of the Theatre Royal, loyal backing by the local Newnham Council has been reduced by central government pressure to cut spending on the arts which, coupled with the withering of support from those central resources, has made the economic crisis in contemporary theatre look more and more grave. Already, two theatres with strong ties to Stratford – the Tricycle in Kilburn and the New Victoria in Newcastle-under-Lyme – are threatened with 'closure or drastic curtailment'. As Manchester prepares to become the Arts Council's City of Drama, the local council have announced plans to close one of the two civic theatres, the

Wythenshawe Forum, to save the £200,000 they need to help finance the City's honouring; and news of the death of several other regional theatres in the near future will come as no real surprise. As the recession takes hold, audiences with money to spend on tickets are harder and harder to find, as are sponsors – the great free-enterprise hope of the 80s – to underwrite the costs.

For although the Association for Business Sponsorship of the Arts figures for 1992 reveal an almost 30 per cent increase in sponsorship over the year, the situation is looking progressively grimmer. That this increase has been largely to support sporting rather than cultural organizations makes them a rather unhelpful guide to current trends in theatre economics; they disguise the actual drop of 37 per cent in corporate memberships, a rather cheaper form of sponsorship relied on by the less prestigious and regional companies. The RSC had already lost an earlier sponsor, British Telecom, and are now faced with the end of Royal Insurance's three-year arrangement, leaving them to find £700,000 per year to offset the loss.[1]

What makes the gamble with the transfer of *The Invisible Man* the more problematic is that the London non-subsidized West End theatre is itself in a parlous state. A survey by the *Investors' Chronicle* discovered that 25 out of the 60 new 'backed' shows that opened between 1978 and 1990 failed, taking all the financial backing with them; and it is becoming progressively more difficult to get any kind of new production mounted at all. It is estimated that 15 out of the 40 London main-houses will go dark in the first quarter of 1993, seven musicals having closed in January alone, as audience figures drop alarmingly. Josephine Hart: 'There is an ever-decreasing number of serious plays. The antidote is well-produced but safe classics and revivals. What scares producers off is the risk involved. A play going straight into the West End will cost at least £200,000 and could close in three weeks.'[2]

What this means is that it is getting harder and harder for even an established writer, let alone a new writer, to get a production on stage. David Edgar has calculated that new work constituted roughly 12 per cent of the repertoire in London and regional main-house theatres between 1970 and 1985; between 1985 and 1990 the figure dropped to about 7 per cent,[3] and the proportion continues to fall.

Philip Hedley, the Artistic Director of the Theatre Royal, recently wrote chillingly about the state of the theatre, and his words will have the ring of familiarity to theatre administrators all over the country. He talked about the need to refer everything to the possibility of a West End transfer; in itself an uncertain game, and one that can have disastrous results on the selection of plays for performance, encouraging a safe line that positively discriminates against new writing.

> However, becoming dependent on the West End is not the most serious danger facing Stratford East and what it now stands for. The recession and government policy have brought bigger dangers which are affecting the whole theatre community. Problems of other educational and dramatic enterprises are having a direct affect on our work. No performing arts organization can survive as an island complete unto itself.[4]

From the mainstream perspective I have been considering in this book, Hedley's point can be put the other way around. The commercial theatre depends upon the subsidized theatre not only for transfers of successful productions, but for the life-blood that comes from the incorporation of the new and the experimental into the mainstream tradition, and without which it would be left in a moribund form. It depends on it as surely as have the writers discussed in this book depended on the strategies that oppose their theatrical models; the relationship between the mainstream and the *avant-garde* is more parasitic than symbiotic.

The effective removal of this *avant-garde* was a matter of history as I started this book. What is now seriously in question is any meaningful sense of the perpetuation of a contemporary mainstream tradition – a mainstream that had previously opposed that *avant-garde*, but is itself now threatened by the conscious construction of a theatre that sees productions only in the crudest terms of commercial product, and that looks to the past rather than to the present for its occasional forays into serious drama. Of course there are exceptions – the work of the Traverse, for instance, and of the Theatre Royal, as well as the heroic efforts of a great number of underfunded and undervenued companies of what is left of a meaningful 'alternative' circuit – but basically British theatre today is living on a combination of escapism and nostalgia. It has not only become a museum, it offers a vision of the nation itself as a museum.

That the two Sheffield theatres, the Crucible and the Lyceum,

should be offering revivals of two plays from that mainstream
tradition – Frayn's *Donkeys' Years* and Gray's *Quartermaine's Terms*
in their 1993 spring programmes – would not seem in the least
surprising in view of the argument I have advanced through this
book. It would be taken as evidence of the success of the new
mainstream in taking over the repertoire of main-house theatre.
But by now, these rather safe revivals look positively adventurous
when compared with the productions that surround them. That
they are revivals, rather than new works, is in itself significant;
but that they are now to be seen as simply token glances towards
what can scarcely be regarded as a consideration of contemporary
issues – both concerned with the ridiculed past values of an elitist
Oxbridge world – is far more important. The mainstream as it
developed through the 70s and 80s may have relied heavily on the
incorporation of oppositional strategies to convince an audience
that it had something of real matter to impart. As we enter the 90s
this is no longer the case. Arthur Miller, one of the two playwrights to have a new play currently on in London's West End,
has written of the current malaise on Broadway:

> The problem is not that people can't write plays any more, the
> problem is that the audience's relationship to the theatre has
> simply dribbled away. We are a kind of church. And if the
> parishioners are no longer interested in that church, you know
> what happens. It becomes a garage or a grocery store.[5]

Miller compares the situation in America with that in the
heavily subsidized Swedish theatre, and the point – the references
to ritual aside – is not without relevance to Britain. In a decade in
which Drama has been removed from the National Curriculum in
schools, and that Curriculum insists on a rigidly applied uniformity of literary reading over the entire country, how is the
theatre to find consumers sufficiently informed or educated into
demanding a drama that offers any real challenge to the simple
reduction of all matters to the values of the market-place: a
process of reductionism, the practical workings of which have
precisely created the theatre as we now have it?

It is hard to avoid the invocation of a conspiracy theory. The
process of centralization of power must also be seen in terms of
the imposition of a kind of cultural totalitarianism, in which even
to question the details of the programme is to open oneself to the

charge of heresy. It is a process which the theatre has half embraced, and half submitted to on grounds of financial necessity.

In contrast to other European countries the amount of government spending on the Arts generally in this country is derisory, and increasingly so. At the 1993 Olivier Awards, the new artistic director of the Royal Court Theatre, Stephen Daldry, responded to his receipt of awards for his National Theatre production of J. B. Priestley's An *Inspector Calls* with an angry diatribe against government policy. In a part of his speech that, curiously, the television company was unable to find space for in their transmission of the event, he pointed out that the 'theatre subsidizes the government'; he accepted the awards 'on behalf of all the productions that are not going to be made next year'. In a subsequent interview he noted that Berlin offers more financial support for cultural activities in its city than the UK Arts Council offers for the entire country.[6]

Given the resultant pressure towards self-sufficiency in economic terms, and the particular pressure thus felt on politically committed companies and writers, it is scarcely surprising that the theatre should not be offering the necessary radical critique to the thoughts and practice of contemporary politics; from a government point of view, it might be felt that it is 'convenient' that this is so. What is even more alarming as an overall register of the state of affairs is that the mainstream tradition which, through a process of incorporation, did at least make liberal gestures in that direction, should also find itself progressively excluded from the new theatrical market-place.

The Royal Court is currently actively pursuing commercial sponsorship from American and British companies. Elsewhere, in the regions, such sponsorship is harder to attract. The Arts Council has already announced a cut of £5 million in funding for 1994, and the result will not simply be a thinner slice of the cake all round, but a selective closure of venues and disbanding of companies at a regional level. To argue, as Stephen Daldry has, that 'when the tributaries are cut off, the general reservoir is diminished',[7] is, perhaps, to view the situation from an essentially centrist position, with the potential of a regional theatre being tapped by London; but the general point remains. Where is the new work to come from, how are new writers to find companies able to work with them, or theatres prepared to take a risk on contemporary plays, when all that is increasingly sought is a safe commercial product? And it is in this sense that the latest news from the British mainstream is so depressing.

For, in a 1992 survey of the autumn programmes of 164 of mainland Britain's regional theatres, there was very little evidence of this kind of incorporation.[8] Plays by Ayckbourn, Bennett and Frayn do feature in the listings but, with the exception of a single production of *Henceforward* at the New Victoria, Newcastle-under-Lyme – a theatre still struggling to work as a theatre, and not just as a provider of commercial product, for which it may be about to pay the ultimate cost – they are all productions of plays that do not impinge on post-79 political issues. And there is a certain irony in that that one production should be sponsored by the New Vic Business Support Group.

Of these writers, Ayckbourn is pre-eminent, remaining easily the most produced contemporary playwright and, if it were not for the continuing existence of Shakespeare on the examination schedules – and in particular currently, *Macbeth* – he would be unchallenged. For all his current success on television there was not a single regional production of a play by Simon Gray; and not a play by Peter Nichols or – less surprisingly perhaps in view of his change of direction – Tom Stoppard. Peter Nichols has recently vented (in verse this time) his anger at not getting new or revived works on in London,[9] but there seems little doubt that both Gray and Stoppard would find a warm welcome onto the National stage with new work (as indeed Stoppard has as I finish writing, *Arcadia* opening at the Lyttelton in April 1994, before embarking on a national tour). Thus the lack of regional productions might seem to point to the importance of perceived distinctions within the new mainstream writers that I have been discussing.

Alan Bennett's *The Madness of George III* was chosen as the previous winter's National Theatre touring production, to be followed this winter by Stephen Daldrey's production of Priestley's *An Inspector Calls*, to give some idea of the thinking behind the decisions. Bennett and Frayn, and most obviously Ayckbourn, are felt to have a populist appeal in a way that is now less obviously so for Gray and Stoppard – who look more 'National' than national as writers. For the regional theatre has fallen into a state of financial panic in which even the proven products of the established mainstream appear a dangerous risk. Whilst *Noises Off* continues to go the rounds, there are no revivals of *Forget-Me-Not-*

Lane or *Joe Egg* – although the latter does have a late spring run at the King's Head in London.

To look at the autumn programmes collectively is to look at a theatre desperate for the onset of the Christmas season, and not only the pantomime (particularly if it can find a national sponsor like Cadburys, as many did), but a whole plethora of children's shows and festive related events. The pantomime season has now become so stretched as to effectively dominate the entire winter programme in the majority of theatres, although the Novello Theatre, Sunningdale, with a run of *Snow White* from November 17 to January 30 easily holds the record! In the light of the recent movie *Hook*, and the re-release of *Peter Pan*, it is not surprising to find the latter jostling with *Aladdin* as the most popular story on offer; to which can be added the many versions of *Beauty and the Beast* and *A Christmas Carol* (or *Scrooge*), as well as a major tour of *Robin of Sherwood*, all a testament to the importance of a movie tie-in.

Television provides another key to the selection of work for the season, with all the major tours of the ever more present children's shows featuring characters from that medium – Sooty, Postman Pat, Fireman Sam, Thunderbirds, the Care Bears, the Mr Men and Button Moon. It also has a heavy influence on the adult programme, with George Cole (currently of *Minder* fame) touring with *Natural Causes*, and Adam Faith with *Alfie*, for instance, amongst a number of safely commercial productions heading from or to the West End. The tour of Sue Townsend's *Bazaar and Rummage* is clearly predicated on the success of her television version of *Adrian Mole*, and frequently the establishment of a television connection has seemed vital – the Nuffield, Southampton, for example, advertising its production of *Building Blocks* (by Bob Larbey) as by the man who wrote *The Good Life*, *Brush Strokes* and *A Fine Romance*.

As well as a heavy reliance on musicals, many of which were effectively subsidized by the use of local amateur companies (an increasing formula in the regional theatre), there was overall a steady drift away from drama towards dance and music. British Telecom, the RSC's erstwhile sponsor, is now turning away from drama and towards dance in its sponsorship, presumably as a result of a discovery of a more useful cultural identification by its market researchers. The majority of touring productions, and the accompanying subsidies, were to be found in this area. Musicals, in particular, are a very marketable commodity. Their appeal to the ticket-buyer lies not only in their predominantly escapist or nostalgic tone. They are safe in that as revivals or as nostalgic anthologies of pop history they can deliver a product the main components of which, the songs, are already familiar to their audiences, have already been marketed in other mediums. And, as seen most impressively at the Palace Theatre, Manchester, which has one production, the Cameron Mackintosh backed *Les Misérables*, for the entire autumn and spring season, their very success acts as a further block on the introduction of real drama into the programme.

The standard diet of formulaic thrillers and comedies (either coming from or on their way to London's West End) was predictable, but the regional bases of these theatres were also highlighted by the frequency with which plays by such as Willy Russell, Bill Naughton and Keith Waterhouse were to be found (either on tour or as in-house productions), and by the fact that the most frequent touring productions were by John Godber, the second most produced contemporary playwright, and Hull Truck.

A predominant theme was nostalgia, with strong evidence of the Noel Coward revival well under way – *Hay Fever* on its way to London, and a tour of *Fallen Angels*, featuring Hayley and Juliet Mills – with presumably a Terence Rattigan one to follow. *An Ideal Husband* was touring, as was Pinero's *Trelawney of the Wells*, both on their way to the West End. There were tours of Steele's *A Tender Husband* and Sheridan's *The Rivals*; and two touring productions of *Cyrano de Bergerac*; with plenty of interest in what can be generally labelled 'costume-drama' of all kinds. As I write, Wilde's *An Ideal Husband* had just been joined by his *The Importance of Being Earnest* in London's West End. It takes over at the Aldwych from *The Rise and Fall of Little Voice* by Jim Cartwright, a National transfer which had been the only significant example of new writing in the entire London commercial theatre.

This nostalgia theme was most frequently associated with memories of the 50s and 60s, and a popular culture connectable with the youth of older and more affluent theatre patrons; there were touring productions of *Tutti Frutti*, *Elvis* and *Buddy*. The last example is instructive. An uncomplicated celebration of the life and music of Buddy Holly – made easier for an audience in that it gets the unfortunate fact of his death out of the way half-way through the second act, so that Buddy can then join the cast for some more good old Rock 'n' Roll – it started life in a regional theatre, Plymouth's Theatre Royal. Now, with a London base, and touring productions in England, over Europe and as far away as Japan, it is bringing a steady income to its home; a pleasant undemanding commodity that has found a public prepared to pay for a product that is marketed like a Rock Concert, with all the paraphernalia of T-shirts, mugs and recordings for sale in the foyer. A measure of its economic importance is that it has caused a hastily reissued collection of Buddy Holly's hits to top the album charts as I write.

The full implications of sponsorship are in evidence in this autumn programme, although the mere fact of sponsorship is not always as significant as it appears. A comparatively small financial outlay will merit an advertising credit at regional level, and the resultant 'support' by more than one company for a single production is a measure not only of the desperate attempts being made to get funding, however minimal, but also of the urge to be seen to be so doing. One theatre, the Watermill at Newbury, had succeeded in finding sponsorship for all of its productions, and others were close behind, and it is hard to ignore the way in which local insurance companies and the like have been matched with appropriate productions.

Finding the Ceramics and Allied Trades Union sponsoring *The Jolly Potters*, a revival of the New Victoria's first drama-documentary, is refreshing. More characteristic is the financial support offered for a five-week run of what is described as an English classic, Priestley's *When We Are Married*, by English Estates at the West Yorkshire Playhouse, Leeds – Britain's newest theatre; of Bennett's *Single Spies* by the English Country Courtyard Association at the Salisbury Playhouse; or, indeed, of the national tour of Christie's *Witness for the Prosecution* sponsored by the privatized British Telecom. It is in all a dismal set of offerings, the occasional bright spot like the evident continuing popularity of more adventurous touring companies such as Trestle, Millstream and Compass notwithstanding. More usually, the heavy reliance on touring productions – the Mayflower at Southampton, for instance, had *The Sound of Music* as the only self-created production in its autumn season – was not such as to encourage the showing of innovative work. Its prime aim was to reduce the costs of production, and its immediate result a levelling of theatrical product, creating an increasing sense of dull uniformity from region to region.

I started this book by talking about a general sense of crisis in the British theatre that began in the early 80s, and discussing the ways in which the new mainstream was particularly equipped to use the crisis for its own recovery and regeneration. The agents of that regeneration are still to be found but in the present economic climate as it is affecting British theatre there can no longer be much confidence in its ability to develop. And if the efforts of the mainstream are increasingly under pressure, what is the likelihood of any really new developments, developments that might just push the theatre into some kind of contact – I dare not say conflict – with a world beyond that of escapism and nostalgia?

Given the complete collapse of the British film industry, and the increasing impossibility of writers finding television space for their work, the potential role of the theatre in a debate about the state of the nation has never seemed more urgent. In the UK the recession continues to worsen; the manufacturing base continues to wither, and unemployment continues to rise – the official figures of 3 million plus masking a far worse situation. As revenue from North Sea oil begins to run out, the government is faced with a mounting financial deficit, and plans for further speculative privatization look increasingly desperate. Britain is now at the very bottom of the league of the 22 major industrialized nations in terms of its manufacturing base,[10] and the temporary relief brought by the enforced devaluation of the pound will have no long-term effect. To look into the future is to see an entire younger generation employed, in as much as they will be, in selling each other hamburgers in fast-food franchises. The whole spectrum of education, welfare and public spending looks set to face further cut backs and, not a million miles away, the terrible, unresolved problems of Ireland are kept uneasily on hold by the presence of the British army.

Internationally, of course, the problems of Britain pale into insignificance, as the first euphoria at the disintegration of the Russian Empire has been followed by the realization of the dreadful economic and nationalistic agonies that lay in its wake – agonies that must be measured in human terms as Europe bloodily readjusts its borders, a process that is having a rippling effect, further aggravating already existing conflicts to the east.

On all these matters, and many more, the theatre is silent.

Effectively closed to radical voices, it can scarcely find space any longer for real dialogue of any kind. This is not only true of native playwrights; we will look in vain for any real representation of contemporary problems by those foreign dramatists who had previously not only brought us news from elsewhere but with that news many exciting dramatic innovations. In its insularity and in its ruthless pursuit of commercial product, it is doing no more than echoing the demands of the ideology of the market-place that have come to dominate what public political debate there is. That the struggle to thus continue will nevertheless result in failure, with theatrical 'lame ducks' going to the wall as surely as their industrial and commercial counterparts, will be savagely ironic. A theatre which, to use Miller's analogy, sells its products like those of a garage or a grocery store, is in very real danger of being transformed into buildings that do actually sell petrol and groceries.

Given the undoubted talent in the British theatre at all levels such closures would seem tragic; but given the way in which such talent is currently being deployed it would be hard to gather together a group of serious mourners. What is required, and required with an urgency almost beyond belief, is a movement that will challenge the ideological assumptions upon which the contemporary theatre has been reconstructed, and once again offer the public a drama that offers to enter the political debate directly. In 1989 John McGrath dedicated his *The Bone Won't Break* to the 'Resistance, to those who have had their lives distorted or destroyed so others could consume', and called at the end of it for a Carnival 'that will enrich lives, raise spirits and prepare the way for the future'.[11] In *The Second Time as Farce*, a year earlier, David Edgar had talked of the problems of producing a theatre of opposition at this time:

> Do we attempt through our work seriously to participate in the debate that is going on on the left after the serious reverses it's suffered – a contribution which would involve a fair amount of dirty political washing, left twisting slowly in the wind? Or do we view our function as socialist artists as being the palm court orchestra on the *Titanic* – providing at least a little cheer and comfort, a bit of confirmation and even celebration of the old ideals – as our comrades call for lifeboats and the waters lap about our heels?[12]

In a 1993 survey by the Association for Business Sponsorship of the Arts, it was revealed that the typical theatre-goer, like the typical concert and museum-goer, is a relatively high earner and middle-aged. Commenting on the report, Richard Orgill, the corporate communications manager of Clerical Medical Investment Group (a sponsor of the survey), expressed his surprise:

> We wouldn't have expected such an upmarket audience. Manual, administrative and clerical, housewives and the unemployed represent up to 60 per cent of the population, but they are only 20 per cent of people attending. The arts are still a middle and upper-middle class activity, with the audience from the top quarter of the population as far as income goes.[13]

It is hard to comprehend the surprise. More interesting would be a breakdown in audience attendance in terms of conventional parameters of cultural respectability, considering, for instance, the difference in audience structure at the opening of a Stoppard play at the National Theatre to that of a typical evening at the London production of *Starlight Express* or, indeed, to a regional revival of an Ayckbourn play. But what is quite evident is that the audience for British theatre has narrowed in ways that are comparable to the situation immediately prior to the 1950s theatrical revival, that the vast majority of theatre audiences are as unrepresentative of the total population as are the social worlds depicted in the plays they pay to see.

And what is perhaps particularly disturbing is that an entire younger generation has now effectively ceased to attend the theatre at all, although given what is generally on offer, this again cannot be a source of much wonder. According to the same report, fewer than 10 per cent of arts-attenders are between 18 and 24, and only 3 per cent under 18, for most of whom the obligatory school trip to see the prescribed Shakespeare text will presumably be virtually the sum total of their theatrical experience.

Furthermore, what little remains of an alternative theatre tradition can now only problematically be so named. The London guide *Time Out* recently removed half the venues from its 'Fringe' section and created a new listing, 'Off-West-End', in recognition of the fact that such venues were now offering nothing more than the mainstream, albeit on a more modest scale. That they had considered scrapping the 'Fringe' heading altogether is the more disturbing in that it was that publication which first introduced the term into general theatrical parlance in the heady days of 1969.

The prestigious annual publication, *The British Alternative Theatre Directory*, took the decision this year that the distinction between mainstream and alternative can no longer be seriously maintained:

> At the moment one of Britain's oldest and most respected 'Fringe' companies, Hull Truck, is presenting *On the Piste*, a lightweight comedy . . . mainly of interest to white middle-class couples who holiday in the Alps . . . [and] set for a long run at London's Garrick Theatre. Meanwhile, in the fifty-odd smaller theatres, which, for want of a better word . . . still constitute London's 'Fringe', a counter-culture to the new mainstream has yet to emerge. At the time of going to press a third of the venues are occupied by classics (four Shakespeares, plus Ibsen, Schiller, Sophocles, Lorca and Chekhov) and other revivals (two Mamets, two Sartres, a Beckett and a Willis Hall). A further eighteen plays are historical dramas.[14]

And meanwhile, in the private sector, Christopher Hampton is busily at work with Andrew Lloyd Webber on the latter's latest extravaganza, a musical version of *Sunset Boulevard* that already has advanced bookings worth approaching £5,000,000! Whilst, in the government sector, the new offices of one of the members of the audience at the Olivier Awards referred to earlier, Peter Brooke, the Secretary of State for National Heritage, have been refurbished at a cost of around £3,000,000.

What is clear is that without some kind of reanimation the British theatre will continue its march towards total irrelevance, and yet another avenue of opposition and of debate will be lost to a perpetuation of the present parade of bland product uniformity. Social and political pressures virtually unconsidered by the contemporary theatre must eventually find a platform. There is another world outside that of the burglar-proofed and lavishly furnished box sets of the contemporary theatre; and other unironic voices, less wittily articulate, but more urgent, than those of the mainstream I have been considering, waiting in the wings.

Notes

Place of publication London unless otherwise stated. There are no notes provided for published works by playwrights considered in more detail in Part II of the book, and details can be found in the bibliography.

Chapter 1   Whither Britain?

1. Brian Appleyard, *The Culture Club: Crisis in the Arts* (Faber, 1984), p. 9.
2. The *Guardian*, 1 November 1968.
3. D. Keith Peacock, *Radical Stages: Alternative History in Modern British Drama* (Westport: Greenwood Press, 1991), pp. 67–8.
4. Howard Brenton, *Revenge* (Methuen, 1970).
5. John Bull, *New British Political Dramatists* (Macmillan, 1984; third edition 1991), cf. in particular, the first chapter.
6. Peacock, *Radical Stages*, p. 68.
7. Malcolm Hay and Philip Roberts, 'Interview with Howard Brenton', *Performing Arts Journal*, III, no. iii (1979), 138.
8. Quoted in Sheridan Morley, 'The man behind the Lyttelton's first new play', *The Times*, 10 July 1976.
9. Howard Brenton, *How Beautiful With Badges* in (ed. and introduced) John Bull, *Howard Brenton: Three Plays, Critical Stages I* (Sheffield Academic Press, 1989).
10. Howard Brenton, *The Churchill Play* (Methuen, 1974).
11. *Plays and Players* (June 1984), 46–7.

Chapter 2   The Gamblers' Den

1. Parts of this chapter are based on my 'Left to Right: English Theatre in the 1980s', *Englisch Amerikanische Studien. Zeitschrift für Unterrricht, Wissenschaft & Politik*, 3 (April 1986), 401–10, and on a lecture given at Loughborough University the same year.
2. Nicholas de Jongh, 'Welcome to the Culture Casino', *Guardian*, 12 February 1991.
3. *Plays and Players* (October 1981), pp. 46–7.
4. Michael Billington, 'The arts in the eighties', *Guardian*, 28 December 1985.
5. Economists' Advisory Group, *Overseas Earnings of the Arts 1988–9*, produced for the British Invisibles' Cultural Sector Working Party (HMSO, 1991).
6. John Vidal, 'The selection of the fittest', *Guardian*, 7 April 1988; cf. also Michael Billington, 'Cash and Carrie', *Guardian*, 4 July 1988.

7.   'The Official London Theatre Guide', *The Observer*, 17 August 1986, and *Society of West End Theatres Newsletter*, June 1992.
8.   Sheridan Morley, 'Tills are alive to the sound of music', *The Times*, 12 April 1986.
9.   *Variety* (New York), 24 September 1990.
10. Michael Church, 'A song in their heart', *Independent on Sunday*, 7 October 1990.
11. *Guardian*, 2 June 1986.
12. John Bull, *New British Political Dramatists* (Mamillan, 1984, 3rd edition 1991), p. 25.
13. Quoted in Sheridan Morley, 'The man behind the Lyttelton's new play', *The Times*, 10 July 1976.
14. Clive Barker, 'From Fringe to Alternative Theatre', *Zeitschrift für Anglistick und Amerikanistick*, 26, no. 1 (Wilhelm Peck University, Rostock, 1978), 62.
15. 'Theatre from the deep-freeze', *Plays and Players* (July 1985), 11.
16. Quoted in Vera Lustig, 'Look Back in Anger?', *Plays and Players* (April 1991).
17. Cf. David Edgar, 'Political Theatre, Part I and II', *Socialist Review*, 1 April and 2 May 1978.
18. For a scathing critique of the activities of the Arts Council from a very different perspective to mine see Brian Appleyard, *The Culture Club: Crisis in the Arts* (Faber, 1984).
19. *Guardian*, 26 January 1981.
20. *Guardian*, 11 February 1991.
21. *Guardian*, 24 January 1986.
22. Quoted in *Guardian*, 27 January 1988.
23. Quoted in *Guardian*, 7 August 1990.
24. Michael Billington, 'Something rotten in the state', *Guardian*, 25 March 1992.
25. Ibid.
26. In his account in the *Guardian*, 7 February 1991, Nicholas de Jongh, whilst defending their work at the same time recommends a politically expedient change of name!
27. Paul Tyler, 'Art for art's sake', *The Independent*, 22 October 1988.
28. Michael Billington, 'Serious money', *Guardian*, 29 December 1987.
29. Martin Hoyle, 'Combing the Fringe', *Plays and Players* (January 1985), 50.
30. Robert Hewison, 'Caution keeps creativity in the wings', *Sunday Times*, 9 October 1988.
31. Nicholas de Jongh, 'Courtship across the Atlantic', *Guardian*, 20 February 1985. In this context, it is instructive to note the increase in productions of American plays in the period since 1979 as Anglo-American co-operation came generally to become part of the economics of survival.
32. Anthony Howard, 'Rolling up the map of broadcasting', *The Independent*, 9 December 1989.
33. 'The Late Show', BBC TV, 15 January 1992.
34. Nicholas de Jongh, 'Cash that eases the pain', *Guardian*, 5 October 1985.

35. The estimates are those of Frank Rich, drama critic of *The New York Times*, quoted in Michael Billington, 'A crisis up west', *Guardian*, 20 June 1987.
36. Ibid.
37. Michael Billington, *Guardian*, 2 November 1990.
38. David Edgar, 'Why pay's the thing', *Guardian*, 28 June 1985.

Chapter 3   *Private Rooms and Public Spaces*

1. Arthur Adamov at session on 'Commitment v the Absurd', International Drama Festival, Edinburgh, 1963.
2. I do not intend to look in detail at these events. Good accounts are to be found in John Russell Taylor, *Anger and After* (Methuen, 1962) and Michael Anderson, *Anger and Detachment* (Pitman, 1976). The liveliest debate took place in *Encore*, and a useful compilation is Charles Marowitz, Tom Milne and Owen Hale (eds), *The Encore Reader* (Methuen, 1965).
3. Kenneth Tynan, 'Preface', *Observer New Plays* (1958).
4. Kenneth Tynan, *Curtains* (Longman, 1961), pp. 83–4.
5. Ibid., p. 85.
6. Robert Rubens, 'Conversations at the Royal Court: William Gaskill', *Transatlantic Review*, no. 8 (Winter 1961).
7. The fullest account of the reception of Brecht's work in Britain is to be found in Nicholas Jacobs and Prudence Ohlson, *Bertolt Brecht in Britain* (TQ Publications, 1977). See also Mario Germanou, 'Brecht and the English Theatre', in Graham Bartram and Anthony Waine (eds), *Brecht in Perspective* (Longman, 1982), pp. 208–24.
8. Howard Brenton, 'Petrol bombs through the proscenium arch', *Theatre Quarterly*, V, no. vii (1975), 20.
9. Tom Milne, 'And the time of the great taking over: an interview with William Gaskill', *Encore*, IX, no. iv, (July/August 1962).
10. Martin Esslin, 'Brecht and the English theatre', *Tulane Drama Review*, II, no. ii (Winter 1966).
11. Quoted in *The Times*, 26 March 1961.
12. Adamov's *All Against All and Professor Taranne* played at the Twentieth Century Theatre, Notting Hill Gate, in April 1959. Interest in Frisch was such that *The Times* carried features on him on 16 January and 8 May 1958, even though *The Fire-Raisers* was not produced in London until December 1961.
13. Eugene Ionesco, 'Le rôle du Dramaturge', *Notes et Contre-Notes* (Paris, Gallimard, 1962), p. 72. Published originally in Donald Watson's translation in *The Observer*, 29 June 1958. I quote the translation by Julian Wulbern in his *Brecht and Ionesco: Commitment in Context* (USA, University of Illinois Press, 1971), p. 13. This remains the best discussion of the debate.
14. Eugene Ionesco, *The Physician's Panorama*, quoted in *The Times*, 11 February 1963.
15. 'Playwrights on commitment', *The Times*, 4 September 1963.
16. *The Times*, 3 July 1962.

17. Ibid., 9 March 1960.
18. Ibid., 16 November 1960.
19. Arnold Wesker, 'One Room Living', *New Theatre Magazine*, III, no. ii (University of Bristol, 1962).
20. John Russell Taylor, *The Rise and Fall of the Well-Made Play* (Methuen, 1967), p. 9, p. 139 and p. 163.
21. *The Sunday Times*, January 1967.
22. *The Times*, 14 October 1967.
23. Ibid., 10 November 1967.
24. Hugh and Margaret Williams, *Past Imperfect* (Evans, 1965).
25. Irving Wardle, 'The pendulum of taste', *The Times*, 26 October 1968.

Chapter 4   Enter the Smooth Men

1. Kenneth Tynan, 'Withdrawing with style from the chaos', *Gambit*, X, no. 37 (1981), 19–20.
2. David Campton, *The Lunatic View* (Scarborough Studio Theatre Ltd, 1960).
3. Cf. John Bull and Frances Gray, 'Joe Orton', in Hedwig Block and Albert Wertheim (eds), *Essays On Contemporary British Drama* (Munich, Max Hueber Verlag, 1981), p. 81.
4. *The Times*, 12 October 1960 and 6 May 1961.
5. Joe Orton, *Funeral Games* and *The Good and Faithful Servant* (Methuen, 1970).
6. John Lahr, *Prick Up Your Ears: the Biography of Joe Orton* (Penguin, 1980), pp. 157–8.
7. *The Times*, 30 March 1965.
8. Ibid., 7 April 1965.
9. Ibid., 10 January 1966.
10. *Guardian*, 29 November 1969.
11. Tadeusz Rozewicz, *The Card Index (Kartoteka)*, in *The Card Index and other plays* (New York, Grove Press, 1970).
12. Joe Orton, *Loot* (Methuen, 1967).
13. Giles Cooper, *Everything in the Garden* (1962), in *New English Dramatists 7* (Penguin, 1963).
14. Quoted in John Russell Taylor, *Anger And After* (Penguin, 1963), p. 177.
15. Although the play's title is actually borrowed from an earlier, abandoned play, the connection remains.
16. Henry Livings, *Eh?* (Methuen, 1965).
17. Michael Billington, *Alan Ayckbourn* (Macmillan, 1983), p. 1.
18. Quoted in Kenneth Tynan, 'Withdrawing with style from the chaos', *Gambit*, X, no. 37 (1981), 20.
19. Quoted in Thomas Whitaker, *Tom Stoppard* (Macmillan, 1983), p. 43.
20. The scene was included in the first published edition of the play (Faber, 1968), but is not included in the altered text available since the second edition in 1968.
21. Kenneth Tynan, 'Withdrawing with style', p. 20.
22. Thomas Whitaker, *Tom Stoppard*, p. 45.

23. James Saunders, *Next Time I'll Sing to You* in *Four Plays* (Penguin, 1971).
24. Vaclav Havel, *Redevelopment; Or, Slum Clearance* (Faber, 1990).
25. Christopher Innes, *Avant Garde Theatre 1892–1992* (Routledge, 1993), p. 229.
26. *The Times*, 21 July 1967.
27. Ibid., 8 April 1968.
28. Michael Billington, *The Times*, 11 October 1967.
29. Quoted in Tynan, 'Withdrawing with style', p. 20.
30. Christopher Hampton, 'Introduction', *The Philanthropist and Other Plays* (Faber, 1991), pp. xi–x.
31. Ibid.

Chapter 5   Set in Rooms

1.   Howard Brenton quoted in Catherine Itzin and Simon Trussler, 'Petrol bombs through the proscenium arch', *Theatre Quarterly*, V, no. 17 (1975).
2.   John Lahr, *Prick Up Your Ears* (Penguin, 1980), p. 315.
3.   David Edgar, 'Theatre and fiction', *The Second Time as Farce* (Lawrence & Wishart, 1988), p. 165.
4.   Michael Billington, *Tom Stoppard* (Macmillan, 1987), p. 147.
5.   Jill Dolan, *The Feminist Spectator as Critic* (Ann Arbor: UMI Research Press, 1988), pp. 3–4.
6.   Susan Bennett, *Theatre Audiences: A Theory of Production and Reception* (Routledge, 1990), p. 105.

Chapter 6   Peter Nichols

1.   Brian Miller, 'Peter Nichols', in George Brandt (ed.), *British Television Drama* (Cambridge University Press, 1981), p. 110.
2.   Irving Wardle, 'A second shot at life', *Independent on Sunday*, 25 March 1990.
3.   Peter Nicols, 'Introductions', *Plays I* (Methuen, 1987).
4.   Cf. Kenneth Tynan, *Curtains* (Longman, 1961), pp. 83–4.
5.   James Allister, 'All Passion Spent', *Plays and Players* (June 1984).
6.   Malcolm Hay, 'Piece of mind', *Plays and Players* (January 1987).

Chapter 7   Simon Gray

1.   Simon Gray, 'Introduction', *Plays I* (Methuen, 1986).
2.   Ibid.
3.   Simon Gray, *Hidden Laughter* (Faber, 1990).
4.   Simon Gray, 'Introduction'.
5.   Mark Steyn, *Plays and Players* (May 1988).
6.   Steve Grant, *Plays and Players* (August 1984).
7.   Simon Gray, 'Introduction'.
8.   Frank Marcus, *Plays and Players* (July 1979).
9.   Ian Hamilton, 'Interview with Simon Gray', *The New Review*, III (January/February 1977).

Chapter 8   Alan Ayckbourn

1.   Ian Watson, *Conversations with Alan Ayckbourn* (Faber, 1988), p. 90.
2.   Ibid., pp. 159–60.
3.   Ibid., p. 113.
4.   Ibid., p. 36.
5.   Ibid., pp. 85–6.
6.   Michael Billington, *Alan Ayckbourn* (Macmillan, 1990), p. 83.
7.   Ibid., p. 141.
8.   Ian Watson, *Conversations with Alan Ayckbourn*.
9.   Michael Billington, *Alan Ayckbourn*, p. 38.
10. Ian Watson, *Conversations with Alan Ayckbourn*, p. 117.
11. Ibid., p. 87.
12. Jean Rafferty, 'Hit Man by the Sea', *Plus Magazine* (24 October 1990).
13. Ian Watson, *Conversations with Alan Ayckbourn*, p. 141.
14. Ibid., p. 125.
15. Ibid., pp. 147–8.

Chapter 9   Michael Frayn

1.   Michael Frayn, 'The theatre of magic', *The Observer*, 8 December 1985.
2.   Michael Frayn, 'Introduction', *Plays I* (Methuen, 1985).
3.   Peter Ansorge, *Plays and Players* (September 1976).
4.   John Bull, *New British Political Dramatists* (Macmillan, 1984), p. 211.
5.   Michael Frayn, 'Introduction'.
6.   Felix Barker, *Plays and Players* (June 1984).
7.   Michael Frayn, 'Introduction'.
8.   W. J. Weatherby, 'Manhatten Transfer', *Guardian*, 2 January 1986.
9.   John Russell Taylor, 'Art and commerce: The new drama in the West End marketplace', in C. W. Bigsby (ed.), *Contemporary English Drama*, Stratford-upon-Avon Studies 19 (Arnold, 1981), p. 118.

Chapter 10   Alan Bennett

1.   Alan Bennett, 'Introduction', *Forty Years On and Other Plays* (Faber, 1991).
2.   Alan Bennett, 'The Writer in Disguise', *The Writer in Disguise* (Faber, 1985), pp. 23–4.
3.   Alan Bennett, 'Introduction', *Forty Years On and Other Plays*.
4.   Alan Bennett, 'The Writer in Disguise', p. 10.
5.   Alan Bennett, 'Introduction', *Objects of Affection and Other Plays for Television* (BBC, 1982), p. 7.
6.   Alan Bennett, 'Introduction', *Single Spies* (Faber, 1989).

Chapter 11   Tom Stoppard

1.   Tom Stoppard, 'Something to declare', *The Sunday Times*, 25 February 1968.

2. Tom Stppard, 'Introduction', *Every Good Boy Deserves Favour and Professional Foul* (Faber, 1978).
3. Tom Stoppard, 'Dirty linen in Prague', *The New York Times*, 11 February 1977.

Chapter 12   Into the Nineties

1. Claire Armistead, 'Risky business', and Adrian Noble, 'A sponsor's farewell', *Guardian*, 13 January 1993.
2. Figures and quotation from Maurice Chittendon, 'West End curtains come down', *The Sunday Times*, 10 January 1993.
3. David Edgar, 'New state of play', *Guardian*, 1 March 1993.
4. Philip Hedley, 'Invisible dangers', *Guardian*, 10 February 1993.
5. Arthur Miller, 'Death of a theatre', *Guardian*, 1 February 1993.
6. E. Jane Dickson, 'The court of new appeal', *The Sunday Times*, 15 August 1993.
7. Ibid.
8. John Bull, 'The 1992 autumn season in Britain's regional theatres', unpublished.
9. Peter Nichols, 'The Rime of the Ancient Dramatist', *The Independent*, 23 January 1993.
10. Ruth Kelly, 'Britain sinks towards the bottom of the world wealth league', *Guardian*, 22 June 1993.
11. John McGrath, *The Bone Won't Break: On Theatre and Hope in Hard Times* (Methuen, 1989), p. x and p. 166.
12. David Edgar, *The Second Time as Farce: Reflections on the Drama of Mean Times* (Lawrence & Wishart, 1988), p. 166.
13. David Lister, 'Arts-goers are mainly old and rich', *Independent on Sunday*, 6 June 1993.
14. David McGillvray (ed.), *The British Alternative Theatre Directory 93–94* (Rebecca Books, 1993), pp. 11 and 13.

Bibliography

Place of publication London unless otherwise stated

PETER NICHOLS

Published Plays

(Published by Faber unless otherwise stated.)
Promenade, in *Six Granada Plays* (1960)
Ben Spray, in *New Granada Plays* (1961)
A Day in the Death of Joe Egg (1967)
Plays I: Forget-Me-Not-Lane, Hearts and Flowers, Neither Up nor Down; Chez Nous, The Common, Privates on Parade (Methuen, 1987)
The Gorge, in Robert Muller (ed.), *The Television Dramatist* (Elek, 1973)
The National Health; or, Nurse Norton's Affair (1970)
The Freeway (1975)
Born in the Gardens (1980)
Passion Play (Methuen, 1981)
Poppy (Methuen, 1982)
A Piece of My Mind (Methuen, 1987)

Secondary Sources

Peter Nichols, *Feeling You're Behind: An Autobiography* (Weidenfield & Nicholson, 1984)
John Russell Taylor, *The Second Wave* (Methuen, 1971), pp. 16–35
'Interview' in Ronald Hayman, *Playback 2* (Davis Poynter, 1973)
Oleg Kerensky, *The New British Drama* (Hamish Hamilton, 1980)
Brian Miller, 'Peter Nichols', in George Brandt (ed.), *British Television Drama* (Cambridge University Press, 1981), pp. 110–36
June Schluter, 'Adultery is next to godliness: dramatic juxtaposition in Peter Nichols' *Passion Play*', in John Russell Brown (ed.), *Modern British Dramatists* (Englewood Cliffs NJ: Prentice-Hall, 1984)

James Allister, 'All Passion Spent', *Plays and Players* (June 1984)

Richard Foulkes, '"The cure is removal of guilt": faith, fidelity and fertility in the plays of Peter Nichols', *Modern Drama*, XXIX, no. 2 (1986), 207–15

Malcolm Hay, 'Piece of mind', *Plays and Players* (January 1987)

Irving Wardle, 'A second shot at life', *Independent on Sunday*, 25 March 1990

Peter Nichols, 'Casting the audience' and 'Introductions', *Plays I* (Methuen, 1987)

Peter Nichols, 'The Rime of the Ancient Dramatist', *The Independent* (23 January 1993)

SIMON GRAY

Published Plays

(Published by Methuen unless otherwise stated.)

Wise Child (Faber, 1968)

Sleeping Dog (Faber, 1968)

Spoiled (1971)

Dutch Uncle (1969)

The Idiot (1970)

Dog Days (1975)

Otherwise Engaged, Two Sundays and *Plaintiffs and Defendants* (1975)

Stage Struck (1979)

Close of Play (1979)

Close of Play (revised) and *Pig in a Poke* (1980)

Plays I: Butley, Otherwise Engaged, The Rear Column, Quartermaine's Terms, The Common Pursuit (revised) (1986)

Melon (1987)

After Pilkington (1987)

Hidden Laughter (Faber, 1990)

Secondary Sources

Simon Gray, *An Unnatural Pursuit and Other Pieces* (Faber, 1985)

John Russell Taylor, 'Three farceurs', *The Second Wave* (Methuen, 1971), pp. 155–71

Peter Ansorge, 'Simon Gray, author of *Butley*, talks to *Plays and Players*' (August 1972)

Ian Hamilton, 'Interview with Simon Gray', *The New Review*, III (January/February 1977), 39–46

Sophia Blaydes, 'Literary allusion as satire in Simon Gray's *Butley*', *Midwest Quarterly*, XVIII (July 1977), 374–91

Frank Marcus, Review of *Close of Play*, *Plays and Players* (July 1979), 20–1

Bryan Nelson, 'The unhappy men in Simon Gray's *Otherwise Engaged*', *Modern Drama*, XXII (1980), 365–73

Rudiger Imhof, 'Simon Gray', in Hedwig Bock and Albert Wertheim (eds), *Essays on Contemporary British Drama* (Munich: Max Hueber Verlag, 1981), pp. 223–52

Simon Gray, 'Otherwise enraged: a paranoid view of reviewing', *Times Literary Supplement*, 2 September 1983

Richard Boston, 'The private quarrel that moved centre stage', *Guardian*, 24 September 1983

Simon Gray, 'Introduction', *Plays I* (Methuen, 1984)

Steve Grant, Review of *The Common Pursuit*, *Plays and Players* (August 1984)

Mark Steyn, Review of *The Common Pursuit*, *Plays and Players* (May 1988), 29–30

Simon Gray, 'Broadway malady', *Independent on Sunday*, 25 February 1990

ALAN AYCKBOURN

Published Plays

(Published by Samuel French unless otherwise stated.)

Mr Whatnot (1964)

Relatively Speaking (Evans Plays, 1968)

Mixed Doubles (Methuen, 1970)

How the Other Half Loves (1972)

Ernie's Incredible Illucinations (1969)

Time and Time Again (1973)

Three Plays: Bedroom Farce, Absurd Person Singular, Absent Friends (Penguin, 1979)

The Norman Conquests (Penguin, 1977)

Confusions (1977)

Joking Apart and Other Plays: Just Between Ourselves, Ten Times Table, Joking Apart, Sisterly Feelings (Penguin, 1982)

Taking Steps (1981)

Suburban Strains (1982)
Season's Greetings (1982)
Way Upstream (1983)
Intimate Exchanges (1986, two volumes)
A Chorus of Disapproval (1985)
Woman in Mind (1986)
A Small Family Business (1987)
Henceforward (Faber, 1988)
Mr A's Amazing Maze Plays (Faber, 1989?)
Man of the Moment (Faber, 1990)
The Revengers' Comedies (Faber, 1991)
Invisible Friends (Faber, 1991)

Secondary Sources

Books

Ian Watson, *Conversations with Ayckbourn* (Faber, 1988)
Malcolm Page, *File on Ayckbourn* (Methuen, 1989)
Michael Billington, *Alan Ayckbourn* (Macmillan, 1983, revised edn
    1990)
Sidney White, *Alan Ayckbourn* (Boston, Mass: G. K. Hall, 1984)
John Russell Taylor, 'Three Farceurs', *The Second Wave* (Methuen,
    1971), pp. 155–71
Guido Almansi, 'Victims of circumstance: Alan Ayckbourn's
    plays', in John Russell Brown (ed.), *Modern British Dramatists:
    New Perspectives* (Englewood Cliffs NJ: Prentice-Hall, 1984), pp.
    109–20
Richard Alan Cave, *New British Drama in Performance on the London
    Stage, 1970 to 1985* (Garrards Cross: Colin Smythe, 1987), pp.
    65–71
Oleg Kerensky, *The New British Drama* (Hamish Hamilton, 1977),
    pp. 115–31

Articles and interviews

Joan Buck, 'Alan Ayckbourn', *Plays and Players* (September 1972),
    28–9
Robin Stringer, 'Scarborough Fayre', *Sunday Telegraph*, 5 April
    1974, pp. 27–32

Michael Coveney, 'Scarborough Fayre', *Plays and Players* (September 1975), 15–19

Russell Miller, 'The Hit-Man from Scarborough', *The Sunday Times*, 20 February 1977, pp. 22–6

Sheridan Morley, 'British farce, from Travers to Ayckbourn', *The New York Times*, 25 March 1979, pp. 1, 4

Harold Hobson, 'Alan Ayckbourn – playwright of ineradicable sadness', *Drama* (Winter 1982), 4–6

Paul Allen, 'Interview with Alan Ayckbourn', *Marxism Today* (March 1983), 39–41

Elmer Blistein, 'Alan Ayckbourn: Few jokes, much comedy' and Malcolm Page, 'The serious side of Alan Ayckbourn', *Modern Drama*, XXVI, no. 1 (March 1983), 26–35, 36–46

Michael Leech, 'National Ayckbourn', *Drama*, no. 4 (1986), 9–10

Peter Roberts, 'Ayckbourn on the South Bank', *Plays International* (February 1987), 18–20, 36–7

John Russell Taylor, 'Scarborough's prodigy', *Plays and Players* (April 1987), 8–10

Jean Rafferty, 'Hit Man by the sea', *Plus Magazine*, 24 October 1990, pp. 6–8

Michael Gray, 'No business like show house business', *Guardian*, 2 July 1991, p. 34

MICHAEL FRAYN

Published Plays and Screenplays

(Published by Methuen unless otherwise stated.)

Jamie on a Flying Visit and *Birthday* (1990)

The Two of Us (Samuel French, 1970)

The Sandboy (1971)

Alphabetical Order (Samuel French, 1976)

Plays I: Alphabetical Order, Donkey's Years, Clouds, Make and Break, Noises Off (1985)

Benefactors (1984)

Clockwise (1986)

Balmoral (1987)

First and Last (1989)

Look Look (1990)

Translations/adaptations

Chekhov, *The Cherry Orchard, Three Sisters, The Seagull, Uncle Vanya, Plays* (1968)
Chekhov, *Wild Honey* (1984)
Chekhov, *The Sneeze* (1969)
Tolstoy, *Fruits of Enlightenment* (1979)

Secondary Sources

Michael Frayn, 'Preface', *Jamie on a Flying Visit and Birthday* (Methuen, 1990)
Michael Frayn, 'Introduction' and 'Credits', *Plays I* (Methuen, 1985)
Michael Frayn, 'The theatre of magic', *Observer*, 8 December 1985
Michael Frayn, 'Introduction', *The Complete Beyond the Fringe* (Methuen, 1987)
John Russell Taylor, 'Art and commerce: The new drama in the West End marketplace', in C. W. Bigsby (ed.), *Contemporary English Drama*, Stratford-upon-Avon Studies 19 (Arnold, 1981)
Katharine Worth, 'Farce and Michael Frayn', *Modern Drama*, XXVI, no. 1 (March 1983), 47–53
John Frayn Turner, 'Desperately funny', *Plays and Players* (December 1984)
W. J. Weatherby, 'Manhatten Transfer', *Guardian*, 2 January 1986
Mark Lawson, 'The man who isn't Ayckbourn', *Independent Magazine*, 17 September 1988, pp. 40–3
Vera Gottlieb, 'Why this farce?', *New Theatre Quarterly*, VII, no. 27 (August 1991), 217–28

ALAN BENNETT

Published Plays and Screenplays

(Published by Faber unless otherwise stated.)
The Complete Beyond the Fringe (with Peter Cook, Jonathan Miller and Dudley Moore) (Methuen, 1987)
Forty Years On and Other Plays: *Getting On, Habeas Corpus, Enjoy* (1991)
The Old Country (1978)
Office Suite (1981)

Objects of Affection and Other Television Plays: Objects of Affection, Our Winnie, A Woman of No Importance, Rolling Home, Say Something Happened, A Day Out, Intensive Care, An Englishman Abroad (BBC, 1982)

A Private Function (1984)

The Writer in Disguise: Me I'm Afraid of Virginia Woolf, All Day on the Sands, One Fine Day, Afternoon Off (1985)

Two Kafka Plays: Kafka's Dick and *The Insurance Man* (1987)

Talking Heads: A Chip in the Sugar, Bed Among the Lentils, A Lady of Letters, Her Big Chance, Soldiering On, A Cream Cracker under the Settee (BBC, 1988)

Singles Spies: An Englishman Abroad and *A Question of Attribution* (1989)

The Madness of George III (1992)

Secondary Sources

'Introduction', *Office Suite* (Faber, 1981)

'Introduction', *Objects of Affection and other Plays* (1982)

'The writer in disguise', *The Writer in Disguise* (1985)

'Introduction', *Talking Heads* (BBC, 1988)

'Introduction', *Single Spies* (1989)

'Introduction', *Forty Years On and Other Plays* (1991)

'Introduction', *The Madness of George III* (1992)

Matt Wolf, 'Alan Bennett speaks', *Plays and Players* (March 1992), 10–11

TOM STOPPARD

Published Plays

(All published by Faber unless otherwise stated.)

Enter a Free Man (1969)

Rosencrantz and Guildenstern Are Dead (1968)

The Real Inspector Hound (1968)

Albert's Bridge and *If You're Glad I'll Be Frank* (1969)

After Magritte (1971)

Jumpers (1972)

Artist Descending a Staircase and *Where Are They Now?* (1973)

Travesties (1975)

Dogg's Our Pet and *The 15 Minute Dogg's Troupe Hamlet*, in Ed

Berman (ed.), *Ten of the Best British Short Plays* (Inter-Action Imprint, 1979)

Dirty Linen and *New-Found-Land* (1976)

Every Good Boy Deserves Favour and *Professional Favour* (1978)

Night and Day (1978)

Dogg's Hamlet, Cahoot's Macbeth (1980)

The Dog it was that Died and other Plays: The Dissolution of Dominic Boot, M is for Moon Amongst Other Things, Teeth, Another Moon Called Earth, A Separate Peace, Neutral Ground (1983)

The Real Thing (1982)

Squaring the Circle (1984)

Hapgood (1988)

In the Native State (1991)

Arcadia (1993)

Adaptations

Slawomir Mrozeck, *Tango* (first published in *Dialog No. 11*, 1964), translated by Nicholas Bethell and adapted by Stoppard (Cape, 1968)

Arthur Schnitzler, *Undiscovered Territory* (1980)

Johann Nestroy, *On the Razzle* (1981)

Ferenc Molnar, *Rough Crossing* (1985)

Vaclav Havel, *Largo Desolato* (1987)

Secondary Sources

Books

Michael Billington, *Stoppard the Playwright* (Methuen, 1987)

Tim Brassell, *Tom Stoppard: an Assessment* (Macmillan, 1985)

Victor Cahn, *Beyond Absurdity: the Plays of Tom Stoppard* (NJ: Farleigh Dickinson University Press, 1979)

Anthony Jenkins, *The Theatre of Tom Stoppard* (Cambridge University Press, 1987)

Thomas Whitaker, *Tom Stoppard* (Macmillan, 1983)

Articles and interviews

Tom Stoppard, 'Something to declare', *The Sunday Times*, 25 February 1968

Tom Stoppard, 'Dirty linen in Prague', *The New York Times*, 11 February 1977

Tom Stoppard, 'The face at the window', *The Sunday Times*, 27 February 1977

Tom Stoppard, 'Prague: the story of the Chartists', *New York Review of Books*, 4 August 1977

'Introduction', Vaclav Havel, *The Memorandum* (Methuen, 1981)

Philip Roberts, 'Tom Stoppard: serious artist or siren?', *Critical Quarterly*, XX (1978), 84–92

Enoch Brater, 'Parody, travesty and politics in the plays of Tom Stoppard', in Hedwig Block and Albert Wertheim (eds), *Essays on Contemporary British Drama* (Munich: Max Hueber Verlag, 1981), pp. 117–30

Gambit, 37 (1981), 'Tom Stoppard Issue': includes 'Interview' with David Gollob and David Roper, and Kenneth Tynan, 'Withdrawing with style from the chaos' (reprinted from *New Yorker*, 1977)

Andrew Kennedy, 'Tom Stoppard's dissident comedies', *Modern Drama*, XXV, no. 4 (December 1982), 469–76

Hersh Zeifman, 'Comedy of ambush: Tom Stoppard's *The Real Thing*', *Modern Drama*, XXVI, no. 2 (June 1983), 139–49

'Profile: Tom Stoppard, a wordsmith of wit', *The Independent*, 13 June 1987

Janet Watts, 'Stoppard's half century', *The Observer*, 28 June 1987

Michael Billington, 'Stoppard's secret agent', *Guardian*, 18 March 1988

David Edgar, 'Public Theatre in a Private Age', *The Second Time as Farce* (Lawrence and Wishart, 1988)

PUBLISHED PLAYS NOT INCLUDED IN THE SPECIFIC BIOGRAPHIES
(excluding Musicals, Pantomimes, etc.)

Arthur Adamov, *Paoli Paoli* (Paris: Gallimard, 1978)

Tariq Ali and Howard Brenton, *Moscow Gold* (Nick Hern Books, 1990)

Samuel Beckett, *Waiting for Godot* (Faber, 1956)
Endgame (Faber, 1957)
All that Fall (Faber, 1957)
Act Without Words, in *Breath & Other Shorts* (Faber, 1971)

Robert Bolt, *The Flowering Cherry* (Heinemann, 1958)

A Man for all Seasons, in *New English Dramatists VI* (Penguin, 1963)

Edward Bond, *Saved* (Methuen, 1966)

The Sea, Plays II (Methuen, 1978)

Bertolt Brecht, *Mother Courage and Her Children* (Methuen, 1962)

The Caucasian Chalk Circle (Methuen, 1963)

Trumpets and Drums, Collected Plays IX (New York: First Vintage Press, 1972)

The Life of Galileo (Methuen, 1963)

The Threepenny Opera (Methuen, 1979)

The Good Person of Szechwan (Methuen, 1965)

Mr Puntila and his Man Matti (Methuen, 1977)

The Exception and the Rule, in *The Measures Taken and other Lehrstucke* (Methuen, 1977)

Howard Brenton, *Revenge* (Methuen, 1970)

The Romans in Britain (Methuen, 1980)

Weapons of Happiness (Methuen, 1976)

The Churchill Play (Methuen, 1974)

How Beautiful with Badges, in John Bull (ed.), *Howard Brenton: Three Plays*, 'Critical Stages I' (Sheffield: Sheffield Academic Press, 1989)

Howard Brenton and David Hare, *Brassneck* (Methuen, 1974)

Pravda (Methuen, 1985)

David Campton, *The Lunatic View* (Scarborough: Studio Theatre, 1960)

Four Minute Warning and View From the Brinks (Leicester: Campton, 1960)

Marc Camoletti and Beverley Cross, *Boeing-Boeing* (Evans, 1967)

Happy Birthday (Evans, 1979)

Jim Cartwright, *Road* (Methuen, 1986)

Agatha Christie, *The Mousetrap* (French, 1954)

Witness for the Prosecution (French, 1958)

Caryl Churchill, *Top Girls* (Methuen, 1982)

Serious Money (Methuen, 1987)

Brian Clark, *Whose Life Is It Anyway* (French, 1978)

Can You Hear Me at the Back? (Derbyshire: Amber Lane Press, 1979)

William Congreve, *The Double Dealer, Collected Plays* (Chicago: University of Chicago Press, 1967)

Giles Cooper, *Everything in the Garden*, in *New English Dramatists VII* (Penguin, 1963)

Noel Coward, *Fallen Angels* and *Hay Fever*, *Plays I* (Methuen, 1979)
  Cavalcade, *Plays III* (Methuen, 1979)
Sarah Daniels, *Masterpieces* (Methuen, 1984)
Shelagh Delaney, *A Taste of Honey* (Methuen, 1959)
William Douglas-Home, *The Chiltern Hundreds* and *The Reluctant Debutante*, *Collected Plays* (Heinemann, 1958)
  The Secretary Bird, *Plays of the Year XXXVI* (Elek, 1969)
David Edgar, Destiny (Methuen, 1976)
  Maydays (Methuen, 1983)
  Nicholas Nickelby, *Plays II* (Methuen, 1990)
  The Shape of the Table (Nick Hern Books, 1990)
Peter Flannery, *Our Friends in the North* (Methuen, 1982)
Dario Fo, *Accidental Death of an Anarchist* (Pluto, 1980
T. M. P. Frisby, *The Subtopians* (French, 1964)
John Gay, *The Beggar's Opera* (Arnold, 1968)
Jean Genet, *The Balcony* (Faber, 1958)
  The Maids (Faber, 1957)
Trevor Griffiths, *The Party* (Faber, 1974)
  Comedians (Faber, 1976)
  Real Dreams (Faber, 1984)
  The Gulf Between Us or, The Truth and Other Fictions (Faber, 1992)
Christopher Hampton, *When Did You Last See My Mother?* (Faber, 1967)
  The Philanthropist (Faber, 1970)
David Hare, *The Great Exhibition* (Faber, 1972)
  Knuckle (Faber, 1974)
  Teeth 'N' Smiles (Faber, 1976)
  Plenty (Faber, 1978)
  A Map of the World (Faber, 1982)
  The Bay at Nice and *Wrecked Eggs* (Faber, 1986)
Vaclav Havel, *The Memorandum* (Cape, 1967)
  Largo Desolato (Faber, 1987)
  Redevelopment, or Slum Clearance (Faber, 1990)
Eugene Ionesco, *The Chairs* and *The Bald Prima-Donna*, *Plays I* (Calder & Boyars, 1958)
  The New Tenant, *Plays II* (Calder & Boyars, 1958)
  Rhinoceros, *Plays IV* (Calder & Boyars, 1960)
Barrie Keefe, *Gotcha*, in *Gimme Shelter* (Methuen, 1977)
  Killing Time, in *Barbarians* (Methuen, 1978)
Tom Kempinski, *Duet for One* (French, 1981)

Arthur Kopit, *Oh Dad, Poor Dad, Mamma's Hung You in the Closet and I'm Feelin' So Sad* (Methuen, 1961)

Kevin Laffan, *It's a Two-Foot-Six-Inches-Above-the-Ground World* (Faber, 1970)

Henry Livings, *Stop It Whoever You Are, New English Dramatists V* (Penguin, 1962)

Nil Carborundum, New English Dramatists VI (Penguin, 1963)

Kelly's Eye (Methuen, 1964)

Eh? (Methuen, 1965)

The Ffinest Ffamily in the Land (Methuen, 1973)

John McGrath, *The Cheviot, the Stag and the Black Black Oil* (Isle of Skye: West Highland Publishing, 1974)

Anthony Marriott and Alistair Foot, *No Sex Please We're British* (French, 1973)

Somerset Maughan, *For Services Rendered* (Heinemann, 1932)

Mark Medoff, *Children of a Lesser God* (Oxford: Amber Lane Press, 1982)

Arthur Miller, *A View from the Bridge* (Penguin, 1985)

Julian Mitchell, *Another Country* (Oxford: Amber Lane Press, 1982)

After Aida (Oxford: Amber Lane Press, 1986)

Molière, *The Misanthrope* (Penguin, 1959)

John Mortimer, *The Dock Brief* and *What Shall We Tell Caroline?* (Penguin, 1982)

The Wrong Side of the Park (Heinemann, 1960)

Slavomir Mrozeck, *Tango* (Cape, 1968)

Bill Naughton, *Alfie* (MacGibbon & Kee, 1970)

Mary O'Malley, *Once a Catholic* (Derbyshire: Amber Lane Press, 1978)

Joe Orton, *Ruffian on the Stairs, Loot* and *What the Butler Saw, Collected Plays* (Methuen, 1970)

John Osborne, *Look Back in Anger* (Faber, 1957)

The Entertainer (Faber, 1957)

Luther (Faber, 1961)

Déjà Vu (Faber, 1992)

Pinero, *Trelawny of the Wells* (Methuen, 1985)

Harold Pinter, *The Birthday Party, The Room, The Dumb Waiter, A Slight Ache* and *A Night Out, Plays I* (Methuen, 1976)

The Caretaker, Plays II (Methuen, 1977)

The Homecoming, Plays III (Methuen, 1978)

Old Times (Methuen, 1971)

No Man's Land (Methuen, 1975)

Betrayal (Methuen, 1978)

Luigi Pirandello, *Rules of the Game* (Penguin, 1959)

Six Characters in Search of an Author (Heinemann, 1954)

Bernard Pomerance, *The Elephant Man* (NY: Grove Press, 1987)

J. B. Priestley, *An Inspector Calls* (Penguin, 1969)

When We Are Married (Heinemann, 1971)

Terence Rattigan, *Separate Tables, Plays II* (Methuen, 1985)

Edmond Rostand, *Cyrano de Bergerac* (New York, 1921)

Tadeusz Rozewicz, *The Card Index* (New York: Grove Press, 1970)

James Saunders, *Next Time I'll Sing to You, Four Plays* (Penguin, 1971)

Bodies (Derbyshire: Amber Lane Press, 1979)

Alas Poor Fred (Scarborough: Studio Theatre, 1960)

Anthony Shaffer, *Sleuth* (Calder & Boyars, 1971)

The Case of the Oily Levantine (Faber, 1979)

Peter Shaffer, *Five Finger Exercise* and *Equus, Three Plays* (Penguin, 1962)

The Private Ear, The Public Eye (Hamish Hamilton, 1962)

Black Comedy (French, 1967)

Amadeus (Deutsch, 1980)

William Shakespeare, *Macbeth, Hamlet* and *Richard III* (Collins, 1983)

G. B. Shaw, *Heartbreak House* and *The Philanderer* (Odhams, 1934)

R. B. Sheridan, *The Rivals* (Penguin, 1988)

Martin Sherman, *Bent* (Derbyshire: Amber Lane Press, 1979)

N. F. Simpson, *A Resounding Tinkle* (Samuel French, 1958)

The Hole (Samuel French, 1958)

One Way Pendulum (Samuel French, 1960)

The Form (Samuel French, 1961)

Sir Richard Steele, *The Conscious Lovers* (Lincoln, Nebraska: Regents, 1967)

Sue Townsend, *Bazaar and Rummage* (Methuen, 1990)

David Turner, *Semi-Detached* (Heinemann, 1962)

Arnold Wesker, *The Kitchen* (Penguin, 1960)

Roots (Penguin, 1959)

Chips With Everything, New English Dramatists VII (Penguin, 1963)

Hugh Whitemore, *Pack of Lies* (French, 1983)

Breaking the Code (French, 1986)

Oscar Wilde, *The Importance of Being Earnest* and *An Ideal Husband*, *Plays* (Penguin, 1954)
Hugh and Margaret Williams, *The Grass is Greener* (Evans, 1960)
The Irregular Verb to Love (Evans, 1961)
Let's All Go Down the Strand (Evans, 1969)
Past Imperfect (Evans, 1964)
The Flip Side (Evans, 1969)

SELECTED GENERAL BIBLIOGRAPHY

Michael Anderson, *Anger and After* (Pitman, 1976)
Brian Appleyard, *The Culture Club: Crisis in the Arts* (Faber, 1984)
H. C. Baldry, *The Case for the Arts* (Secker & Warburg, 1981)
Graham Bartram and Anthony Waine (eds), *Brecht in Perspective* (Longman, 1982)
Susan Bennett, *Theatre Audiences: A Theory of Production and Reception* (Routledge, 1990)
Eric Bentley, *The Theatre of Commitment* (Methuen, 1967)
C. W. Bigsby (ed.), *Contemporary English Drama*, Stratford-upon-Avon Studies 19 (Arnold, 1981)
Hedwig Bock and Albert Wertheim (eds), *Essays on Contemporary British Drama* (Munich: Max Hueber Verlag, 1981)
George Brandt (ed.), *British Television Drama* (Cambridge: University Press, 1981)
Broadcasting in the 90s: Competition, Choice and Quality (HMSO, 1988)
John Russell Brown (ed.), *Modern British Dramatists* (NJ: Prentice-Hall, 1984)
Terry Browne, *Playwright's Theatre* (Pitman, 1975)
John Bull, *New British Political Dramatists* (Macmillan, 3rd edn 1991)
John Bull, 'Left to Right: English Theatre in the 1980s', *Englisch Amerikanische Studien. Zeitschrift für Unterricht, Wissenschaft & Politik*, 3 (April 1986), 401–10
Jill Dolan, *The Feminist Spectator as Critic* (Ann Arbor: UMI Research Press, 1988)
Gresdna Doty and Billy Harbin (eds), *Inside the Royal Court Theatre, 1956–81* (Baton Rouge, Louisiana State University Press, 1990)
Bohdan Drozdowski (ed.), *Twentieth Century Polish Theatre* (John Calder, 1979)
Economists' Advisory Group, *Overseas Earnings of the Arts 1988/9* (HMSO, 1991)

David Edgar, *The Second Time as Farce: Reflections on the Drama of Mean Times* (Lawrence & Wishart, 1988)

John Elsom, *Post-War British Theatre* (Routledge, 1976)

John Elsom (ed.), *Post-War British Theatre Criticism* (Routledge, 1981)

Martin Esslin, *The Theatre of the Absurd* (Penguin, 1961)

Martin Esslin, *Brief Chronicles: Essays on Modern Theatre* (Temple Smith, 1970)

Barbara and Gareth Lloyd Evans (eds), *Plays in Review 1956–80* (Batsford, 1985)

Richard Findlater, *The Unholy Trade* (Gollancz, 1952)

Richard Findlater (ed.), *At the Royal Court: Twenty Five Years of the English Stage Company* (Derbyshire: Amber Lane Press, 1981)

Andrew Gamble, *Britain in Decline* (Macmillan, 1981)

Daniel Gerould (ed.), *Twentieth Century Polish Avant-Garde Theatre* (Cornell: University Press, 1977)

J. S. Harris, *Government Patronage and the Arts in Britain* (Chicago: University of Chicago Press, 1970)

Ronald Hayman, *British Theatre Since 1955* (Oxford University Press, 1979)

Ronald Hayman, *The Set Up: An Analysis of the English Stage Today* (Methuen, 1973)

A. P. Hinchcliffe, *British Theatre 1950–70* (Oxford: Blackwell, 1974)

A. P. Hinchcliffe, *The Absurd* (Methuen, 1969)

Harold Hobson, *Theatre in Britain: A Personal View* (Phaidon, 1984)

Christopher Innes, *Avant Garde Theatre 1892–1992* (Routledge, 1993)

Eugene Ionesco, *Notes et Contre-Notes* (Paris: Gallimard, 1962)

Stephen Joseph, *Theatre in the Round* (Barrie & Rockliff, 1967)

Olga Kerensky, *The New British Drama* (Hamilton, 1977)

Laurence Kitchin, *Mid-Century Drama* (Faber, 1960)

John Lahr, *Prick Up Your Ears* (Penguin, 1980)

J. W. Lambert, *Drama in Britain 1964–73* (Longman, 1974)

Justin Lewis, *Art, Culture and Enterprise: The Politics of Art and the Cultural Industries* (Routledge, 1990)

Edward McFayden, *The British Theatre 1956–77: A Personal View* (National Book League, 1977)

David McGillivray (ed.), *The British Alternative Theatre Directory 93–94* (Rebecca Books, 1993)

Charles Marowitz (ed.), *Tom Milne & Owen Hale, The Encore Reader* (Methuen, 1965)

Charles Marowitz, *Confessions of a Counterfeit Critic* (Methuen, 1973)

E. H. Mikhail, *Contemporary British Drama 1950–1976* (Macmillan, 1976)

Bart Moore-Gilbert and John Seed (eds), *Cultural Revolution: The Challenge of the Arts in the 1960s* (Routledge, 1992)

Prudence Olson, *Bertolt Brecht in Britain* (TQ Publications, 1977)

D. Keith Peacock, *Radical Stages* (NY: Greenwood, 1991)

Philip Roberts, *The Royal Court Theatre* (Routledge, 1986)

John Russell Taylor, *Anger and After* (Penguin, 1963)

John Russell Taylor, *The Second Wave* (Methuen, 1971)

John Russell Taylor, *The Rise and Fall of the Well-Made Play* (Methuen, 1967)

Simon Trussler (ed.), *New Theatre Voices of the Seventies* (Methuen, 1981)

Kenneth Tynan, *Curtains* (Longmans, 1961)

Kenneth Tynan, *Tynan Right and Left* (Longmans, 1967)

Kenneth Tynan, *A View of the English Stage* (Methuen,

Walter Wager (ed.), *The Playwrights Speak* (Longman, 1969)

Michael White, *Empty Seats* (Hamish Hamilton, 1984)

World Competitiveness Report 1993 (Lausanne, Switzerland: International Institute for Management Development, 1993)

Katharine Worth, *Revolutions in English Drama* (Bell, 1972)

Julian Wulbern, *Brecht and Ionesco: Commitment in Context* (Illinois: University Press, 1971)

Index

Adamov, Arthur 37, 47, 49
  Paoli Paoli 47
Addison, Joseph 5
Aladdin 213
Albery, Donald 46
Aldwych Theatre, London 43, 62, 63, 73, 82, 117, 202, 214
Alhambra Theatre, Birmingham 25
Anouilh, Jean 191
  Beckett 191
Ansorge, Peter 162–3
Apollo Theatre, London 3
Arden, John 37, 43, 49, 52
Arts Council, the 20, 23–30, 207
Arts Council (Scotland), the 28
Arts Theatre, London 46, 61, 83, 139
Arts Theatre Club 91
Associated Television (ATV) 69
Association for Business Sponsorship of the Arts 208, 218
Ayckbourn, Alan 30, 33–4, 36, 57, 70–1, 73–4, 83, 127, **137–55**, 158, 212, 218, 229–31
  Absent Friends 138, 140
  Absurd Person Singular 11, 70–1, 138, 146, 150, 156
  Bedroom Farce 83, 99, 137–8
  Chorus of Disapproval, A 34, 74
  Henceforward 140, 154, 212
  How the Other Half Loves 99, **142–8**, 150
  Intimate Exchanges 149
  Joking Apart 83
  Just Between Ourselves 141–2
  Man of the Moment 151
  Mr Whatnot 70, 139
  Norman Conquests, The 99, 150
  Relatively Speaking 156
  Revengers' Comedies, The 151
  Sisterly Feelings 148–50
  Small Family Business, A 90, 91, 94, 98–101, 139, 154–5
  Taking Steps 143
  Ten Times Table 137
  Way Upstream 138, 152–4
  Woman in Mind 152

Balustrade Theatre, Prague 63–4
Barclays Bank 26
Barker, Clive 21
Barker, Felix 175
Barker, Howard 31, 34
Barnstaple Festival of Arts 43
Bates, Alan 124
Beamish Stout 32
Beauty and the Beast 213
Beckett, Samuel 49, 50, 57, 61, 62, 63, 68, 75, 82, 121, 129
  Acte Sans Paroles 47
  All That Fall 47
  Endgame (Fin de Partie) 47
  Waiting for Godot 46, 47, 48, 50, 63, 75
Behan, Brendan 37
Belts and Braces Theatre Company 21
Bennett, Alan 36, 121, **178–91**, 202, 212, 232–3
  An Englishman Abroad 188
  Beyond the Fringe (with Peter Cook, Dudley Moore and Jonathan Miller) 3, 14, 57, 179
  Day Out, A 184, 187
  Enjoy 181–3, 187
  Forty Years On 3–7, 9–12, 179
  Getting On 178–81
  Habeus Corpus 78, 180–1
  Insurance Man, The 190
  Kafka's Dick 189–90

243

Office Suite 184
Old Country, The 187–8
Private Function, A 187
Question of Attribution, A 188–9
Madness of George III, The 190–1,
    212
Single Spies 215
Talking Heads 184–6
Bennett, Susan 103
Beyond the Rainbow 84
Billington, Michael 16–17, 18, 27,
    28, 34–5, 73, 137, 140, 142, 147
Billy Liar 37
Birmingham University Guild
    Theatre Group 43
Blackboard Jungle 41
Blake, William 3
Bleasdale, Alan
    Monocled Mutineer, The 32
Boeing-Boeing 55, 84
Bolt, Robert 58, 75, 121
    Flowering Cherry, A 75
    Man for all Seasons, A 44, 191
Bond, Edward 29, 140
    Saved 35, 140
    Sea, The 140
Brecht, Bertolt 42–4, 75
    Caucasian Chalk Circle, The 42, 44
    Exception and the Rule, The 43
    Galileo 43, 45
    Good Woman, The 43
    Mother Courage 43
    The Threepenny Opera 43
    Trumpets and Drums 42
Brenton, Howard 8, 13, 36, 74, 87
    Churchill Play, The 8, 9, 84
    How Beautiful with Badges 9
    It's My Criminal 62–3
    Revenge 7–8
    Romans in Britain, The 8
    Weapons of Happiness 8, 20
    (with David Hare):
        Brassneck 8
        Pravda 8, 35
    (with Tariq Ali):
        Moscow Gold 205
Brickman, Mark 25
Briers, Richard 11
Bristol Old Vic Theatre 25, 198

British Broadcasting Corporation
    (BBC) 4, 11, 32, 43, 47, 61, 66,
    69, 114, 139, 142, 157, 184, 201,
    203
British Telecom 27, 208, 213, 215
Brooke, Peter 219
Brown, Tim 19
Buddy 214–15
Bull, John 8, 13, 19–20, 35–6, 172,
    178
Burton, Richard 38
Bush Theatre, Hammersmith 22

Cambridge Theatre 29
Camden Town Council 24
Campton, David 58–60, 139
    Four Minute Warning 139
    Lunatic View, The 58–60, 69
    View From the Brinks 139
Carr, J.L. 136
Carrie 17
Cartwright, Jim:
    The Rise and Fall of Little Voice
        214
    Road 30
Ceramics and Allied Trades Union
    215
Charter 77 192, 196
Chekhov, Anton 160, 219
    Cherry Orchard, The 160
Chicago 84
Chichester Festival, the 10, 11
Christie, Agatha 27, 103
    Mousetrap, The 28, 84, 108
    Witness for the Prosecution 27,
        215
Christmas Carol, A 213
Churchill, Caryl 102
    Serious Money 8, 102
    Top Girls 8, 90
Clark, Brian
    Can You Hear Me At The Back?
        83
    Whose Life Is It Anyway? 83, 93,
        113
Cleese, John 157
Codron, Michael 21, 78, 134, 158,
    166, 202
Cole, George 213

Compass Theatre Company 215
Congreve, William:
  Double Dealer, The 84
Conservative Party, the 14, 23, 28,
  29, 83, 84, 105, 137, 178
Cooper, Giles:
  Everything in the Garden 67, 109,
  145
Coward, Noel 41, 214
  Cavalcade 6
  Fallen Angels 207, 214
  Hay Fever 214
Crenna, Richard 201
Criterion Theatre, London 46, 83,
  124
Crucible Theatre, Sheffield 25, 209
Curteis, Ian 32
Cyrano de Bergerac 214

Daldry, Stephen 211, 212
Dallas 93
Dalton, Timothy 26
Daniels, Sarah 102
  Masterpieces 120
*Day in Hollywood, A; Night in the
  Ukraine, A* 84
Dean, James 41
de Jongh, Nicholas 14
Delaney, Shelagh 37
  Taste of Honey, A 37–8
Dennis, Nigel 58
Dolan, Jill 103
Dolphin Theatre Company 24
Duchess Theatre 61
Dunant, Sarah 32

Eddington, Paul 11–12
Edgar, David 21, 35, 36, 74, 93–4,
  195, 208, 217
  Destiny 8
  Maydays 8, 30–1
  Nicholas Nickelby 35, 93
  Shape of the Table, The 205
Edinburgh Festival, the 48
Eliot, T. S. 40, 134
Elvis 84, 214
English Country Courtyard
  Association 215
English Estates 215

English National Opera 28
Esslin, Martin 44, 48, 66

Fainburg, Victor 196
Faith, Adam 213
Falklands crisis, the 12, 23, 32, 104
Farquhar, Sir George:
  Recruiting Officer, The 42
Fenton, James 183
Five Guys Named Moe 207
Flannery, Peter:
  Our Friends in the North 8, 31
Fo, Dario:
  Accidental Death of an Anarchist
  21
Foco Novo Theatre Company 26
Forty Second Street 18
Forum Theatre, Wynthenshawe
  208
Frayn, Michael 21, 36, 69, 84, 121,
  150, **156–77**, 210, 212, 231–2
  Alphabetical Order 157, 158, 160–
  1
  Balmoral (Liberty Hall) 164–5
  Benefactors 156, 166, 172–7
  Birthday 157
  Clockwise 157, 158
  Clouds 156, 157, 164, 165–72
  Donkey's Years 160, 161–4
  First and Last 157
  Jamie on a Flying Visit 157
  Look Look 165, 177
  Make and Break 90–1, 98, 166–
  72, 177
  Noises Off 11, 77–8, 162, 165,
  176, 177, 212
  Sandboy, The 160
  Two of Us, The 157–60
  Zounds! 157
Frisby, T. M. P.:
  Subtopians, The 67
Frisch, Max 47
Fry, Christopher 40

Garrick Theatre, London 140, 157,
  219
Gaskill, Bill 41, 44
Gay, John:
  Beggar's Opera, The 74

Gay Sweatshop 27
Genet, Jean:
  Balcony, The 46
  Maids, The 46
Gielgud, Sir John 3, 4, 11
Giradoux 40
Globe Theatre, London 84, 151
Godber, John 142, 214
  On the Piste 219
Good Life, The 11, 213
Gowrie, Lord 24
Granada TV 69
Grant, Steve 130
Gray, Simon 36, 57, 69, **123–36**, 212, 228–9
  After Pilkington 136
  Butley 80, 124–5
  Close of Play 84, 131–2
  Common Pursuit, The 80, 128–31, 136
  Dutch Uncle 80
  Hidden Laughter 126, 134–5
  Melon 89, 97–8, 123–4, 132–4
  Month in the Country, A 136
  Otherwise Engaged 123, 162
  Quartermaine's Terms 80, 125–8, 131, 210
  Rear Column, The 125
  Stage Struck 77
  Wise Child 79
Greater London Council, the 24, 25
Greenwich Theatre 114, 202
Griffiths, Trevor 32, 34, 36, 74
  The Party 8
  Comedians 8, 31, 35
  Fatherland 32
  God's Armchair 32
  Gulf Between Us, The 32
  Real Dreams 31
  Tom Paine 32
Grossman, John 64
Gulbenkian Theatre, Newcastle 25
Guys and Dolls 18

Hair 55
Hall, Sir Peter 3, 7, 71, 72, 137–8
Hall, Willis 219

Hampshire, Susan 54
Hampton, Christopher 57, 80–2, 121, 219
  Philanthropist, The 80–2, 156
  When Did You Last See My Mother? 82
Hancock, Sheila 138
Hands, Terry 17
Happy Birthday 84
Hare, David 21
  Bay at Nice, The 35
  Great Exhibition, The 179
  Knuckle 8
  Map of the World, A 165–6
  Plenty 8, 35
  Teeth 'N' Smiles 21, 124, 162
  Wrecked Eggs 35
Hart, Josephine 208
Havel, Vaclav 196, 198
  Garden Party, The 64
  Largo Desolato 198
  Memorandum, The 64, 198
  Redevelopment; Or, Slum Clearance 76
Heath, Edward 110, 178
Hedley, Philip 208–9
Herr, Michael:
  Despatches 84
Hewison, Robert 29
Highsmith, Patricia:
  Strangers on a Train 151
Hird, Thora 185
Holmes à Court, Robert 33
Home, William Douglas 55
  Chiltern Hundreds, The 55
  Reluctant Debutante, The 55
  Secretary Bird, The 55
Hook 213
Hornchurch Theatre 67
Howard, Anthony 32
Hoyle, Martin 28
Hull Truck Theatre Company 142, 214, 219

Ibsen, Henrik 40, 219
Innes, Christopher 79
Inspector Morse 32
Intimacy at Eight 46

Invisible Man, The 207–8
Ionesco, Eugene 45, 46–8, 49, 57, 58, 63, 64, 65, 69, 82
   The Bald-Headed Prima-Donna 46, 57, 58
   Chairs, The 46
   Lesson, The 46
   New Tenant, The 46, 50
   Physician's Panorama, The 48
   Rhinoceros 45, 47, 48

Jellicoe, Ann 37
Jolly Potters, The 215
Joseph, Stephen 139, 142

Kafka, Franz 65, 189–90
   The Trial 190
Kahout, Pavel 64–5, 192
Keefe, Barrie:
   Gotcha 24
   Killing Time 24
Kempinski, Tom:
   Duet For One 94
Keith, Penelope 11
Keller, Don 28
Kendal, Felicity 11
Kidd, Robert 62
Kind of Loving, A 37
King and I, The 84
Kings Head Theatre, London 213
Kopit, Arthur
   Oh Dad, Poor Dad, Mumma's Hung You in the Closet and I'm Feelin' So Sad 61

Labour Party, the 14, 23, 41, 110, 137, 178
Laffan, Kevin:
   It's a Two-Foot-Six-Inches-Above-the-Ground World 68
Lahr, John 88
Larby, Bob:
   A Fine Romance 213
   Brush Strokes 213
   Building Blocks 213
Le Carré, John 202
   Tinker Tailor Soldier Spy 202
Les Misérables 18, 19, 31, 33, 214
Lewenstein, Oscar 88
Levin, Bernard 49

Littlewood, Joan 43, 49
Livings, Henry:
   Eh? (Work is a Four-Letter Word) 71–2
   Ffinest Ffamily in the Land, The 73
   Kelly's Eye 77
   Nil Carborundum 71
   Stop It Whoever You Are 72–3
Loneliness of the Long-Distance Runner, The 37
Lorca 219
Luce, Richard 28
Lyceum Theatre, Sheffield 209
Lyric Theatre, Hammersmith 25, 34, 57, 143, 166

McCarthy, Desmond:
   Waiting Room, The 61
John McGrath 21, 28, 217
   Cheviot, The Stag and the Black Black Oil, The 8
Mackintosh, Cameron 17, 18–19, 33, 207, 214
Macmillan, Sir Harold 12, 41
Major, John 14, 28
Mamet, David 219
Marcus, Frank 132
Marowitz, Charles 62, 75
Maughan, Somerset:
   For Services Rendered 84
Mayflower Theatre, Southampton 215
Medoff, Mark:
   Children of a Lesser God 94
Miller, Arthur 38, 45, 75, 210
   View from the Bridge, A 34
Miller, Brian 113
Mills, Hayley 214
Mills, Juliet 214
Millstream Theatre Company 215
Minder 213
Miners' Strike, the 12, 31, 104
Miss Saigon 18, 19
Mitchell, Julian 121
   After Aida 176
   Another Country 176, 202
Molière:
   Le Misanthrope 80

More, Kenneth 179
Morley, Sheridan 18–19
Mortimer, John 57–8, 61, 69, 73, 121
   Dock Brief, The 57
   What Shall We Tell Caroline ? 57
   Wrong Side of the Park, The 60
Mrozeck, Slavomir:
   Let's Have Fun 63
   Tango 63
   What A Lovely Dream 63

National Theatre, the 3, 9, 16, 20, 22, 34, 35, 73, 74, 79, 83, 84, 98, 101, 109, 117, 131, 137, 138, 139, 142, 146, 148, 149, 152, 189, 190, 191, 205, 212, 214, 218
National Youth Theatre, the 24
Naughton, Bill 214
   Alfie 213
New Arts Theatre Club, London 70
Newnham Council 207
New Lindsey Theatre, London 46
New Vic Business Support Group 212
New Victoria Theatre, Newcastle-under-Lyme 207, 212
New Victoria Theatre, Stoke-on-Trent 215
Nichols, Peter 36, 68, 69, **105–22**, 212, 227–8
   Born in the Garden 105, 106–9, 116, 120
   Chez Nous 68, 116
   Day in the Death of Joe Egg, A 69, 79, 93, 105, 113, 116, 156, 213
   Feeling You're Behind 121
   Forget-Me-Not-Lane 114–16, 121, 212–13
   The Freeway 109–13
   Hearts and Flowers 69, 114
   National Health, The 105, 114
   Passion Play 90, 116–17, 120
   Piece of My Mind, A 121–2, 207
   Poppy 120
Northern Ballet Theatre, the 27
Novello Theatre, Sunningdale 213
No Sex Please, We're British 55, 84

Nuffield Theatre, Southampton 213

O'Casey, Sean 40
Old Vic Theatre, London 73, 74, 109
Olivier, Sir Laurence 45, 46
O'Malley, Mary:
   Once a Catholic 102
Open Space Theatre, London 55
Orgill, Richard 218
Orton, Joe 57, 62, 79, 83
   Entertaining Mr Sloane 62
   Funeral Games 62
   Loot 62
   Ruffian on the Stairs, The 59, 62
   What the Butler Saw 83, 88
Osborne, John 37, 52–3, 58, 121
   Déjà Vu 36
   Entertainer, The 35
   Look Back in Anger 36, 37, 41, 50, 75
   Luther 44

Palace Theatre, Manchester 214
Papp Theatre Company, the Joe 17, 30
Parry, David:
   Stuff and Nonsense 61
   Trouble With Our Ivy, The 61, 67
Peter Pan 213
Phoenix Theatre, London 83
Picadilly Theatre, London 83
Pieces of Eight 60
Pinnock, Winsome
   Hero's Welcome, A 29
Pinter, Harold 29, 41, 51, 56, 57, 58, 60, 61, 63, 73, 80, 84, 87–8, 124, 131
   Betrayal 84, 91–2, 117, 131
   Birthday Party, The 50, 52, 57, 59, 60, 74, 75
   Caretaker, The 60, 61, 75, 87–8, 91, 92
   Counterpoints (with David Campton and James Saunders) 61
   Dumb Waiter, The 50, 60
   Homecoming, The 62

Night Out, A 61
No Man's Land 73, 117
Old Times 73, 82
One to Another (with
     N.F.Simpson and John
     Mortimer) 60, 61
Room, The 50, 51, 60
Slight Ache, A 62
Pirandello, Luigi 40, 82, 121
Rules of the Game, The 82
*Six Characters in Search of an
     Author* 82
Piscator, Erwin 44
Pit Prop Theatre, Wigan 25
Playhouse, Salisbury 215
Playhouse Theatre, Liverpool 25
Polish Contemporary Theatre
     Company 63
Pomerance, Bernard:
Elephant Man, The 94
Previn, André 196
Priestley, J.B.
An Inspector Calls 211, 212
When We Are Married 215
Prince, Hal 19
Prince of Wales Theatre, London
     83, 138
Pryde, Bill 29

Queen's Theatre, London 10, 141

Rattigan, Terence 40, 41, 52, 56, 214
Separate Tables 46
Reach for the Sky 179
Rebel Without a Cause 41
Redgrave, Vanessa 26
Richmond Theatre 25
Ridley, Arnold:
Ghost Train, The 61
Riverside Studios, London 25
Roberts, Peter 16
Robin of Sherwood 213
'Rock Around the Clock' 41
Rocky Horror Show, The 30
Room at the Top 37
Roper, David 10
Royal Court Theatre, London 17,
     20, 21, 26, 29–30, 37, 38, 43, 45,
     46, 47, 50, 60, 61, 62, 68, 82,
     102, 189, 211

Royal Insurance Company 26, 208
Royal Opera House 24
Royal Shakespeare Company, the
     9, 17, 22, 24, 26–7, 30, 32–3, 34,
     43–4, 45, 62, 72, 73, 80, 117,
     120, 138, 205, 208
Royal Variety Performance, the 11
Rozewicz, Tadeusz 65–6
Card Index, The 65–6
Russell, Willy 214

St James's Theatre, London 46
Sartre, Jean Paul 219
*Saturday Night and Sunday
     Morning* 37
Saunders, James 61, 75–6
Alas Poor Fred 69, 139
Bodies 83
Next Time I'll Sing to You 75–6
Savoy Theatre, London 83
Scnitzler, Arthur:
Undiscovered Country, The 84
Seaford, Jeremy:
Cathy Come Home 69
Schiller 219
Scrooge 213
7:84 Theatre Company 21, 27, 28
Shaffer, Antony:
Case of the Oily Levantine, The 77
Sleuth 77
Shaffer, Peter 34, 58, 121, 176–7
Amadeus 16, 19, 20, 115–16, 177,
     191
Black Comedy 79
Equus 30, 79, 93, 115–16, 176–7
Five Finger Exercise 79
Public Ear, The; Private Eye, The
     79
Shakespeare, William 27, 30, 65,
     137, 212, 218, 219
Coriolanus 65
Hamlet 74, 192
Julius Caesar 65
Macbeth 65, 192, 212
Richard III 27
Shaw, George Bernard 40
Heartbreak House 88
Philanderer, The 84
Shaw Theatre, London 24

Shell Petroleum 28
Sheridan, R.B.:
  Rivals, The 214
Sherman, Martin:
  Bent 27
Simon, Neil:
  Brighton Beach Memoirs 35
Simpson, N.F. 37, 58, 62
  Form, The 58
  Hole, The 58
  One Way Pendulum 58, 61
  Resounding Tinkle, A 38, 47, 58,
    60–1
Snow White 213
Social Democratic Party, the 23,
  137
Solidarity 66, 200–1
Sophocles 219
Sound of Music, The 215
Stalker, John 25
Steele, Sir Richard
  Tender Husband, A 214
Stephen Joseph Theatre,
    Scarborough 69–70, 74, 101,
    139, 140, 141, 142, 143, 146,
    148, 149, 151, 152
Stevas, Norman St-John 24
Steyn, Mark 129
Stoppard, Tom 13, 36, 56, 57, 63,
    64, 66, 74–8, 80, 84, 100, 121,
    189, 192–206, 212, 218, 233–5
  After Magritte 76
  Albert's Bridge 66, 76
  Arcadia 205–6, 212
  Cahoot's Macbeth 64–5, 192–3
  Dirty Linen 83, 193
  Dissolution of Dominic Boot, The
    75
  Dogg's Hamlet 192–3
  Dogg's Our Pet 192
  Dog It Was That Died, The 203–4
  Enter a Free Man 75
  Every Good Boy Deserves Favour
    196–8
  Gamblers, The 75
  Hapgood 202–5
  If You're Glad I'll Be Frank 66, 76
  In the Native State 201
  Jumpers 11, 78, 81, 205

  *M Is For Moon Among Other
    Things* 76
  Night and Day 83, 193–6
  Professional Foul 195, 199–200
  Real Inspector Hound, The 76, 77,
    192
  Real Thing, The 94–7, 100, 117
  *Rosencrantz and Guildenstern Are
    Dead* 74–6, 81
  Squaring the Circle 200–1
  Travesties 74, 78, 82, 193
  *Walk on the Water, A (Enter a Free
    Man)* 75
Strand Theatre, London 45, 94,
  151
Swift, Jonathan 68
Synge, J.M. 40

Taylor, John Russell 51–3, 105,
  176, 177
Temba Theatre Company 26
Thacker, David 26
Thatcher, Margaret 12, 14–15, 23,
  25, 31, 100, 104, 110, 136, 151,
  154, 155, 156, 181, 190, 193
Theatre Royal, Haymarket 82, 88,
  166
Theatre Royal, Plymouth 25, 215
Theatre Royal, Stratford East 37,
  104, 207–9
Theatre Royal, York 25
This Sporting Life 37
Thorndike Theatre, Leatherhead
  207
Tolstoy, Leo:
  Fruits of Enlightenment, The 84
Topper, Jenny 22
Townsend, Sue:
  Adrian Mole 213
  Bazaar and Rummage 213
Traverse Theatre, Edinburgh 104
Trestle Theatre Company 215
Tricycle Theatre, Kilburn 207
Turner, David:
  Semi-Detached 67–8
Tutti Frutti 214
Tyler, Paul 28
Tynan, Kenneth 38, 39, 40, 48, 57,
  75, 116

Unity Theatre 43

Vaudeville Theatre, London 134, 140, 152, 207

Wallace, Philip Hope 6
Wardle, Irving 64, 79, 114
Waterhouse, Keith 214
Watermill Theatre, Newbury 215
Watson, Ian 150
Weatherby, W.J. 176
Webber, Andrew Lloyd 17, 18–19, 30, 33
  Aspects of Love 18
  Cats 18
  Evita 19, 84
  Jesus Christ Superstar 84
  Phantom of the Opera, The 18–19
  Starlight Express 18, 218
  Sunset Boulevard 219
Welles, Orson 45
Wesker, Arnold 37, 51, 52
  Chips With Everything 35
  Kitchen, The 41, 72
  Roots 41, 45, 89–90

West Yorkshire Playhouse, Leeds 32, 215
Whitemore, Hugh:
  Breaking the Code 176
  Concealed Enemies 202
  Pack of Lies (Act Of Betrayal) 176, 202
Wilde, Oscar 74, 121
  An Ideal Husband 214
  Importance of Being Earnest, The 74, 87, 214
Williams, Hugh and Margaret 53–5, 102
  Flip Side, The 53, 55
  Grass is Greener, The 53
  Irregular Verb to Love, The 53
  Let's All Go Down the Strand 53, 54–5
  Past Imperfect 54–5
Williams, Tennessee 45
Wilson, Sir Harold 54, 110, 178
Wilson, Lanford 94
Wood, Charles 121

Young Vic Theatre, London 25–6